DYNAMICS OF CRIME PREVENTION AND CRIMINOLOGY

READINGS IN CRIME AND CRIMINOLOGY SERIES

DYNAMICS OF CRIME PREVENTION AND CRIMINOLOGY

Edited by
PARVESH K. ATRI

ANMOL PUBLICATIONS PVT. LTD.
NEW DELHI-110 002 (INDIA)

ANMOL PUBLICATIONS PVT. LTD.
4374/4B, Ansari Road, Daryaganj
New Delhi-110 002

Dynamics of Crime Prevention and Criminology

First Edition 1998

ISBN 81-7488-815-2

PRINTED IN INDIA

Published by J. L. Kumar for Anmol Publications Pvt. Ltd., New Delhi-110 002 and Printed at Mehra Offset Press, Delhi.

CONTENTS

PREFACE

An accepted fact of modern criminology is that crime statistics do not draw a relevant and accurate picture of criminality. As a corollary, it can be stated that any type of criminology based on available data and statistics on crime will, at the best, only point out to the diligence and perseverance of the people involved in enforcement and combating crime. Other important facts have come into play over the past few decades: As cities have grown along with populations and migrants from rural areas, crime has escalated into near-unmanageable proportions. Developed nations have distinct patterns of criminality, hence have evolved and developed appropriate approaches to criminology and criminal rehabilitation. Developing countries have to cope with the burgeoning disparities in economic well-being among diverse groups and segments of their populations. It is not uncommon to find the term (in social criminology) in frequent use: 'socially alienated.' Crime and criminality, penology and prison reform, rationalisation of approaches to anti-crime efforts and criminal rehabilitation as a relevant social action component—all are factors that require continuing study and research for fruitful and dedicated application in the area of crime and criminology.

The attempt in the following collections has been to bring together selected and useful materials in the forms of articles, papers, documents and extracts to provide the student, researcher and professional in crime studies and criminology a strategic window onto the vast landscape the subject commands. The treatment is under four thoughtful heads, namely, Sociology of Crime and Criminality, Dimensions of Crime in India, Dynamics of Crime Prevention and Criminology, and Policy and Planning in Criminology. Together, these collections deal with a vast range of subjects, including historical perspectives in crime and criminality, country experiences in approaches to criminology, crime and social environment, state and the anti-social individual, science and science practice in criminology, law and basic rationale, crime and criminal behaviour, economic offences and approaches to their curtailment, urban crime profile, police and police system reform, crime prevention and realities, criminal psychology and fear of crime, criminology and rehabilitation, and factors in the causation of crime and criminal behaviour. Of special interest are the appendices dealing with perceptions of crime in medieval and colonial India, and also the most recent papers on aspects of crime in India, including heinous offences such as child rape and kidnapping as well as white collar crime such as the stock scam and drug abuse. In putting together such diverse materials, the focus, nonetheless, has not been blurred: to provide a lucid and cogent picture of the vital aspects of crime and criminology in wide-angle perspective.

Editor

1

STATE AND THE INDIVIDUAL

Relation between the State and the Individual

The relation between the State and the individual is, in a sense, a relation based on the ground of the convenience or safety of the individual; it is also conceived with reference to the protection of its constituents from anti-social individuals and the aggression of other rulers or nations; but above all it is sought to, or it ought to, exist on the ground of the necessity for helping individuals to partake in all that in best in life and to promote the material and moral welfare of its subjects. The State is not a mere police force for the protection of its members; it is, or it ought to be, something far more, far subtler, are nobler than that. The State is meant to provide the individual that higher liberty which he could not expect to get otherwise than in and through social well-being; the State should provide the individual with conveniences for his health, education and other wherewithals of good life. No State can prosper when the individual citizens starve or go without the barest necessaries of life; for it is in the welfare of its citizens that the strength of a State lies, it is in the welfare of its subjects that the welfare of the State is found. If the State is regardless of the liberties, rights and welfare of its subjects, the subjects must come in conflict with the State; they must regard the State as hostile; the result of all this would be dissatisfaction and heart-burning leading the citizens to a disregard for the laws. Every State is known by its laws and the benevolence and wisdom of its administrators; if these are wanting, what regard can be expected of the individual for the State! Such a state of affairs in a State would probably lead some of its citizens to commit crimes. Bad laws and bad governance may tend to product criminals, under the laws of the State, but martyrs under the laws of God. Or, on the other hand, intense poverty, misery, ignorance of the laws of health, marriage and procreation, illiteracy, lack of moral and compulsory State education, alcoholism, immorality—all such evils which arise out of the ignorance or negligence of the citizens would lead to crimes and other miseries known most among the uncared for, the ignorant and the exploited. The State should be held responsible for the health, education and other conveniences of its subjects; a good State promotes the efficiencies in life by creating and facilitating a healthy environment. Exploitation, unchecked or unrestricted, leads to conflict and variance between groups. Disputes and hostility between capital and labour, variance and conflict of interests between the governors and the governed, defiance, disrespect and disregard for unfair or unjust laws,— all these provoke the dissatisfied majority to turn against oppression. Justice, benevolence and freedom from oppression must be the watchwords of a good State.

A State which exists for the welfare of its members, with its benevolent and efficient services, is like a family to which the interests of its members are always dear at heart; like a family which would not be happy if its members are in difficulty, want or trouble; like a family which would not interfare unnecessarily with the free choice of its members, allowing them their just rights and liberties and interceding only when necessary or desirable for the good of its members. Such should be the harmonious relation between the State and the individual in at least an ideal State.

For establishing harmonious and ideal relations between the State and its members, it is necessary that the governance of the affairs of the State should be left in the hands of wise rulers. No wiser or better remark was made in this regard than the one made by Socrates when he said, "Until either philosophers become kings, or kings philosophers, States will never succeed in remedying their shortcomings". Every constitution must provide reasonable safeguards for the liberties of the subjects. The origin of the State lies in the necessity for regulating the social relations of man to enable him to live well, and for promoting its subjects' social well-being in addition to their material and economic welfare. In this respect the State is one of the most essential and important social institutions. And for the services rendered by the good

State the individual is bound to pay taxes and to render due regard and obedience to the just laws made by the State and thus to co-operate with it so as to enable the political aggregate to continue promoting his and his fellow-citizens' welfare.

State and Personal Liberty

What about the liberties of the individual in the State? Does the State seek to take away the liberty of the individual? Far from taking away the rights and liberties of the individual, the State vests, and ought to vest, if it is a good State, those rights and liberties which the individual could not have enjoyed in a bare State of Nature. The State protects those rights through the enforcement of its laws which ought to be meant to so regulate the subjects' liberties as to be just to all in the State. As interpreted in the Declaration of the Rights of Man(1879) liberty consists in the "power to do everything that does not injure another."Liberty is not inconsistent with the idea of State control, legislation and political sovereignty. It is the State which gurarantees, or which ought to guarantee, liberty to its citizens by recognising their liberties and vesting in them rights.

Legislation should be effected wherever necessary and beneficent. Even marriage, though a personal matter for the individual, has a great bearing on social welfare; maladjustment in married life, caused by unsuitable marriages, have led so often to commission of crimes. If only our law ordinarily prohiblted marriages between persons with too heavy a difference in their ages, so many foul and unpleasant reactions, even crimes, would not take place; there ought to be a law providing for marriage licenses to be given before solemnizing marriages. For instance, a man of 60 should not be allowed to marry a woman between the ages of 20 and 35, unless he is really healthy and strong enough.

In England, there is what is known as the Red of Law. According to Professor Dicey, the Rule of Law involves: (1) that no man is "punishable or can lawfully made to suffer in body or goods except for a distinct breach of law established in the ordinary legal manner before the ordinary Courts of the land;" (2) that every person "is subject to the ordinary law of the realm and amenable to the jurisdiction of the ordinary tribunals;"[1] (3) that the "general principles of the constitution (as for example the right to personal responsibility or the right of public meeting) are....... the result of judicial decisions determining the rights of private persons in particular cases brought before the Courts."[2]

In France, there is the Droit Administratif, under which officials are tried by special administrative tribunals for any breach of the law. An interesting feature of the French and the American Constitutional Law and of the Judiciary is that the Courts can declare the unconstitutionality of any law which, in their opinion, is ultra vires under the constitution. In the Unites States of America, the Supreme Court has become, in many respects, the most powerful factor in the American political system and the greatest judicial organization in the world;[3] it ensures the liberty of the subjects which the Executive cannot violate; this Court protects the just rights of the citizens within the States. In India we have the Supreme Court of India to declare void laws ultra vires the legislature.

The Modern State

In the words of Laski, the State is an "organisation for enabling the mass of men to realise social good on the largest possible scale."[4] And citizenship, according to him, means the contribution of instructed judgement to the public good.[5] By liberty he means "the eager maintenance of that atmosphere in which men have the opportunity to be their best selves......A State built upon the conditions essential to the full development of our faculties will confer freedom upon its citizens. It will release their individuality. It will enable them to contribute their peculiar experience to the common stock....It will prevent that frustration of creative impulse which destroys the special character of man. Without rights there cannot be liberty, because, without rights, men are the subjects of law unrelated to the needs of personality........Where restraint becomes an invasion of liberty is where the given prohibition acts so as to destroy that harmony of impulses which comes when a man knows that he does something it is worthwhile to do. Restraint is felt when it destroys the life of spiritual enrichment.[6]

A government is worthy or unworthy, according as it does or does not discharge its social obligations.The first element of a good State is the promotion of the moral life and intelligence of its citizens.[7] The ideal State is like a social service agency. And the State should help in the procuring of 'full employment,' 'social security' and 'freedom from want.' The Varna-Dharmas and Asharama-Dharmas stressed social well-being rather than individual gain. Dharma Rajya was the Rajya in which the citizen was to do his duty not for Artha but for Dharma.[8]

Indian Context

It is the duty of the State to provide facilities for living well. What the actual state of maternal and child welfare work in India is and what yet remains to be done is therefore relevant for our consideration. Besides, labour welfare work done by the labour welfare departments of our State Governments and municipalities help in occupying the mental energies of their workers. Certainly our municipal government also should do all the best it can for the betterment of the conditions of living and for fostering good health, compulsory education, maintaining of public gardens, recreation places, good sanitation, and doing, within the scope of its functions, its duties in an ideal manner. The municipalities will then surely contribute to the minimising and preventing of crime. Every municipality has a social side of its duties. In ancient India, it was the ideal of self-governing and local bodies to provide for the citizens opportunities and conveniences for living a healthy, decent and moral life. And our local bodies to-day must cherish these ancient ideals and emulate them. The nation as a whole must also co-operate with these; for without such co-operation nothing can be achieved. Co-operation by the citizens and the Social Service Bodies with the Municipalities and District Local Boards would certainly help a better functioning of the Municipalities and would ensure greater good.

Quoting Brahspati, Sir Masani discusses what functions the local bodies in ancient India carried out.The Vedas show the existence of the monarchical system; but self-governing institutions came into prominence in the Post-Vedic age. The scope of function of these local boards was very wide indeed, embracing many benevolent activities. There was self-government by right, and not merely by delegation of powers and duties as at present. The aim of the Municipality in old days was to make the "village or the city healthy, happy and holy...... its range of social service embraced problems affecting the material as well as the spiritual welfare of the people.[9] The local bodies were interested in and concerned with the following among other concerns:-

(1) Construction of places of worship;

(2) Preservation and maintenance of public places, temples, wells, inns, rest-houses;

(3) Construction of water-courses;

(4) Protection from crime; Santika, i.e., police work;

(5) Relief of the distressed;

(6) Administration of estates and property, including those of minors;

(7) Judicial work concerning municipal administration; and

(8) Other works which contributed to the welfare of the people (the Paushtika works done by the urban corporation 'Paura').[10]

The local boards paid all necessary attention to their duty of providing medical aid and relief and the care of the disabled and the diseased. Orphans were well provided for and not left to fall to crime because of destitution and starvation.

In the civilized countries of the West, the modern municipality has taken up and is carrying out many social activities. Public health and safety, police and fire brigade, city planning, street and road construction, drainage, supply of electricity, water, transport facilities, public parks, play-grounds, education, adult education, the provision and maintenance of libraries, art galleries and museums, the rendering of charity and of correctional services, public loan offices, and saving banks, employment bureaus—all these are accepted as the functions of modern municipalities in the Western countries.

In India, what do the Municipal bodies do? There are Public Health Department; in some places police work is also done. In Bombay, until the middle of the eighteenth century, the Municipality was responsible for police work and also for magisterial work. Thereafter a divesting of such control took place. Our municipalities do the work of supplying water, and are also responsible for the provision of markets, road lighting and local transportation. They are sometimes concerned with the work of rendering compulsory education. They maintain schools in which the teachers should be better paid, and more satisfactory attention to moral education should be devoted. In our schools, moral education is not provided in quite an efficient way. Lack of funds stifle the progress of the municipalities. For lack of funds we have not been able to fight and prevent tuberculosis and other diseases, as also the high death-rate among infants and mothers. Whereas in Europe and America there are municipal houses and shelters for the poor and the homeless, sanatoria for the treatment of patients suffering from tuberculosis, and hospitals and nurseries for mothers and their babies, assistance to women before and after childbirth, we have made, in these matters, a beginning. In India, we have still slum areas, *e.g.* in Bombay City, which require prompt and immediate attention for their improvement. The possibility of living in a decent manner that would lead to living hygienically—on a decent level, physically, mentally and morally—is minimised wherever we have such slums. The municipalities have at times taken up schemes for the abolition of slums; they have executed some of these schemes, but lack of money has prevented them from carrying out other such schemes. As long as slums and/or want of proper sanitation persist, so long would there be a serious drawback to the physical, intellectual and spiritual living by those affected. We want poor laws also, and we want more of factory and labour legislation to secure for the worker in the smoke of the town and for the woman worker with a child or children healthier conditions of labour.

Some of the Municipal primary schools are accommodated in chawls and buildingss hired for the purpose; most of these buildings are far from satisfactory. There is over-crowding of children in class-rooms. This state of things tells upon the health of school children. Schools should be built on hygienic principles, in different parts of the City.

Though Maternity and Child Welfare Movement is still in its infancy in India, there are some organization for promoting the welfare of the family. We have, in Bombay, associations such as the Maternity and Child Welfare Council, the Bombay Presidency Infant Welfare Society, the Bombay Presidency Baby and Health Association, the Maternity and Child Welfare Bureau of the Red Cross Society. Pre-natal and post-natal clinics in rural and urban areas are needed.[11]

Social Welfare Work

The special branch organised under the Public Health Department of the Bombay Municipality has labour centres in the city of Bombay. Social welfare work is done by private bodies also: such as the Bhagini Samaj (Centre at Bellasis Road), The Hindu Sevak Samaj (Centre at Valpakhady), the Municipal Scouts Local Association (Centre at Kasarwadi).

Welfare work includes; (1) Recreational Activities, (2) Educational Activities, (3) Health Work, and (4) Labour Officer's Work. Men, women and children are taken to picnics and to educational and social films. Attempts are made to allow the people's aesthetic development. Social gatherings are held to celebrate feasts and festivals, under the auspices of the Bhajan Mandalis.

At each of the Welfare Centres, literacy classes are held Lessons are "accomapanied by and alternated with cultural instructions in the form of lectures with the help of lantern slides, maps, charts and pictures, story-telling, reading of interesting passages from books and magazines." For women, classes in sewing, embroidery, literacy and elementary home-nursing are conducted.

Chawls are visited by part-time workers who advise on matters of hygienic living. Lectures are delivered on personal hygienic, the care of the body and mind. Prizes are given to encourage cleanliness. Women are taught the mode of preparing healthy diet dishes and are persuaded to take advantage of the Municipal Maternity Homes. Labour Officers are appointed to redress the grievances of the workers.

An account of the labour welfare work done by the Labour Welfare Departments of the State Governments is given in a later chapter.

The conclusion is that in the midst of a growing population, a very large part of which is noted for its poverty and lack of education, leagues and bodies like Social Service Leagues should help the State, and should render door-to-door social relief and education work. The Annual Reports of the Bombay Social Service League show the scope of its activities. Preaching in prisons is one of its principal activities. Its other activites include promotion of education and useful information, through magic-lantern shows, lectures, libraries and night-school, boys' clubs and activities such as the scouts', promotion of public health and hygiene, work amongst women, recreation and sport and securing of compensation for workmen. There should be more of philanthropic voluntary social aid workers to spread education, to remove the colossal ignorance and to train the people to good habits and proper care of the family. Charities should lend money and lease farms to agriculturists, thus relieving them from the money- lender. Technical training should also be substantially helped by charities and the wealthy capitalists. More social centres, and, what is more important, more zealous social workers rendering door-to-door aid and advice are necessary.

The problem of crime is a problem for every citizen, and not merely for the State or the Municipality. Every citizen should step forward and do his best towards helping the spread of good education and relief of distress. Those who have money should help by money, as also by service; and those who are poor can serve and help and thus contribute towards bettering the lot of an erring and suffering humanity.

Conclusion

A good State is not only necessary but also highly beneficial. Even from the earliest times man has found the great need of the State: for, without association and unity, man could not find strength, protection, convenience or progress. The good State is not a mere police force to protect its citizens from aggression by outsiders or from anti-social acts by fellow-citizens ; it is a potent force of enabling its citzens to attain a fuller and happier life and for providing such environment as prevents crime. It affords not only economic but also social services. The State should not merely protect its citizens from aggression and crime; it must prevent aggression and crime. The State that has good laws prospers, and its members are less susceptible to crime than in a State that operates merely as a punishing agency. A good State prevents poverty, provides an equitable distribution of wealth, arranges for social insurance and devises some satisfactory scheme of provision against wants; a good State affords adequate facilities for compulsory education. The education that a State must provide should be such as may culture the sentiments in order to mould the qualities of the head and the heart and to develop the powers of the head and the senses and the faculties, so as to facilitate the rearing of good citizens who carry within the desire and the enthusiasm to do good and to live in human fellowship and love and to fight disease, ildeness, ignorance, avarice, hatred, sexual perversion and vengeance. The State should provide not only ideal methods of dealing with its criminals but also a satisfactory environment that would be unfavourable to crime. By minimising the causes that lead to crime and by acting like a family to help and to look to the welfare of its members, a good State should seek to serve those for whom it claims to exist.

REFERENCES

1. Dicey, A. V.: Law of the Constitution, p. 188.
2. *Ibid.*, p. 123.
3. Haskin, F.J. : The American Government, p. 285; cited by Ram, Ashirvatham and Sharma,; Political Theory and Modern Government, p. 63.
4. Laski, H.: A Grammer of Politics, p. 25.
5. *Ibid*, p. 29.
6. Laski, H.: A Grammer of Politics, pp. 142, 143.
7. Mill, J.S. Representative Government, Chapter 2, cited by Dr. Garner, in his "Political Science", at p. 236.
8. Anjaria, J.J.: Article in the Social Service Quarterly, April 1944 at p. 138.
9. Masani, R.P.: Art.: The Social Function of Municipal

Government, in "Bombay looks Ahead," p. 6.

10. Masani, R.P. : Art.: The Social Function of Municipal Government, in "Bombay Looks Ahead," pp. 7, 8.

11. Kumarappa, J. M.: *Mobilizing Social Services in Wartime*, p. 10 (Article entitled: Social Services for Family Security).

2

CRIME PREVENTION AND REALITIES

The following subjects are considered in this paper:

(1) the necessity,

(2) material possibilities,

(3) non-material possibilities,

(4) legal regulation and

(5) classification into the appropriate category of crime prevention.

1. The Necessity of Prevention

Today crime prevention is a concept that is extremely widespread. The view that crime prevention is the most important means of combating crime is coming very much into the picture in studies as well as in debates on crime. But even journals and magazines that have nothing to do with the issue, the daily papers as well as the means of mass media tend to use the notion of crime prevention and the related phrases ever more frequently. Moreover ''Kek feny'' or Blue Light in English, a popular monthly programme on Hungarian Television on crime and crime fighting with the inclusion of the viewers and the public at large has also changed its tone and attitude : instead of the previous rather harsch approach, the programme is now adopting a tone and formulation displaying more understanding (but not one of approval!) of the perpetrator and the offence he/she has committed, and posing a demand for measures designed to prevent crime. The most significant development in this context, however, is the first draft of new provisions of the law, a document that has been drawn up by the Hungarian Ministry of Justice and contains the importance, fundamental principles, means and organizational framework of crime prevention.

It is, therefore, quite obvious that many people pose the questions : what is lying behind this rapid change in the approach, what is the reason for crime prevention working its way so strikingly into the focus of attention ? The direct answer to the questions lies first and foremost in the substantial increase in crime. In connection with this, however, it must be repeatedly underlined that the idea of crime prevention and the demand for its implementation had arisen in both science and legislation long before the rising trend in crime was identified.

In Hungarian criminal sciences the concept of criminal human behaviour being influenced through the personality by the objective conditions, first and foremostly the prevailing code circumstances became quite general way back in the 1960s and 1970s. If this is true, then measures designed to prevent crime must be the most effective means of combating crime. This truth, came to be generally recognized in a few years following a very sharp increase in crime figures which came in the wake of the unfavourable changes that took place in social conditions and as a consequence of the proliferation of social injustices, tensions and contradictions. At the same time it also became quite obvious that in spite of being supported by multiple decriminalization, the administration of penal justice is incapable of providing for a decrease at a stagnation of crime, retaining public security which is basically favourable in the face of criminogenic factors growing ever stronger and multiplying under the prevailing social conditions.

Obviously, social changes should not be considered as negative ones out of necessity because they bring about an increase in crime. They are not to be regarded negative from an objective viewpoint if the point at issue is a transition lasting for a couple of years only, or from a subjective aspect if someone takes the position that any increase or decrease in crime is independent of the development of society, a view which is wrong in my opinion.

In its Directives issued for its 13th Congress the Central Committee of the Hungarian Socialist Workers' Party states that ''phenomena running counter to the law and violating moral norms are now on the increase; they include the loosening of discipline, irresponsible approach, negligent handling of public property, making profit against the law and an attitude that is too lenient towards these phenomena.

By relying on the support of public opinion the party, state and social organs should take definite and firm action in order to curb these negative phenomena, prevent criminal offences and to achieve that the law is abided by. It is particularly important to safeguard the purity of public life and to wage consistent struggle against the abuse of power, personalties maintained to promote each other's ends, string pulling and corruption and against all of their manifestations.[1]

In my opinion the development of crime and other types of deviant behaviours can be essential characteristics of a society, especially if they are examined in the long run (over a period of 20 to 30 years). The position taken by Soviet criminologists is much the same: ''An increase in the breaches of the law and lasting deterioration of the quality of their structure offer evidence to the effect that there are unfavourable processes taking place in the organization of society.[2]

If we take a look back on the development made by our socialist society we can see that in the postwar years, and particular in the initial stages of the major transformation, when the conditions were in a disarray and desperate struggle was being waged between the new and the old, both openly and in a concealed fashion, crime assumed unprecedented dimensions and the tendency began to decrease only after the social order had been stabilized and excesses were eventually brought to an end.

Although there has been no change in our policy of building socialism, we have been involved in the substantial transformation of our society over the past fifteen years or so. In this connection the question arises whether the increase in crime is only a provisional element accompanying social transformation or it is bound to go hand in hand invariably with the new social conditions that are in the make.

According to our knowledge accumulated so far, increase in crime in the long run is incompatible with the idea of socialism. The classics of Marxism linked the concept of the socialist social order with the idea of such a social order in which, apart from some brief spells of transition, social injustices are reduced or make their appearance at a low level.

In the studies, documents and the like relating to crime prevention the common demand is voiced that concerning the social means of crime prevention.

(a) family education must be made more effective and families with many children must be given increased support,

(b) the educational standards of the primary schools must be raised,

(c) greater attention should be paid to the lot of children exposed to danger,

(d) more attention should be devoted to creating favourable opportunities for people in general, but especially for young people to spend their leisure time usefully, to participate in organized entertainment programmes and to go in for some sport,

(e) social injustices prevailing in the wages, at work and in the social benefits must be reduced as much as possible,

(f) socialist awareness, collective spirit and the awareness of responsibility should be developed,

(g) the struggle for better labour discipline should be intensified,

(h) increased struggle should be waged for reducing corruption.

The measures voiced and to be taken to prevent crime could make up a long list, but it is obvious from the ones presented above that they are actually measures the overwhelming majority of which have material implications.

2. Material Possibilities of Prevention

Under the present difficult economic conditions in which prices continue to rise considerably, real wages decrease and production is at a comparatively low level, the efforts designed to prevent crime are bound to pose the question whether or not material investments can be intensified at all particularly in spheres from which it is expected to contribute to crime prevention. There are people maintaining that it is practically impossible or they even suggest that the state of affairs is more likely to deteriorate. Others, however, including myself, are of the opinion that following a certain regrouping of the national income an amount of money can be set aside to be spent on social projects that can serve the ends of crime prevention quite favourably. (There are examples to this effect already.)

However, no major progress can be made in this field even if a system of more just distribution has been introduced, because we can only distribute in a more just manner what we have already produced. If we make a judgement of the words uttered and statement made by Hungarian economists and politicians, it would be unreasonable to expect any major improvement regarding the nation's economic conditions in the not too distant future.

It follows then that criminogenic factors associated with the social situation and the economic circumstances will continue to prevail rendering further increase in crime probable. We must be fully aware of the fact that we cannot satisfy our day-to-day needs by drawing infinte supplies from the horn of plenty according to our own liking, but by waging a hard struggle for our subsistance, or for a better subsistence or by adopting the method of fiddle and cunning, and very often the extent to which the demands are met is very limited.

All this could be accepted with a sober mind since there are also necessary limits set to the pace of social development. In other words, it is impossible to create conditions resembling those in the Garden of Eden overnight, or in a decade or two in a backward country what Hungary was.

Considering the conditions it is a fact of historic importance that in a matter of ten or twenty years the country which used to be described as the land of three million beggars rose to a level at which the citizens lead a life worthy of man.

The core of the problem is that the rate of economic growth has come to a standstill, or worse than that, compared to the leading market economy countries the gap between them and Hungary is widening. Under the present conditions the bright prospects which were outlined in the years that followed the Second World War practically dimmed if we think of a statement made by Lenin in his work bearing the title *The Great Initiative* and which is most certainly true. He said that in the final resort it is the productivity of labour that is vital and the most important from the point of view of the victory of the new social system. He added that capitalism established such standards of the productivity of labour which had been unknown in feudal society. Socialism can only defeat and will score eventual victory over capitalism if it can achieve a new and much higher level of productivity.[3]

Thus we cannot afford to be misled by day-dreaming in respect of our social development ; we cannot ignore reality, nor can we ignore the expected development of crime. Therefore, we have to make a realistic approach towards the possibility of crime prevention. Regarding the prospects of Hungary's economy.[4]

3. Non-material Possibilities of Prevention

The means of prevention associated with material costs and investments constitute only one group of crime prevention. Even if one is poor and one's needs are satisfied only to a limited extent, one can lead an honest life. A person living under such conditions may well pay due respect to the material wealth, corporal integrity and personality of others. There are and will be examples to this effect in sufficient number. To this end, however, several factors are indispensable at the present standards of our social development. They include just distribution based upon broad democracy, purposiveness of a definite level and last but not least calling to account which is enforced consistently.

Let me discuss the latter point first. So far as calling to criminal account is concerned it is a burning social issue today. The idea that in calling to criminal account not the strictness of the sanction but the fact that calling to account is unavoidable has the decisive role to play in preventing crime has been reiterated so many times that part of the meaning is almost lost. By contrast, let me mention that almost half of the criminal offences that have become known are left to be detected, meaning that there is a high probability of calling to criminal account being dropped altogether. Calling to criminal account is either scarcely used, or if adopted, it is not sufficiently firm ; it is characteristic not only of criminal offences but also of other types of negative behaviours. For example, it is unwise to make people feel uncomfortable ever so often because of the unprecedented frequency of price rises which, in turn, weakens their belief in the socialist system, for incompetence and irresponsibility cause considerable damage to the country. (In this respect examples can be listed in large numbers.)

I do not want to assert that the strengthening of the system of calling to criminal account does not have material implications (for any increase in the number of the police staff or in the means at their disposal is a costly business), but in my opinion, they do not constitute an unbearable burden even under the adverse economic conditions of today and the additional expenses can be recovered as a result of a decrease in the damage caused by crime. Consolidation of discipline is primarily a matter of organization and setting an example.

I only want to refer to the question that whenever the issue of responsibility is considered in literature on law, what the authors have in mind is, as a rule, calling to account linked with some sort of sanction. The interpretation of responsibility, which recognized and demands that positive responsibility, that is, activity carried on with full responsibility be recognized, moreover, it should be recognized to an increasing extent is something that began to spread quite recently.[5]

In addition to responsibility to be borne by the person who has committed a criminal offence, the responsibility of the circumstances, the family, group of friends, colleagues or fellow-workers, leaders must also be established and they must also be called to account under the new interpretation of the concept of responsibility. It means taking measures in an effort to prevent similar events from occurring in the future. The latter is termed "the indirect way of calling to account" and as such it does not necessarily mean calling to criminal account penal law. (Expansion and the new interpretation of signalization.)

While listening to people discussing the related problems, you can often in hear the argument that like in the leading industrialized countries the rise in crime figures in attributable to the "abundance of goods" to the more favourable situation prevailing in Hungary than in the other socialist countries in several respects. In my opinion, the view discussed above is much more of a means of compounding with one's own conscience than of portraying the actual implications. We do not have to go far to be able to find an opposite example. In Austria, for instance, one of Hungary's neighbouring countries in which the economy is a capitalist one and it is market-oriented, there has been no increase in crime figures recently.[6] Or if we go far to the east to take Japan as an example, one of the leading countries of the capitalist world, until quite recently crime revealed marked decrease in that country for over two decades.[7] I know only too well that the highly disciplined way of life which is characteristic of Japan is not attractive for Hungary, but it has been proved by several evidence that the too loose way of life adopted in this country is no adequate path either for the Hungarians to tread along.

Quite the contrary : owing to the low of productivity, it is liable to bring about conflicts. It is my firm conviction that a more disciplined way of life could help us make progress and it would also contribute to a decrease in crime.

A more just system of distribution is another major group of the means of crime prevention not founded upon material means. In theory, it is generally accepted that distribution according to the quality and quantity of the work performed is a just principle. Although this principle contains certains types of injustice stemming from the fact that people's needs are not adjusted to their ability to work, nevertheless it is more just than any other principle to govern distribution as a basic concept at the present level of development. However, we grossly violate it because wages and salaries, or incomes in general, are not differentiated according to the level of training, higher level of knowledge or better performance in several fields. Generally differentation is made according to the position held and it is very often completely independent of the quality of the work done. Accordingly, most of the social injustices can be identified today in the fields of incomes, wages amd salaries. It is true that attempts are being made to improve the situation, but it is also true that it is no easy job at all since a practice extending to several years has to be changed.

Besides, the demands of productivity must be brought into harmony with the system and extent of social assistance, and it cannot be permitted that we should be left to learn the value of the work have performed from the incalculable changes in the market in every case. It is quite difficult to establish a management and decision system, a political mechanism which can ensure very broad democracy.[8] It follows that the social injustices revealed in this field will not be eliminated overnight. As a result, no rapid and favourable changes can be expected from these factors of crime prevention either.

The loss of ideological and political prospects and increasing uncertainty are very serious criminogenic factors in the present phase of our social development. It can frequently be heard or read that we have landed in a "value crisis". Magnificent values of old fade away, values that have been believed to be outdated assume fresh brightness and new values arise. Quite a few people donot simply know what the real values are and in seeking values they do not have an appropriate compass on hand to guide them. In this atmosphere of increasing uncertainty social interests necessarily lose much of their importance, while individual interests and their enforcement to the greatest possible extent come very much into the picture. Pursuing individual interests may well lead to resorting to unjust means more frequently than before. This applies, in particular, when there is increased probability that calling to account can be evaded.

Today a substantial proportion of people set excessive material goals for themselves, objectives that cannot be accomplished in general at the present stage of our social development. This is attributable, on the one hand, to the fact that after the liberation of Hungary from fascist rule in 1945, which was the initial period of socialist construction characterized by a large measure of enthusiam, the complete building of socialism was predicted to be round the corner or at least within comparatively easy reach and socialism which was being built and which was to be accomplished was painted in colours much brighter and richer than those used at present to portray it. In other words, our demands were dimensioned to be very much in excess of our potentials. On the other hand, in recent years there has been a considerable increase in the number of people who, as a result of more intensive tourism and our broadening economic and cultural relations with the capitalist countries, tend to focus their attention first of all on the standards of the material and technological development of the states they have visited and come to know and this is the level from which they pose their demands to be met by socialist social conditions.

And pursuing excessive material goals especially under our difficult economic conditions of today, stimulates many people to satisfy their demands in a manner running counter to the law.

The economic policy that has been pursued in recent years and which has "opened the gates to the capitalist countries" and as such it wishes to provide for an ever wider scope for individual initiatives and individual enterprising approach renders several principles that have been emphasized and believed to be socialist ones quite dim. They are, for instance, the principle of collectivist attitude, the superiority of social property to individual property, or the market anarchy of capitalist society being inferior to planned economy—to mention but a few of them. Ference Kozma is quite right in stating in his work that has already been quoted "In an effort to promote our ability to see things clearly, to act correctly and to put our ideological conscience back on the right tract again we have to re-think whether or not our concept of the dialectics of the forces of production and the relations of production still correspond to today's reality in the form in which we have been teaching and learning them for several decades."[9]

It goes without saying that development renders previous values gradually obsolate and it also paves the way for seeking new values. Once they are found, they are placed into the focus of attention. All this is a natural process and in this context Robert Hoch's conclusion is quite noteworthy. He suggests that "society can only be regarded as having been firmly established in case the received system of values coincides by and large with what is accepted by the individuals and groups of people, or it becomes part and parcel of their system of ethical values and norms.

Justified or not, the criticism, voiced against the social conditions prevailing in the 1950s and the efforts to find a way out of our present difficult social conditions have been greatly polarizing people's views about socialism, planned economy, the market, capitalism, as well as the desired and unwanted tendencies of our development. The future image of society has been narrowed down considerably especially in respect of collective forms, and the individualistic approach of "make maximum use of what is offered to you today" is gaining increasing ground. The tense international situation which is aggravated with the danger of war looming on the horizon largely contributes to the complete loss or dimming of prospects as the case might be. The shadow of the arms race which has been imposed on the world by the leading western powers and its material implications have a very depressive influence to exert on the social life of our age. In the midst of economic, political and ideological uncertainties people accommodate themselves to the idea of individual survival during hard times in very large numbers. The representatives of individual interests and the people professing individualistic, egoistic and selfish views are prevented from satisfying their demands against the law by possible sanctions to be faced and not by the recognition that any breach of law is harmful to society and that it causes damage and sufferings to others.

The very large measure of "privatization" taking place in our society necessarily brings about endeavours advocating a decrease in possible end to centralized power and central ideological. The representatives of these endeavours maintain that prospects extending to the whole society, the central adminstratives machinery as well as the guiding ideas have become unnecessary and as such they should be replaced by local administration based upon local specificities and by the views elaborated by small groups of people. The advocates of views of this kind have in my view, launched an offensive on the very foundations of the socialist system even if they are not aware of what they are doing. Opinions of this kind are commonn mainly to people who, under the pretext of trying to find a way out, engage in a sort of underrating the national self-esteem instead of creative patriotism and they do so in favour of the highly developed western societies, above all, of the United States of America. At the same time they also reveal nationalism of the belittling type towards the neighbouring socialist countries, first of all towards the Soviet Union—as it was very correctly stated by one of the theoretical experts. There seems to be no appropriate intellectual reaction on the part of the competent people to the ideological distortions and their consequences. It is virtually impossible to perform efficient crime prevention activities without firm ideological views of principle and prospects and without consistent endeavours to implement them, since the moulding of the mind and education have a fundamental role to play in crime prevention.

It has been verified by history that considerable development could only be made in countries in which, and in historical periods during which, there were guiding ideas and there was an organized force which was waging consistent struggle for translating them into practice. Obviously it is no indifferent an issue what ideas come to be predominant. Increased implementation of the socialist ideas which are concentrated around a decrease in social injustices, ensuring human dignity, humanizing social co-existence, democratic government and the administration of affairs can act by themselves against crime and every kind of negative social phenomenon. However, ideas and objectives are not sufficient for performing creative and efficient work. It is also necessary to be more than familiar with the means, methods and organizations necessary for achieving them and for operating them appropriately.

The long term ideology of the further development of our society and outlining them very definitely constitute the basis on which better harmony can be created between the interests of society as a whole and those of the individuals.

Re-thinking of the socialist doctrines that have been professed so far, determination of the means of the development of society and moulding people's minds adequately are processes that obviously take more than 24 hours. Likewise, curbing egoistic endeavours and deviant behaviours also takes a considerable time.

It is obvious from what has been said thus that if we want to be realistic, we have to reckon with further increase in crime in the near future. But is equally obvious from the foregoing that in case we organize our society more adequately and if we consider crime prevention a task to be accomplished not only by the organs which are assigned the duty of combating crime and the adminstration of justice, if we endeavour to increasingly ensure collective and individual interests on the basis of socialist democracy, and work performed properly is given appropriate recognition, if calling to (criminal) account is made unavoidable and social injustices are reduced in harmony with the possibilities, then we shall be in a position to offer again a clear prospect for our social development and it will also bring the rising trend of crime to a halt to be followed eventually by a decreasing tendency.

4. Legal Regulation

Recognition of the necessity of crime prevention over a broad range holds out the hope that in addition to words, recognition and estimation of the magnitude of the issue effective measures will also be taken to prevent crime.

There are different views as to the forms and organisational framework in which intensive crime prevention activities should be launched or carried on as the case might be. On the basis of extensive debates held in 1984 the concept that the tasks ahead of crime prevention, the related means and organisational forms should be contained by legal provisions of the highest level has become fairly general. Several people are of the opinion that high level legislation should take the form of a resolution to be passed by the Council of Ministers, while others suggest that a resolution to be passed by the Presidential Council would be even wiser. In the course of these debates it was impossible to identify the importance of the level at which the resolution should be made with adequate accuracy. But the case is quite different today when the issue is seen quite clearly. It is generally accepted that the present social conditions as well as people's awareness of and mood in connection with crime and the deterioration of public security call for legal provisions of the highest level.

By making legislation of this kind the leaders of the country would express, among other things, that they are completely determined to wage a relentless struggle against social injustices and that they attach great importance to securing the citizens' quiet and overall good feeling. In any case crime prevention is a task to be accomplished to a very large extent by the government ; but there is more than that to it, because all the social organisations and all citizens must join in the effort. That is why it is extremely important that a body the members of which have been elected by the people or an organ representing it should make a resolution on crime prevention, and this job should not be assigned to an organ entrusted to perform the work of execution. In this manner implementation of the resolution would be obligatory for everyone and for every organ equally but obviously not to the same extent.

5. Appropriate Classification

The question of the category into which crime prevention should be classified occupies a central position in the set of the organisational problems of prevention ; in other words, the point at issue is the organ or authority which should be made responsible for crime prevention.

It emerged from the relevant debates as a general opinion that a central organ of nation-wide authority should be set up straight away to be entrusted with the job of designing, organizing and co-ordinating all the state and social activities that are concerned with crime prevention. In addition, the national organ is to be given the following tasks to accomplish:

(1) It should regularly examine and evaluate the situation of crime and define the most important tasks next in line for prevention in co-operation with state and social organs of nation-wide authority and fighting crime and other types of deviant behaviours.

(2) It should guide and offer advice to the local (city and county) committees on crime prevention which are existing already and mushrooming all over Hungary.

The organs of crime prevention and the measures proposed to be taken to promote prevention obviously serve not only for the prevention of crime as such and in general, but also for the prevention of other deviant behaviours. Crime prevention that is translated into practice as part and parcel of the social policy pursued necessitates harmonious co-operation within the whole system of organisations. The organs of crime prevention to be set up are not designed to participate in this co-operation activity as professional (health, educational, and so on) administrative units, but as organs promoting the administrative organisation to work more efficiently in performing their co-ordinating and control functions, voicing demands and making available the information in their possession.

The task of recognizing the changes taking place in the tendency, structure, underlying causes and possibilities of crime prevention and of directing crime fighting in the knowledge of the above on the theoretical, organisational and practical areas by relying on the results achieved by science is also to be assigned to the organs of prevention.

So far as the category into which crime prevention is to be classified from an organisational point of view there are three solutions adopted in the socialist countries. In the Soviet Union, for the direction and co-ordination of instance, crime prevention activities are delegated to be under the authority of social organisations named Social Basis for Safeguarding Order. They operate under the supervision of the regional party organisation. In Czechoslovakia, Poland and Romania, the job of directing and co-ordinating crime prevention is assigned primarily to the public prosecutors' offices'. In the German Democratic Republic, crime prevention is the responsibility of the organs of the state and municipal councils. They invite other state and social organs to participate in the work of accomplishing crime prevention tasks.

As it can be seen from the above, crime prevention organs are generally attached to the public prosecutors' offices. It is quite reasonable a method for while performing its general supervisory duties the public prosecutor's office can act as part of the authorities in relation to every state and social organ in an effort to organize crime fighting as effectively as possible. In spite of this, however, I do not consider it an example to follow because crime prevention calls, in the first place, for adminstrative activities. It is not wise for the public prosecutor's office to embark on performing guiding; co-ordinating, valuating and analysing types tasks. It is more advisable to remain to obe a supervisory body and confine its activities to general supervisory work. After considering the problem several times in appropriate depth I am of the opinion that the central and local organs of crime prevention must be attached to the machinery of state administration, an institution which is in charge of a complexity of a activities including those relating to social, education, health and economic affairs, housing and local planning. In other words, I consider, in the final resort, the example of the German Democratic Republic to be followed. I use the term ; in the final resort, because under the conditions prevailing in Hungary at present I do not think it wise to extend the range of authority of the municipal councils to cover crime prevention as well. On the other hand, I completely approve of the idea that the committees in charge of crime prevention should be brought under the supervision of the organs of state adminstration (government, municipal councils) straight away. For the time being these committees could operate as social organs, but since they are designed to ensure the best possible accomplishment of the tasks of state administration, it would be quite reasonable to place them under state guidance as long as an adequate position is found for them in the network of state administration. The position that the Committees (or Councils) on Crime Prevention to act as (central or local) social organs should operate under the guidance of the state was generally accpeted in the course of the debates on the issue. The Preparatory Committees for Entrance to Higher Education, organs which perform their special educational activities under the direction of the Ministry of Culture, are par excellence examples of social organs performing state duties and operating more than favourably under the guidance of the state. However, considering the fact that crime prevention is a highly diverse task (with educational, health, family care and several other implications), it is beyond any doubt that supervision to be exercised by the government and the local municipal councils can be the most suitable means of implementing state guidance. Likewise, it is again the government and the municipalities that can be expected, first of all, to accomplish tasks that appear to be expedient. This is the manner is which it can be achieved most favourably that the obligations coinciding with crime prevention are observed and made to be observed adequately.

Let me list another major argument in favour of the idea that the provisions of the law designed to prevent crime should take the form of a resolution to be passed by the supreme authority of Hungary, the Presidential Council and that the Committees on Crime Prevention, bodies to be set up at a later date, should operate under the supervision of the government or the local municipal councils. In 1976, a resolution was passed by the Council of Ministers (No. 2015/1976.IV.17/MT) which ruled that an Inter-Ministers Committee be set up and operate under the direction of the Council of Ministers in order to improve public order and public security. The resolution was passed in the wake of the very correct criminal policy endeavour which was irradiated from the resolutions made by the Presidential Council in 1973 (No. 14/1973 NET) on the guidelines of legal policies. What inspired these resolutions was not sheer necessity but science. It is still to be identified why the resolution passed by the Council of Ministers has not been implemented to the present day. Today, however, when one of the priority items on the agenda is to prevent a rise in crime and the deterioration of public security, in other words, what we are actually involved is an emergency situation, the approach formulated and political position taken a decade earlier can be an important guidance. It is, therefore, quite reasonable that the resolution made by the Presidential Council should have the way for and underline the importance of intensifying the struggle against crime.

It is quite obvious from the ideas discussed in the paper that crime prevention is very closely linked with the present situation of society and the tendencies of its further development. There can be no doubt about it that a decrease in crime, especially in the long run, is inspearable from a well organised social system which has appropriately established and definite prospects and which is free from accumulated injustices and tensions, besides, it is also closely related to the rational ideological and political outlook of the citizens. I believe that we can reach this stage in the shortest possible time in case we embark on studying the regularities and issues of both past and present without any prejudices and formulate the conclusions we are about to draw without any unnecessary adornments. This is the only way in which we can be true Marxists, because in their time the classics of Marxism also acted in this manner.

So far as the issue of formulating the regularities and issues is concerned it must be repeatedly underlined that criminology must formulate its own theorems on two separate planes.

One of them is the level of pure theory, in other words, the plane of the long-term occurrence of regularities. The other one is the short term plane, or the level of today, which contains the major issues that can be implemented at the moment because the necessary conditions for translating them into practice either exist or can be created in the not too distant future. In the field of crime prevention one of the short-term issues of the above kind is making legislation of the highest level to be followed by the establishment of both the central and local co-ordinating organs at the earliest possible date in an attempt to get the current and possible measures of crime prevention implemented without the slightest delay.

Criminality in the Czechoslovak Socialist Republic does not represent a first-rate social problem. But it is important particularly because it represents the explicit antipode of the socialist way of the life and of the shaping of the socialist man that is being in principle successfully implemented in Czechoslovakia.

In comparison with the Czechoslovak Republic in 1918—1938 criminality has dropped quite distinctly in 1952-1984. In 1918—1937 only in Bohemia and Moravia (that represented about 2/3 of the whole population) 170,000—200,000 citizens were sentenced by courts every year. In 1952—1984 the number of the sentenced did not surpass 140,000 persons annually.

The tendency of the criminality in the Czechoslovak Socialist Republic is the stabilization—in spite of certain fluctuations of the political, social and economic situation (the resistance of the expropriated bourgeoisie after 1948, the social and political crisis in 1968-1969) and (as far as the quantitative following is concerned, in the first place) by the changes of the penal policy in the sphere of the so-called trivial criminality, particularly property criminal activity. In the last years (since 1976) we follow the drop of deliberate as well as careless acts against health (bodily injury, serious body injury, including careless acts in traffic), sexual abuse and other crimes, on the contrary the growth of thefts (particularly of burglaries in the residential districts of towns) and robberies.

A serious problem continues to be the recidivism of the criminal activity (about 30 per cent of persons where recidivism was recognized as an aggravating general circumstance) and criminality under the influence of alcohol (although its percentage is diminishing it represents always about 30 per cent of prosecuted offenders).

A positive tendency is also the fact that there do not exist in general criminal gangs of juveniles.

REFERENCES

1. Directives of the Hungarian Socialist Workers' Party.
2. V. N. Kudryavtzev, V. I. Remenev: *Izutchenie dinamiky pravonarushe i yeo pritchini* (Studying the Dynamism of the Breaches of Law and Their Underlying Reasons). Sovietskoye gosudarstvo i pravo No. 8 (1984), p. 20.
3. V. I. Lenin: *Complete Works.* Vol. 29, p. 394. (Russian edition).
4. F. Kozma: *Egyen, vallalat, allam* (The Individual, the Enterprise, the State). Kossuth Publishing House, Budapest 1984.
5. Felelosseg es szankçio a jogban (Responsibility and Sanctions in the Law). A publication issued by the Faculty of Law and Political Science of Eotvos University. Budapest, Kozgazdasagi es Jogi Konyvkiado. Economic and Legal Publishing House, Budapest 1980.
6. Jogi Tudosito (Legal Information Bulletin). Hungarian News Agency MTI Vol. 15 (November 1984).
7. Government of Japan. Summary of the White Papers of Crime, 1983. Ministry of Justice.
8. L. Bognar: *A felodes dra* (The Price of Development). Kozgazdasag es Jogi Konyvkindo, Budapest 1983.
9. *Ibid.*, p. 26.
10. *Gondolatok szocialista ertekrendxzerunkrol* (Thoughts of

Our Socialist Value System). Tarsadalmi Szemle (Social Review) 1982. Issue No. 11, p. 15.

11. S. Nyiri: *Hungary's Deputy Chief Prosecutor*, Ugyeszsegi Ertesito (Prosecutors' Gazetta). Issue No. 2 (1983), and Issue No. 4 (1984).

12. A *bunmegelozesrol I-II* (On Crime Prevention Vols. I and II). A publication by the Hungarian Ministry of Justice, 1984.

3

FACTORS IN THE CAUSATION OF CRIME

The factors in the causation of crime, are organic or physical defects (organic abnormalities or physical anomalies) coupled with an environment favourable for some anti-social outburst, and, as we shall now see, pathological and other factors. The other factors include the environmental factors.

ORGANIC AND PATHOLOGICAL FACTORS

Conduct is an expression of mental life. A delinquent act may be the result of insanity or of susceptibility to crime by reason of feeble-mindedness coupled with some environmental factor, or in spite of sanity of mind it may be the result of some emotional disturbance in childhood, *e.g.*, the awakening, in an undesirable manner, of the sexual impulse accompanied by some talk or incident of stealing; or it may be the result of "moral insanity" or "moral imbecility." Due to some anomaly, *e.g.*, in the skull or in the cranium formation, the presence of the animal impulses in the man may make him susceptible to crime much more than normally constituted persons.

"Conduct," says Dr. Healy, "may be readily stated in terms of muscular action; the latter activity, in turn, is propagated by currents of nervous force which, for all such complicated processes are known to arise from the co-ordinated energy of cerebral cells. The parts of the brain involved are the higher levels, those which we know are correlated with mental phenomena rising on occasion above the threshold of consciousness. So it seems that all analysis of the dynamics...of conduct leads directly to contemplation of mental activity."[1]

The offender's mental traits, peculiarities and abilities play a very important part in the determination of delinquency. It is really the mind that controls, and if the mind is deranged, defective or feeble, we must turn, for a cure, to the removal of the defect or the fortification of the faculty.

Physical Characteristics and Ailments

Ocular ailments, nose and throat obstructions, ear troubles, teeth ailments, speech defects, enuresis, phimosis, physical irritations, headaches, excess of physical strength, menstrual disorders, ailments of adolescence and other physical ailments and under-nourishment—these must be taken into consideration, as they are factors in the causation of delinquency.

Ocular ailments lead to irritability, discontent, and headache. And, we know, irritability and discontent are the main factors of emotional disturbance and in the causation of crime. Moreover ocular ailments prevent the acquisition of knowledge, which is so useful for making one fit for making a living. Not only that, but the chances of passing leisure hours usefully in some literary activity or in pleasant reading fade away, leaving the person concerned to use his leisure in probably or possibly, an undesirable channel, such as in the drink evil or in sexual perversions. Dr. Healy regards even strabismus as capable of causing a tendency to delinquencies. Good moral results have been produced by straightening of eyes by operation.[2]

Nose and throat obstructions, like occluded pharynx adenoids, very large tonsils, may cause physical weakness and discomfort, and may result in school truancy or dislike work. Breathing may be obstructed, and may result in mouth and other wise.

Ear troubles, such as deafness or difficulty in hearing, making the person concerned inefficient, act as a considerable detriment to efficiency, and makes the person afflicted despondent, or helpless, or generally weak in his ability to work and thus may lead to delinquency.

Bad or decaying teeth cause bodily ailments due to the poisons from the decay of the teeth, getting absorbed constantly.

Speech defects have been found to lead to stealing, vagrancy and bad sexual practices. How? The defective is shunned in society; he gets insulted and offended; he then wishes to move about only in the company in which he is not shunned and thus may get into the company of undesirable friends. An inferiority complex may be developed in the speech-defective.

Enuresis, which involves disorder of the functions of the bladder, sometimes results in shame or discomfort and thus may lead to delinquency.

Phimosis, which involves the condition of an imperfectly retractable perpuce, causes in young children irritability and nervousness, resulting in delinquent behaviour.[3] Apart from that, it is very difficult to say definitely how far phimosis is the cause of delinquency, because it is hardly every found as the sole character in delinquents examined; it is to be found along with other characters which can also be regarded as factors in delinquency.[4]

Physical irritations, caused by ailments such as ringworm, eczema, irritation of sex organs, are important factors. Local irritations lead to irritability of temperament and even to delinquency. Treatment should be in the direction of the removal of the cause of the local irritation and in curing the affected area. Headaches also cause irritability and may result in some sort of outburst or outbursts.

Where a person possesses an excessive amount of physical strength and his mentality is uncultured, abounding in animalism, it is quite probable that he may commit an act of violence. Excessive restlessness resulting from such physical vigour in such a person may lead to delinquent acts. When there is organic over-development, or "over-energizing of related nerve centres," there may result excessive impulsions, perhaps paroxysmal.[5]

Over-development in adolescence may lead to some sort of outburst. The deviation from the normal mental state resulting in or before the menstrual period, or some sort of menstrual disorder, may also lead to delinquency, particularly of a sexual type. It may lead to pathological stealing (kleptomania).

Under-nourishment is a serious matter. It arises out of some sort of dyspepsia, or by reason of inadequacy of good food. It has been found, for example, that lack of vitamin B_1 in diet leads to irritability of temperament, confusion of mental powers, fading of the memory, and even general despondency. This vitamin is found in wholemeal bread, yeast, pure honey (which is very rich in the B vitamins including the B_1), coconut, milk, green vegetables. Lack of calcium, iron, the potash salts, phospherous, iodine, also cause low resistance powers and a decline in health. Artificial stimulants should be avoided.

Hypoglycemia, caused by low level of glucose in the blood, disturbs the mental equilibrium of the person concerned. It makes him irritable, aggressive, sexually depraved, and impairs his will and morality. This condition of health may lead the patient even to murder while he is in an abnormal functioning of the brain.[6] It may make the patient liable to assaults, violent breaches of peace, suicide, homicide, drunkenness, sexual perversions, theft, mischief, arson, slander.[7]

Developmental physical abnormalities such as poor physical development, delayed puberty, general physical over-development—these also play a significant part in the causation of delinquency, as these may lead to social maladjustments. Over-development sexually may lead to sex delinquencies. Erotomania, implying a lack of mental balance, is also an important factor.

Hypersexualism may be a factor in the causation of sexual delinquency, e.g., rape, indecent assaults, co-habitation by deceit or false representation, bigamy, undergoing of fraudulent marriage ceremonies, adultery, enticement, and even unnatural offences. Early experiences and habits of mental imagery also explain delinquencies in many cases.[8]

Mental Development and Ailments

Mental and physical breakdown and the nervous troubles that may result from masturbation are factors in the causation of delinquency "We have particularly noted in connection with masturbation," says Dr. Healy, "such delinquencies as slipping away from home, unwillingness to go to school or to work, recourse to excess of stimulants, petty stealing, vagrancy, constant giving way to desire for exciting amusement (particularly as afforded by moving picture shows).[9] Often perverted sexual practices are the result of bad environmental conditions and bad company. Where caused by environmental conditions, the environment must be changed so as to bring about a cure of the delinquent. Penal sentences and repressions would do no good, and on the contrary, may add to the injury. Where caused by hyper-sexualism, the importance of dietary treatment cannot be over-emphasized. As Dr. William McDougall says, 'temperament is a complete resultant of many factors each of which is in the main natively determined, and they are alterable by disease and the influence of the physical environment, especially by temperature and food." Food, then, is capable of changing and moulding temperament; fruitarian and vegetaran diet would be the best for checking, to an exent, sexual outbursts.[10] Sexual sublimation, i.e., directing of the sexual energy into some healthy non-sexual channel, is also a good remedy.

Mental abnormalities and peculiar mental characteristics include mental weakness (feeble-mindedness—moron, and feeblemindedness that amounts to imbecility; mental aberrations, *e.g.*, epileptic mentality, hysteria, psychoses (paranoia, dementia precox, paresis, amnesic fugues, hypomania), sensuality, stubbornness of an extreme type hypersensitiveness.

Imbecility is a kind of feeble-mindedness. The best way of dealing with the imbeciles is to send them at the earliest possible opportunity to some institution of the care of the feeble-minded.

Morons, or the feeble-minded of an upper grade than the imbeciles, constitute cases of considerable importance.

As regards treatment for feeble-mindedness, Dr. Healy says that remediable physical conditions may increase both physical and mental disabilities, and for that reason, professional care and arrest of development spread evenly over all faculties, must be resorted to.[11] Individual treatment is of the utmost importance. Alcohol should be prohibited.

In cases of epileptic offenders, there is frequently a correlation with "premature development and over-development, both of the general physique and sex attributes."[12] Lombroso has told us of so many cases of epileptic assassins and rapists. Epilepsy may give rise to stealing also.[13] *Cerebral dysrhythmia* may also be the cause of violent offences. Dr. Berg has pointed out how a young man of twenty-one who was sentenced for having quite senselessly in a public place attempted to attack a young woman, failed to recognize his father who interviewed him in prison and how he made an almost murderous attack on him. Though there was no evidence that he had suffered from any definite *grand mal,* yet it was a case of cerebral dysrhythmia.[14] The proper handling of the epileptic offender involves first a diagnosing of the type of epilepsy from which he is suffering. Dietary care and long treatment can give hopes of cure. Segregation of the epileptic is a good social remedy.

Dementia precox, so often found connected with bad sexual habits, is a type of major psychoses, and is found among offenders.

Paresis (Dementia Paralytica) which is a symptom of syphilis of the brain is conducive to delinquency. This disease involves emotional disturbances where the patient finds annoyance with all things, even imaginary things. There are types of this disease; the patient may also be found completely satisfied with all things as he finds them. Impulses may direct the patient to an anti-social act, unless the mental weakness resulting from the disease renders him incapacitated from carrying out any vicious impulse that he may get. Though as a rule, the victims of paresis are found committing petty or less serious offences, there have been cases of homicidal assaults also committed by such persons.

Paranoia is a type of insanity in which the patient gets some sort of delusion. The patient thinks of his own grandeur or of his own persecution. The paranoiac thinks or believes that he has been badly treated; he thinks of vengeance, or he may believe that he is going to relieve society of some wicked person and think of killing him. A misguided political assassin is often a person suffering from paranoia. Paranoia may result from imprisonment also, because a mentally weak person may easily get the idea that he has been persecuted, and that idea would lead him on to this disease.

Melancholia may lead to delinquency by reason of the delusions found to exist in this disease. Suicide, under some hallucination, frequently results in the case of such sufferers, Pathological arson (pyromania) is frequently resorted to by melan choliacs. A melancholiac may even commit murder at home and then follow the act by taking his own life. Such acts are done under the delusions that exist in melancholia.

Hypomania (constitutional excitement) is a type of minor mental aberrations. In the disease though the person concerned does not show apparent symptoms of insanity, yet his mental psychotic condition is such as to make him liable to abnormal social behaviour.

Chorea is another type of mental ailment, in which the patient's mental state is confusional. The delinquencies the frequently arise as the result of chorea are: lying and falsely accusing innocent persons, petty thieving, immoral tendencies, truancy.

Trauma may lead to delinquency, insofar as by reason of some cerebral injury the patient gets his character changed. The injury causing the cranial trauma may produce mental exhaustions after work, and may thus render the person disabled. It may also produce lack of self-control, which is an important cause of crime.

Another type of mental ailment is the *amnesic fugue*, e.g. loss of memory with a wandering. But this sort of psychosis is very rarely a cause of delinquency even of a petty type.

Hysteria, which is found to exist mostly among women (though it may exist among men also), is mental ailment which may lead, though not often, person concerned to make false accusations against innocent persons, simulations attempt at suicide, petty stealing, obscenity.

An effective cure for several types of insanity is the drug developed by Professor Jean-Delay of the Faculty of Medicine, and termed *succinic dinitrile* DNT. This drug is very useful in treatment of obsessions. A woman suffering from an obsession that she was ugly and hideous and would have committed suicide, was treated and cured by six injections of DNT.

Suitable music is very valuable and effective in the treatment of several forms of insanity. Music is very widely and effectively used in neuropsychiatric hospitals. The co-ordinated use of music in hospitals now plays a very important part in the treatment of mental afflictions. It is also used in connection with in sulin shock treatment. As to how music is usable in an insulin shock treatment, first insulin shock is injected intravenously; after that, sedative music—slow in tempo and soft (without sudden accents)—is provided for the sick room so as to enable the patient to relax. After the patient reaches the excited or elated phase of the treatment, fast, loud and strong music is played.

In the phase (which is recovery from coma) glucose is intravenously injected or fruit juice is given as drink ; at this stage, soft, soothing and even music is played as the patient is brought to consciousness.

Fear as a Cause of Crime

Darwin says: "Fear is often preceded by astonishment, and is so far akin to it that both lead to the senses of sight and hearing being instantly aroused.......The heart beats quickly and violently, so that it palpitates or knocks against the ribs......the skin becomes pale due to the vaso-motor centre being affected in such a manner as to cause the contraction of the small arteries of the skin......the hairs also on the skin stand erect, and the superficial muscles shiver....As fear increases into an agony of terror, we behold.......diversified results.[15]

Fear often leads to a criminal act. With a desire for self-protection a person may cause harm to another. A robber, with a view to escaping detection or arrest may even commit an act of homicide. Sometimes abortions are committed as a result of shame, disgrace or fear. There have been several cases in our law courts of new-born babes having been cruelly done away with because of fear and shame. One the 11th day of March, 1943, one Satya Sidhappa committed a premeditated murder of his new-born babe got through a woman (with whom he was not married). He committed the monstrous crime of infanticide by drowning the helpness little babe. He was found guilty by a unanimous vote of the jury, and the judge gave him a proper sentence, *viz.* of transportation for life. Another detestable case of infanticide is that in which a woman, one Shantabai Dhondu, was sentenced to seven years' rigorous imprisonment. On 21st August 1943, the crime was committed; the cause of the offence was fear. The prisoner, who was a woman about 35 years of age, had strangulated her own grandchild. The effect of her daughter having given birth to a child (without having been married) troubled the grandmother who felt so ashamed and frightened about the matrimonial prospects of her daughter that she thought she should conceal the whole affair by doing away with the child. Here fear of disgrace and loss of matrimonial prospects of her daughter led her to take the life (in a brutal manner) of an harmless and innocent babe. The sentence of seven years' rigorous imprisonment passed on her was a proper one.

In his "Maria Murder and Suicide," Dr. Verrier Elwin gives illustrations of homicides caused by fear.[16] A Maria, being very much afraid of witchcraft and sorcery, believes that it is proper to kill one whom he imagines to be a 'witch' or a 'sorcerer'. Dr. Elwin cites the case of one Guma Hunga who left his village and home because he believed that the members of his family had been bewitched by one Burgi. But a year later when Hunga saw Burgi even in the new village where he had shifted, he (Hunga) got into a sudden access of fear and murdered Burgi there.

Emotional Trauma in Childhood

Case No. 71, given by Dr. Healy, in his "The Individual Delinquent,"[17] affords a very good illustration of the effects of emotional disorder. A 12-year-old boy set out on a criminal career after he came to know that the person whom he believed to be his mother was not his mother, and that his own mother had passed away a long time ago. The boy, being sensitive, got highly affected when he came to know of the truth, so much so that he began thereafter to consider this world to be a world of lies. He then decided to embark on a criminal career.

Mental Abnormality Therapeutic Approach

The proper course of treatment in cases of mental abnormality is the study of the delinquent's case individually and thoroughly, and then after diagnosing the cause taking measures to bring about cure and prevention of recurrence. Individualised treatment under expert medical, psychiatric and educational care in necessary.

In all cases of pathological delinquency, a thorough and patient inquiry into the earlier life of the delinquent is absolutely necessary and desirable. The analysing of mental traits should involve an extensive and intensive investigation. The use of mental tests would prove to be of great advantage. The use of psychoanalytic method has given brilliant therapeutic results. The substratum on which the psychoanalytic method rests is the principle that for a solution or explanation of all human behaviour tendencies we must probe into an understanding of the individual's environmental and mental experiences of childhood or early life, because it is in the early formative period that the future of the child, psychologically speaking, is founded. In the psychoanalytic method, induced introspection is the principal method employed. The subject is asked to think back over his past and to remember and give answers to questions put. The inquirer must act as a friend and helper. The friendly inquirer should get disclosed what lies also in the subconscious mind of the person concerned. Dreams may be studied and interpreted in the light of past experiences and in the light of the future, so that dreams and symbols may reveal the truth. Mental conflicts occur even at early ages, and are left unsuspected by the parents and others. Repression of such conflicts may take place, but they are still capable of playing an important part in the formation of character tendencies. Artificial repression of that which needs an expresion will result in serious reaction, and thus produce anomalies. The environment of the delinquent must be changed so that the old disturbing influences could not exist. Re-education and the help of a healthy environment may help in the removal of the irresistible impulse or the defect. Physical culture and health-building should also be resorted to. Restricted diet consisting of milk butter, fruits and raw vegetables would do a great deal of good. Baths and massage treatment may also be used with great benefit. Dr. Havelock Ellis shows how a group of dullards at the U.S. Reformatory, 'Elmira,' were successfully treated and greatly improved by the use, by Dr. Wey of Elmira, of proper treatment which included a special restricted dietary (Dr. Wey being strongly in favour of a diet consisting chiefly of milk, bread and butter), bathing (including vapour baths), massage, gymnastics, and a continuation of the school work (the daily industries of the shop, etc., having been suspended).[18]

Physical defects should be thoroughly detected and eliminated. Otherwise a person may get out of prison, only to return later. Where the removal of a physical defect or abnomal characteristic is a difficult affair, institutional treatment is a good remedy. The delinquent should be treated and kept there as long as it may become necessary.

The value of psychiatry in the prevention of crime by curing mental ailments and by providing proper treatment (after segregation) for individual offenders cannot be overemphasised. Psychiatry can also help our law courts in deciding questions of responsibility, partial responsibility, and irresponsibility. It is not use obstinately holding that the criminal is responsible for his crime; that, really, is a question of fact to be tested and determined by scientific observation in each particular case. Whether a particular offender is responsible, partly responsible, or wholly irresponsible, for the offence committed by him can be determined by psychiatric observations. Psychiatric and psychological guidance clinics can therefore help our law courts in arriving at proper treatment for individual offenders. Psychiatric clinics have been established in Chicago, Baston, New York, and other places, to help the courts in determining the question of responsibility of the offender and in arriving at proper treatment. In India, an intensive and extensive development of such clinics are bount to produce good results.

Every prison should have a psychological clinic attached to it the enabling a proper segregation and treatment of the offenders, if rehabilitation really is to be desired. Reformative treatment, and prevention by wise methods of education and by the practice of the principles of genetics, can bring about substantial solution of the problem of crime.

To facilitate the establishing of psychological clinics we must have able and qualified psychiatrists. Since 1944, there has been instituted, at the Bombay University, a post-graduate diploma course in psychological medicine. The Bombay University has been the first in India to institute the course and the emulation of this by the other Indian Unversities cannot but produce gratifying results. In India, in spite of the great want for qualified psychiatrists, there has been a lack of them yet. For carrying out the various post-war reconstruction schemes, there will be a demand for psychiatrists for mental hospitals and psychiatric and child guidance clinics, it is of the utmost importance that mental diseases be treated rightly, and that child guidance and even adult psychiatric and psychological clinics be established all over India.

Insanity can be treated by the use of hypnotism, insulin-shock treatment, and, in the last resort, by psycho-surgery.

The New York State Commission on State Hospital problems, in a Report, in 1944, stated that the insulin-shock theory, devised in 1936 by Dr. Manfred as a new type of treatment for dementia precox, a kind of insanity, has proved very successful and that is should be utilised in all mental hospitals. After a study of 1,218 cases of dementia precox, treated with insuling shock method, at the Brooklyn State Hospital for the insane, over a period of five years and a half, it was found that, comparing these cases with a group of 876 patients, in other hospitals, who were not treated by the insulin-shock method, patients treated by the insulin-shock method were cured far better than those treated otherwise; 79.5 per cent of the cases of insulin treatment were successful as against the 58.8 per cent treated otherwise. It was also found that the insulin-shock treatment "effected the saving of 286,695 days of hospital care, a saving of 80,274 dollars in the cost of food and clothing, a substantial (though undetermined) saving in maintenance costs and still larger savings, ultimately, in construction costs."

PATHOLOGY OF ABERRATION

Pathological Stealing (Kleptomania)

Dr. Healy prefers the expression "pathological stealing" to the term "kleptomania" which nevertheless is used by writers. It is a peculiar kind of stealing. It implies that the stealing is done not for the purpose of possessing the object of the theft, but for the sake of the act itself, i.e., the act of stealing. Pathological stealing may be the result of epilepsy; or it may be the reactional relief resulting from repressed mental factors. The epileptic, during automatic states, may steal things which are not in themselves desired; that is pathological stealing. Or, it may be act of false sublimation of the sexual impulse, arising, as it often does, through some sort of stirring of the sexual impulse during childhood.[19] Dr. McDougall cites the case of a boy who was repeatedly apprehended for driving away in some buggies that he could find on the road. The case shows that the boy had an experience at the age of eleven, which still worked, with an irresistible impulse, on his mind. At the age of 11, the boy had been invited by a man with a buggy and a horse to go with him for a drive; during the drive the man disclosed to him that the horse and the buggy were stolen by him (the man), and while so telling him he so behaved with the boy that the latter was sexually excited. From that day onwards (because of that sexual excitement which had taken place) the boy got an irresistible impulse for stealing any horse and buggy that he came across and that he could steal; not because he wanted the horse and the buggy (the same might be of no use to him), but because in the act of stealing the horse and the buggy he got sexual excitement which he so desired or craved for. When the sexual instinct is roused in a young person by another young person or by an adult, the former in that experience gets so attracted to, and influenced by, the latter, that he becomes as powerless as an object of hypnosis, and his mind gets readily influenced, even with an effect that lasts, by the other person. Dr. McDougall says: "It would seem that these and similar cases are closely allied to sexual fetichism. Instead of impelling to the possession and repeated contemplation of some fetich object, the sexual impulse drives the patient to a particular kind of action at the time when it was first aroused to activity. Owing to the performance of the act of stealing during a state of obscure sexual excitement, when the sexual impulse is still blind and when circumstances do not lead it on to its natural goal and expression, its energy becomes diverted into the activity of stealing; and thereafter it is apt to follow a similar course, whenever the impulse is excited. The formation of such perversions may, therefore, be regarded as being misdirected processes of sublimation."[20] Dr. Havelock Ellis describes "sexual kleptomania" (or theft associated with sexual excitement) as "kleptolagnia."[21]

In his article : Mental Abnormality and Crime, Jehangir M. Sethna has aptly pointed out that the kleptomaniac and the pyromaniac suffer from 'compulsion neurosis'. He cites Rouke who says that eighty-seven per cent of those engaged in stealing from shops do so because of some urge created by some sort of emotional difficulty.[22] There are some shop-lifters who commit theft for sexual satisfaction of some type. Rouke cites how a woman stole several times from shops for relieving the deep tension she experienced as the result of suppression of the strong impulses she felt toward men other than her husband. She stole things of higher or lesser value according to the intensity of the tension which she experienced. Sethna has well remarked, in this connection, that the woman's acts of stealing were nothing but the "victimisation to the *irresistible impulse* she felt" Sethna adds: "In cases of such neurotic conditions, the kleptomaniac should be considered 'not guilty' and sent to an institution for mental treatment"[23]. We may here mention that a neurotic of the type of the kelptomaniac or the pyromaniac should, even if found 'guilty', be sent to a mental hospital for proper treatment and not to an ordinary prison, or, at least to a prison which possesses an efficient psychological clinic of the genuine type, and segregated for special curative treatment and that the purely punitive attitude of retributive punishment should not be resorted to in his case. Of course, in the modern progressive age, the remedy suggested by Jehangir Sethna is more satisfactory. We should rather agree with him when be says: "In cases of such neurotic conditions, the kleptomaniac should be considered 'not guilty' and sent to an institution for mental treatment."

At the substratum of the impulse to steal are found several other causes also. Dr. Janet found a case in which to obtain relief from melancholia the kleptomaniac committed thefts of the pathological type. By extensive thieving of small articles from shop, Dr. Janet's patient got relief from her tendency to depression. The desire for excitement gives an impetus to the thieving impulse. Not the article that is wanted, but the excitement and the relief from depression that are obtained are the factors in causation.[24] Dr. Gudden found that practically all cases of kleptomaniacs whom he examined revealed that they were in or near their period of menstruation; he found that 99% of the shoplifters were women in or near their menstruation. While at shops, they got some strong irresistible impulse which they could not get over. The thieving resulted subconsciously. Dr. Healy gives instances of thieving occurring during menstruation and instances of pathological stealing during pregnancy also.[25]

According to Schlapp and Smith, "most crimes come about through disturbances of the ductless glands in the criminal and through mental defects caused by endocrine troubles in the criminals mother."[26] He adds that endocrine troubles cause *Kleptomania* also.[27]

Kleptomania Therapy

The person concerned must be studied, and after a diagnosing of the cause of the thieving, the environment should be changed so as to bring about a change of mental activity and habits. Patient and prolonged efforts may be required. If the cause be bad environment leading to unhealthy sex impulses the environment must be so shifted as to cause a fading away of the unhealthy sexual impulse. There should be proper sexual sublimation; or the person concerned may, if desirable, be allowed or recommended marriage.

If the pathological stealing be the result of a desire for excitement or relief from malancholia, the person concerned must be put to some sort of remedial measure in that direction, *e.g.*, he may be put in the company of good friends, or to enter the marriage relationship if he is fit enough for that. If the outbursts take place during or near the menstrual period, or during pregnancy, the disturbing factor must be carefully studied and then eliminated.

Pathological Arson (Pyromania)

Pathological arson, also called "pyromania," involves an impulse for setting fire to property, due to some mental aberration. The act of arson, in a pathological arson, is not an ordinary act of arson, but an act actuated by an abnormal impulse. In cases of mental conflict, the pathological arson is the result of a reactive outlet. It is caused also by feeblemindedness or done by insane and epileptic persons. In the opinion of Dr. Healy, "the discussion of pyromania as given under the head of impulsive insenity in works of psychiatry is extremely unsatisfactory. A much wider view of the subject must be taken."[28] According to him, "pathological arson" is "fire-setting under an abnormally conditioned impulse by a person not determinably insane.'' The pyromaniac knows and understands the nature and quality of his act and knows that what he is doing is wrong, but is *unable* to control the *irresistible impulse* which he experiences.[29]

Treatment

Where epilepsy is the cause, treatment should be in the direction of giving relief from epilepsy. If feeble-mindedness be the factor, treatment for feeble-mindedness should be prescribed.

Suicide and its Causes

Many are the causes of suicide. Often a person under temporary insanity or depression caused by deep grief or loss commits suicide. Failure in love affairs, sometimes, failure in life or in the fulfilment of some cherished ambition, may break the person concerned, emotionally, and may result in act of suicide on his part. It generally arises out of melancholia. It is the result of mental depression, weakmindedness or despondency. Epilepsy, neurasthenia, insanity and borderline cases, fear, fright or disease may lead the afflicted person to suicide.

At about 1-30 p.m., on the June, 1944, the driver of a goods train, seeing a woman (aged 25) with a child lying on the railway track, stopped the train, got down, and took charge of the child and the woman. He handed them over to the police. On investigation, it was found, and the prosecution alleged in Court at the time of her trial (on the charge of attempt to murder her minor daughter and the charge of attempt to commit suicide), that she had quarrelled with her husband and as the result of that she had taken the morbid step. Had the driver not noticed her and her child, they both would have been run over. The cause of this attempted suicide was, to a great extent, the morbidity which had been acquired becuase of ill-treatment by her husband.

The treatment lies in determining the cause and then eliminating the same. If some bad environment is the cause, it should be substituted by a healthy one. If melancholia is the cause, relief should be provided in that direction, i.e. care of melancholia.

Treatment of Neurotic Persons and Psychopaths

As aptly pointed out by Jehangir M. Sethna, neurotic persons, as for example, kleptomaniacs and pyromaniacs, are not psychotics, but at the same time, it must not be forgotten that such persons are not sane persons.[30] "Though not 'insane' within the meaning of the M'Naghten rules, they are yet sufferers from 'compulsion neurosis' and are victims of the irresistible impulse. They should be excused from criminal responsibility, on the ground of the loss of the emotional equilibrium due to emotional difficulties of a very serious and obsessive nature."

In the treatment of neurotics, as also in the consideration of the question of insanity, in the psycho-legal light, we would do very well to follow the test propounded by Jehangir Sethna which runs as follows:

> "No act can be called a crime, if, at the time the act was committed, the doer was suffering from some mental derangement or morbid impulse of a really irresistible type that caused a loss of the mental or emotional equilibrium."[31]

Jehangir Sethna's theory or test accepts as legal excuse cases of emotional difficulties of serious types causing severe neuroses, if not psychoses. He rightly observes that the burden of satisfactory proof should lie on the defence, unless the facts themselves reveal the truth in a clear manner. He adds: "If morbid impulse is resistible and merely not resisted, then, of course, the accused person can be held criminally liable, for his case is that of a *simple psychopathic condition*, and no more. Even in the latter type of cases of mere psychopathic condition, the psychopath needs proper institutional treatment and mental therapy; he should not be sent to an ordinary prison but should be relegated to a *fit and proper* mental hospital or mental institution for proper and *fuller diagnosis and highly individualised psychotherapeutic treatment.*"[32]

OTHER CAUSES OF AND REMEDIES FOR CRIME

The causes of and remedies for crime are as diverse and complex as are the crimes. Maladjustment, or lack of organisation of the traits of personality, suggestibility, imitation, the unwholesome influence of bad company or undesirable environment, lack of reverence and religion, lack of moral culture, alcoholism, addiction to bad drugs, poverty, lack of education and training, unhealthy conditions of work in some of the factories and industrial houses, child labour, mental conflict, society's apathy and lethargy in its relationship with criminals and in its modes of dealing with crime, faulty theories of punishment and defective prison systems, lack of after-care of the criminal, lack of societies for preventing unemployment and helping the deserving poor, neglect and/or delay in checking juvenile delinquency, lack of home training of a proper type, quarrels between parents, broken homes, overcrowding in one-room of verandah residences, disgusting home-environment—too much of interference by parents or too slack a discipline, trouble caused by step-parent, favouritism of a child over the rest of the children, jealousy, lack of love of the parents or a parent in the case of an unwanted child or a defective child, death, imprisonment, detention of a parent, drunkenness at home or on the part of the bread-winner, immorality or cruelty—lack of satisfaction of desires, and avarice (avarice which was the originating cause of sin and crime)—these are the main causes of crime, *i.e.*, causes in addition to those we have considered in the preceding section.

COMBINATION OF FACTORS

Though some causes of crime have been shown by us, yet it is important to remember that in the causation of crime there is usually no single factor but a combination of factors working together, mutually stimulating and supplementing. Thus the weak biological equipment of a person may not lead him to crime, unless there is something more, *viz.*, a tempting environment, in which case the environment would be like a match applied to gunpowder. Likewise an environment of an undersirable type would not in itself be responsible for the causation of crime; crime may be caused if there is a person who by some weakness of mind or lack of organisation of personality traits is susceptible to such environment.

CRIME AND ROLE MODEL

Theory of the French School

'Imitation' is a potent factor in the causation of crime. Most of our culture is transmitted by imitation which is a process of conditioning of responses. The child begins learning mostly by imitation, and this process goes on in youth, adult life, and even in old age. Man, as a rule, conforms to the environments, and follows what is accepted in society. Very much of man's behaviour is adjusted in the environment of society.

Very often the children of parents who smoke also smoke. What is that due to? The child often imitates the parents and forms their habits. Very often parents exhibit faulty habits and modes of living which their children imitate; and parents then attribute the same to heredity while the real factors are faulty environment and imitation by the children. Wherever there is family disorganisation or maladjustment, children are likely to imitate and get corrupted. During the formative period, the parents must be very careful of their children who should be given all scope for developing good habits. But when the parents themselves live in utmost ignorance, misery and a state of want of culture, how can we expect them to give good home education and training in good morals so far as their children are concerned! What is needed is the process of mental and moral transformation. But how can such transformation be effected when the child is trained neither at home (for the parents are too ignorant to do so) nor at school (because often the child is kept at home, though of the school-going age)? The remedies lie in (a) adult education for the parents *i.e.*, not merely making them literate, but making them understand their moral duties and their duties towards their children, making them realise well that their children are not mere took for increasing the family income, but are meant for being grown up as they ought to, with the blessings of an ideal education, and (b) ideal education, which should be free for all poor children, and provided by the State, through its Municipal bodies—nor the "make-believe education," but something really sound, something that would develop character and ennoble and heart, something that would help in the making of good men and women who would serve humanity and live usefully and benevolently.

MEDIA AND PREVENTION OF CRIME

By seeing what is shown sometimes on the screen, the feelings susceptible persons with easily impressionable minds are aroused; sex feelings may be aroused; and inclinations towards adventure may be stimulated or created. The person concerned may desire doing himself what he saw on the screen. The remedy lies in an efficient censorship of films and shows, and parents themselves must be careful in abstaining from taking their young folk to undesirable pictures, especially the crime pictures and even dance pictures.

ADVERSE ENVIRONEMENT

A child starved at home may escape, and, seeing another child or an adult pilfering an article from a street-waggon or a stall, imitate the act and commit the crime of theft. And a first offender, who fell into the committing of a crime simply because of circumstances, may, if kept in prison (where he may be sent) with persons of desperate character, learn from such persons the art of committing desperate and daring crimes. If of a weak character, he may be so inspired and influenced by all the talks of the darings, the criminal's braveries and felicitations in sins and wrong-doings, that after his release he himself would attempt the commission of such daring crimes and imitate those who taught him the mode of living successfully as a desperate criminal.

ALCOHOLISM AND DRUG ADDICTION

Many crimes are caused under the influence of alcohol or drugs.[33] The use of alcohol, in course of time, causes a great and irresistible craving for it. To retian the so-called 'satisfaction,' derived from the use of alcohol of drugs, the drunkard or the drug-addict has got to go on increasing the quantities from time to time; such a state of affairs may lead him even to commit theft or frauds to get the money for purchasing the liquor or the drug, or to get the same otherwise. Now when he is drunk so heavily that he cannot understand the consequences of his acts he is quite likely to do some harmful act—even an act of homicide. Very often, crimes of violence have been committed in a state of intoxication. Dr. Healy is of the opinion that complete elimination of alcohol and harmful drug habits would cause a reduction in crime by at least 20 per cent; not only that, but there would also be cumulative effect on the generations to come, by diminishing poverty, improving home conditions and habits of living and environment, and perhaps even an improvement in heredity itself.

Alcohol may have its value. Brandy—a spoonful—may be given to a sick person to produce warmth in his body or to tone up his stomatch; but the point is that the ignorant may make an unreasonable use—and abuse—of alcohol, and instead of using it as a medicine (only at times) may use it for the intoxicating so-called pleasure derived from the use of it in large quantities. And, in practice, that really is the case; it was so before the introduction of prohibition in India.

The abuse of alcohol ultimately creates heavy damage to the body and mind. The cortex, which is "the seat of reason and judgment and self-control" is affected "earlier than the thalamus,[34] thus producing the factors of delinquency. The abuse of alcohol or the use of harmful drugs can be regarded as a powerful factor in the causation of criminality, insofar as it acts on temperament and creates susceptibilty, to crime. We hear of crimes committed under the direct influence of alcohol, and of crimes where the cause of crime is psychosis or some physical or mental defect caused by the abuse of alcohol or the use of objectionable drugs. Abstinence campaigns carried out efficiently and in the proper manner show how crime drops Dr. Healy cites Baer, who says that Father Matthew's abstinence campaigns in Ireland, during 1837-1842, reduced the use of spirits 50 per cent., and the crimes dropped from 64,520 to 47,027. According to Evangeline Booth, the Commander of the Salvation Army, "In New York before prohibition, the Salvation Army would collect from 1,200 to 1,300 drunkards in a single night and seek to reclaim them. Prohibition immediately reduced the gathering to 400, and the proportion of actual drunkards from 95 per cent to less than 20 per cent." And a decrease of two-thirds in the number of derelicts, coupled with a decrease in the number of drunkards almost to the vanishing point. certainly lightened crime and charity bills. It gave many of the erstwhile drunkards new hope and a new start. So says E. E. Covert, in an interesting article on

Prohibition.[35] And, in India, with the introduction of prohibition we find a good decline in crime. There are, however, some persons who cannot do without liquor. Such persons even go to the extent of making illicit liquor and do not mind drinking harmful rums and spirits. The result is starvation of children at home, assaults and quarrels between husband and wife, between father and child, desertion, and other evils resulting from the abuse of alcohol.

Delirium tremens may be caused by the protracted and inordinate use of alcohol or other ardent spirit. In delirium tremens there may be violent excitement or wild enthusiasm or mad rapture. According to Dr. Taylor, "When alcohol is habitually taken to excess there is liability to an attack of delirium tremens: (a) without other obvious cause than a bout of drink, or (b) on sudden deprivation of drink, or (c) on meeting with some shock or accident, or (d) on being attacked by some disease, e.g. pneumonia."[36] "Patients with delirium tremens are often violent, and prone to commit suicide or murder," continues Dr. Taylor.[37] For an act done by a person in delirium tremens he cannot, and should not, be held responsible. Even a temporary excess in the case of habitual drunkenness may bring on an attack of delirium tremens.[38]

Delirium tremens caused by alcohol or other spirit, though different from drunkenness, relieves the accused from liability, if it rendered him (even for a time) incapable of distinguishing right from wrong.[39] Though voluntary drunkenness is no excuse for the offence,[40] yet voluntary drunkenness which causes insanity is a good excuse.[41] An accused person is said to be insane when he does not, and cannot, understand the nature and quality of his act.[42]

[Small doses of the drug "Acth" has a remarkable sobering effect in cases of severe intoxication, and have a speedy effect in cases of delirium tremens. It is a good remedy.]

Where 'intention' on the part of the prisoner (accused) is an essential ingredient of an offence (such as murder) the fact of intoxication should certainly be taken into consideration, "the intention which would be ascribed to a sober man....must not necessarily be ascribed to an intoxicated man who does the same act. If the accused was so drunk as to be unable to form the intent to kill, the offence would be one of manslaughter, i.e., culpable homicide only (and not murder).[43]

In the matter of punishment, it should be remembered that intoxication forms a reasonably sufficient excuse for not imposing the extreme penalty prescribed by the law.[44]

Whether the offender was intoxicated at the time of the commission of the offence can be determined in a number of way. Some evidence of his behaviour, some overt act done by him, a record of his demeanour, or his handwriting tremors if he had written something at the time of the offence, or if he was arrested soon after the offence, a medical examination of his conditions a trace of alcohol somewhere would lead to a correct conclusion. And we have the "drunkometer" which (invented by Docter Horger of Indianapolis) can determine the presence of alcoholic element in the blood-stream and thus enable or fortify the conclusion that the person concerned was drunk. Such evidence can save an unfortunate man from the extreme penalities of the law and can go a great extent in protecting offenders who reach need protection. The apparatus can indeed be used to detect alcoholic condition and thus to prevent alcoholics from potential mischief.

The introduction of prohibition in India actually caused a considerable fall in the number of crimes caused by intoxication. Before prohibition, one often had to witness the miserable spectacle of poor and ignorant persons—millhands, labourers, and even the unemployed with starving families at home—frequenting the pithas (liquor and adulterated toddy shops) drinking burning and harmful spirits, and *adulterated* toddy which really had no vitamin B value; these persons spent the little they earned after a hard day's toil, or what little that had remained with them, or what they had obtained by some theft, trick, fraud or a borrowing; they spent away all that, and then, at home, left wife and children starving, and without proper clothes, education, and other elementary necessaries of life.

The Labour Welfare Departments of the State Governments and of the Municipalities are rendering valuable service, through their labour welfare officers who work at the centres assigned to them, impressing upon the people how the use of alcohol in ruinous and instructing them also how to live hygienically; there are lectures on the evils of drug and drink habits.

Partial prohibition of hot country liquors was introduced by the Congress

Ministries in Bombay, Bihar, Madras (in Salem, Chitoor, Cuddaph and North Arcot Districts) when they first came into power.[45] In C.P. and Berar, prohibition covered approximately one-fourth of the area and population of the State.[46] In Assam, prohibition is directed mainly against opium.[47] In Deccan Hyderabad, on 3rd January, 1943, a Firman was issued by His Exalted Highness the Nizam, supporting the temperance movement.[48] Jammu and Kashmir are also on the move towards prohibition. Since 1949 State Governments determined the policy of introduction of total prohibition.

On April 10, 1948 the Central Advisory Council for Railways, under the Chairmanship of the Hon'ble Dr. John Matthai, agreed to the proposal to ban the serving of liquor in refreshment rooms at Railway Stations and dining cars.

In Madras, prohibition was inaugurated on 2nd October, 1948, by the Premier, the Hon'ble Mr. O.P. Ramaswami Reddiar who pronounced it a red letter day.

In 1949, West Punjab took steps for the establishment of prohibition. In 1949, nearly half the area of the Central Provinces and Berar got dry, and it was proposed to enforce prohibition throughout the State.

In Bombay the Prohibition Bill was passed and became Act in 1949, and Bombay got dry by April 1950.

The number of offences under the Abkari Act is notoriously high. It shows the craving of some persons for liquor in spite of all good efforts of legal prohibition. The remedy lies in making prohibition successful of legal prohibition. The remedy lies in making prohibition successful *through education* (even at the school stage), suggestion, re-education.

Some persons are so heavily addicted that they cannot do without a bout of liquor once at least in twenty-four hours. Lack of a bout of liquor may cause such a person delirium tremens which may have some terrible consequence, for example, a brutal murder or a violent suicide. One cannot even by institutional treatment or by locking up such a person deprive, him of what he is so terribly craving for. A healer cannot expect the man to give up his deeply-set habit to be got rid off summarily or by coercion. Even a gradual improvement of a lasting character—psychologically well-set—is the proper remedy. One cannot expect, by law alone, (by coercion) to stamp out a habit of a long standing. Let the drink addict be first convinced about the evils of drinking. Even after that he will think of drinking. So an institutional treatment, or other type of attempt to cure the drunkard, must be of a psychological type. The force of law may do no more than repress; but repression may make the habit more confirmed and more deeply rooted. So the person concerned must be re-educated. The evil effects of the alcoholism must be so brought home to his mind that he gives his free consent to giving up liquor. But still if he cannot immediately act to his decision, he should be allowed to volutarily lesson, day by day, the quantity, till it comes to drinking nothing at all. He may be even allowed the smell of liquor, then by a steady (though even a slow) diminution, the addict may reach the stage at which he gets completely cured and rid of alcoholism. Total abstinence then may save him completely.

Morphine, Opium, Cocaine, Addiction

Unlike the use, for the purpose of stimulation, of alcohol or cocaine, morphine is used for the quieting effect ir can produce. Neuropathic persons and prostitutes and social failures generally use this drug. Long use of morphine results in mental weakness, loss of energy, loss of concentration, loss of self-control, and even paralysis of the will. Character deteriorates, and morbid impulses and hallucinations follow its continued use.

Cocaine, like alcohol, is a stimulant in the first instance, insofar as it increases nervous energy, but ultimately to find the victim a wreck. Cocaine delinquents are often found bold enough because of the use of cocaine, but after a time, when the use of cocaine is taken away in prison, they show the weakness of their mental condition. Criminals using cocaine are often very desperate type of criminals—ready to take life of the victims, even on the slightest provocation or resistance.

Use of Tobacco

Tobacco is a bad thing, particularly for young persons. Young persons becomes susceptible to delinquency by the use of tobacco. The use of tobacco soon causes an unstable nervous system, and may lead to delinquency.

In Bengal there is an Act preventing the use of tobacco by young persons. In Bombay, a police officer can prevent a young person or a juvenile smoking on the public road or in a street.

AVARICE: PRIME CAUSE

Avarice is a potent cause of sin and crime. The origin of sin can be traced to avarice; and it is avarice that has dragged, many to their damnation. When the spirit of greed exceeds its tolerable limits, there is great probability of a culmination in an anti-social act. Religions show how sin, and most misery consequential, originated in avarice. Zoroastrianism condemns avarice as satanic, and regards sin and crime as emanating from the Ahraman (the evil mind). In the Bhagavad Gita, Lord Krishna regards avarice as one of the gates of hell. Lust wrath and avarice are, says the Gita, the three gates of darkness, Islam preaches strongly agianst the spirit of avarice. Christianity regards avarice as the originator of sin—the cause of the fall of Lucifer. "How art thou fallen from heaven, O Lucifer, son of the morning! How art thou cut down to the ground, which did not weaken the nations! For thou has said in thine heart, I will ascend into heaven, I will exalt my throne above the stars of God: I will sit also on the mount of the congregation, in the sides of north; I will ascend above the heights of the clouds; I will be like the Most High."[49]

AVARICE, LACK OF REVERENCE AND THE RELIGION

Lack of reverence, and the substitution of religious beliefs and spirituality by "enlightened rationalism" can also be regarded as the factors responsible in the causation of wrongdoing and crime. Where the "nuddling intellect" has become the "supreme arbiter of man's fate," where man has lost belief in the Supreme Being, where man believes only in a material existence, where man is lured by the desire for power and the craving for possessions at all and any costs, where man has no belief in the exitence-to-come-hereafter, where man has forgotten completely his inner and finer being, where the true self is lost, and the longings of matter alone become conspicuously dominant in the desires of man, there is no wonder that there is, and would be, social disorganization and mal-adjustment leading to conflict of interests and crime. In his admirable work: "Modern Man in Search of a Soul," Dr. C. G. Jung says, "The modern man has lost all the metaphysical certainties of his mediaeval brother and set up in their place the ideals of material security, general welfare and humanness.

But it takes more than an ordinary dose of optimism to make it appear that these ideals are still unshaken. Material security, even has gone by the board, for the modern man begins to see that every step in material "progress" adds just so much force to the threat of a more stupendous catastrophe. The very picture terrorizes the imagination. What are we to imagine when cities to-day perfect measures of defence against poison-gas attacks and practise them in "dress rehearsals"? "We cannot but suppose that such attacks have been planned and provided for—again on the principle "in time of peace prepare for war". "Let man but accumulate his materials of destruction and the devil within him will soon he unable to resist putting them to their fated use."[50]

White-Collar Crime

What Professor Sutherland calls: The White-Collar Criminals,[51] is an *avaricious* person.[52] It is his *greed* that is the cause of his crime. White-collar crime is one of the worst types of anti-social conduct, and needs severe repression. Deterrent punishment is indeed desirable for prevention of white-collar crime. Those business-men who indulge in their dirty practices of making money at all costs, even at the risk of life of fellow-men, should not only be imprisoned for long terms so as to serve a lesson unto others dreaming of such acts, *but also their licences should be cancelled,* and, in less serious cases, suspended for sufficiently long periods.

Cause of War

Avarice leads not only to crime by individuals but also to what are known as "war crimes" by nations, the spirit of aggrandisement leading a nation prepared for war to pounce upon other nations and/or to keep other nations under unfair subjectivity. In the words of Dr. Radhakrishnan, "The necessary conditions for work union are available. Our planet has grown to small for parachial patriotism. A capitalist society, a militarist tradition and a world broken up into a number of independent sovereign States, which are greedy for power and domination, have brought about the present distress," and, we should say, the war crime. Narrowmindedness, selfishness and avarice—these have been the cause of man's decline from spiritual eminence to barbarous degradation and miserable decline.

On November 27, 1943, His Holiness the late Pope's letter, exhorting for peace in Europe, addressed to the Cardinal-Secretary of the Holy See, was reported by the Vatican radio. The text of the letter was as follows:

"Even if this gigantic conflict-certainly the greatest that the whole of history has ever witnessed—is daily raging with increasing violence and causing innumerable tragedies and ruin both on land, at sea and in air, we see with sadness that many are living forgetful of their personal duties to God. They ignore, sneer at and violate His holy laws. It is necessary, therefore, that all, through the medium of penitence and virtuous thoughts, turn again to God."[53]

Dr. Hermann Mannheim, writing on the social aspects of crime in England between the wars, points out the contrast between England and Germany. In Germany, he shows how a rapid deterioration, brought about by the military defeat, the inflation and consequent economic distress caused an increase of convictions for murder from 87 in 1918 to 243 in 1921 (1913: 110), for manslaughter from 91 to 383, for robbery from 316 to 1,789, for wounding from 29,000 to 45,000 for assault against officials from 3,000 to 15,000 in 1921 and 24,000 in 1923.[54] And as regards the causes of war, Dr. Hermann mentions the physical economic, social and psychological causes.[55]

The World requires a strong United Nations Organisation, an important function of which should be that of settlement of all disputes through an International Court of Justice. Fit terms of settlement should be capable of being dictated by such lawful authority.

If every child is taught to love his neighbour and to respect the rights of his fellows, there would not be that deplorable rushing of man against man or retaliation by.force. If the demon of destruction could be encaged, no longer would the happiness of man be shattered by any crime of an unjust war International tribunal, we earnestly hope, may succeed in taking the place of settlement of disputes between nations.

It is too much of self-love, self-esteem, self-regard, and it is the spirit of avarice, that can be regarded responsible for the calamity of war. Just for the sake of a little of material acquisition, a nation rushes at the throat of another nation, and humanity thus dehumanised loses every particle of its true value. The demon of destruction set loose causes revages. God feels sorry for what men on earth do, and the unheeding men not listening to the Voice of God, go on till their desire for destruction dooms them to damnation. Overestimation of one's own country and one's things and rights, coupled with the vice of avarice, standing at the substratum of sin, should be removed, and the spirit of brotherhood and universal love should be implanted, if the good of humanity is not to be an unachieved dream but an actual fulfilment. Nationalism and internationalism should go together, and due regard for others' lands, laws and rights should not be parted with. In short, there should be a world organisation for protection of rights of all nations in a just and charitable manner, free from any sense of hatred, oppression of mistrust. Universal regard and brotherhood should be regarded as a true solution.

Conflict and Crime

Conflict is another important factor in the causation of crime. Mental conflict may arise in a number of ways. It may be of the highest and best type, e.g., when the person concerned would not obey an unjust positive law. Such are the examples left to humanity by the prophets, saints, sages and martyrs in the cause of truth and love for humanity. In such cases the breach of the unjust or unethical law in an act of true courage and the fulfilment of the righteous purpose. Such conflict of ideals is the result of moral excellence, soul's loftiness and divinity.

REFERENCES

1. Healy, W.: *The Individual Delinquent*, p. 27.
2. *Ibid.*, p. 128
3. *Ibid.*, p. 226

4. *Ibid.*, p. 225
5. *Ibid.*, p. 231.
6. Podolsky, E. : The Chemical Brew of Criminal Behaviour, Journ. Cr. Law, Vol. 45, pp. 675-679, 1955.
7. Montagu, M. F.: The Biologist Looks at Crime, The Annals, Vol. 217, pp. 50, 51, 1941.
8. Healy, W.: The Individual Delinquent, p. 402.
9. *Ibid.*, p. 408.
10. McDougall, W.: *Social Psychology*, pp. 119, 120.
11. Healy, W. : *The Individual Delinquent*, pp. 456, 460-462.
12. *Ibid.*, p. 419.
13. In his excellent article : Mental Abnormality and Crime, Jehangir M. Sethna discusses the role of epilepsy in crime. He shows how 'automatism' in epilepsy can be a matter of complete excuse from criminality, on the ground that the person concerned could not have understood at all the nature and quality of his act (within the meaning of the M'Naghten rules). The fit of epilepsy, or the resulting amnesia, may deprive the person concerned of the cognitive and conative faculties. He points out how in an epileptic fit, the psychomotor attack causes automatism. He cites Sullivan who has reported how a woman, while cutting bread, got a vertiginous attack, and as the result of automatism, continued the cutting movements and cut the arm of her child, hardly realising what she was doing. It was really not her act. The psychomotor attack, he says, was responsible for what happened. Jehangir Sethna further points out how sleep-walking is often associated with nocturnal epilepsy. The person concerned may, in such a state, be legally insane, as held also in Re Papathi Ammal (A.I.R. 1959 Mad., at p. 241), by Ramaswami J. who said: "...somnambulism, if proved, will constitute that unconsciousness of mind, attracting the application of section 84 of the Indian Penal Code. (Sethna, Jehangir M.:

Mental Abnormality and Crime, p. 245, published in Contributions to Synthetic Jurisprudence, 1962, N. M. Tripathi Pvt. Ltd., Bombay.) See also : Morgan, J. and Lovell, G. D.: The Psychology of Abnormal People, 1953, p. 466, where they show how *amnesia* may follow an epileptic delirium which may cause a clouding of consciousness. They mention the case of a boy involved in burglaries found asleep in the very factory he had broken into, and without any recollection of what he had done or what had happend. The boy was often found wandering away at night involving himself in burglaries of which he did not remember anything. A case of amnesia following epileptic delirium.

14. Berg, C.: Clinical Psychology, 1948, p. 305. See also: Sargant and Slater : An Introduction to Physical Methods of Treatment in Psychiatry, p. 75; cited by Berg, C. *Ibid.*, p. 305.

15. Drawin: Origin of Emotions, pp. 290-292; cited by Professor William James in his ''*Principles of Psychology*'', Vol. 2, at p. 446.

16. Elwin, V.: *Maria Murder and Suicide*, pp. 65, 66.

17. Healy, W.: *The Individual Delinquent*, p. 393.

18. Ellis, H.: *The Criminal*, pp. 329-333.

19. McDougall, W.: *Abnormal Psychology*, pp. 327-330.

20. McDougall, W.: *Abnormal Psychology*, pp. 327-330.

21. Ellis H.: *Studies in the Psychology of Sex*, Vol. VII, p. 477.

22. Rouke, F. L.: J. Soc. Therapy, Vol. I, 1955, p. 95. See also:

Morgan, J. and Lcvell, G.D.: The Psychology of Abnormal People, 1951, p. 513. Professors Morgan and Lovell regard kleptomania as definitely the result of an irresistible impulse to steal. See also Healy, W.: Mental Conflicts and Misconduct, 1923. Dr. Healy considers kleptomania to be the result of some mental conflict. Professor Bridges is of the opinion that kleptomania may involve an uncontrollable impulse to steal. Really the presence of the *uncontrollable* (and not merely uncontrolled) impulse is essential, if a ground of defence of mental abnormality is to be successfully pleaded. See Bridges, Psychology, Normal and Abnormal. There is another group of shop-lifters who, according to Rouke, after strained relations at home with their parents leave their home and take to stealing, for being caught and punished and these for disgracing their parents. For a discussion on such shop-lifters, see Rouke, F.L.: J. Soc. Therapy, Vol. I, 1955, p. 95, et seq.

23. Sethna, J. M.: Mental Abnormality and Crime, pp. 257, 258; Contributions to Synthetic Jurisprudence, 1962. Tripathi, Bombay.

24. Janet: Kelptomania and Mental Depression, Journal die Psychologie Normale et Pathologique, No. 2, March-April, 1911; cited by Dr. William Healy, in his "*Individual Delinquent*, p. 772.

25. Healy, W.: *The Individual Delinquent*, p. 772.

26. Schlapp, M. and Smith, E.H.: The New Criminology, 1928, p. 72.

27. *Ibid.*, p. 218.

28. Healy, W.: *The Individual Delinquent*, p. 774.

29. Morgan, J. and Lovell, G. D.: The Psychology of Abnormal People, 1953, p. 514.

30. Sethna, Jehangir M.: Mental Abnormality and Crime, p. 258, in Contributions to Synthetic Jurisprudence, 1962; N.M. Tripathi Pvt. Ltd.

31. Sethna, Jehangir M.: Mental Abnormality and Crime, p. 255.

32. *Ibid.*, p. 255; also p. 256.

33. Bacon has said: "All the crimes on earth do not destroy so many of the human race, nor alienate so much property, as

drunkenness.''

34. Craig, R. N. and Ors.: *Mental Abnormality and Crime*, p. 165. Article by Dr. G. M. Scott.

35. Cited by E. E. Covert, in an article entitled: ''Did Prohibition really Prohibit? America's Experience'', published in The Oriental Watchman (September, 1944), at p. 4.

36. Taylor, A. S.: *Medical Jurisprudence*, p. 831.

37. Taylor, A. S.: *Medical Jurisprudence*, pp. 831, 832.

38. Mody, J. P. : *Medical Jurisprudence, & Toxicology*, p. 674.

39. Re Davis, 1881, 14 Cox, 563; Emperor v. Bheleka Aham, 1902, 29 Cal. 493.

40. Section 85 of the India Penal Code.

41. Section 84 of the Indian Penal Code.

42. Regina v. Daniel M'Naghten, Law Reports (1843) 4 State Tribes p. 847.; Emperor v. Bheleka Aham, 1902, 29 Cal. 493.

43. 39 Cr. L. J. 689.

44. 1917, Punjab Record No. 28 of 1917.

45. *Social Reform Annual*, 1943, pp. 20-23.

46. *Ibid.*, p. 25.

47. *Ibid.*, pp. 28-30.

48. *Ibid.*, p. 31.

49. Isaiah 14 : 12-14

50. Jung C.: *Modern Man in Search of a Soul*, pp. 235, 236.

51. Sutherland: *Crime and Business, The Annals*, 112, 1941.

52. Sutherland: Is '*White-Collar Crime*' Crime?

53. Reuter; Reported in the Bombay Chronicle of 29th

November, 1943; *Times of India*, 29th November, 1943.

54. Mannheim, H.: *Social Aspects of Crime in England between the Wars*, p. 105.

55. Mannheim, H.: *War and Crime*, pp. 22-61.

4

ORGANISED CRIME: INTERNATIONAL APPROACHES AND NORMS

The theme of the Fifth United Nations Congress on the Prevention of Crime and the Treatment of Offenders having been established as crime prevention and control—the challenge of the last quarter of the century, the programme had been structured in such a manner as to provide the Committee on Crime Prevention and Control with the largest possible amount of information and the largest number of findings and suggestions on the basis of which it could prepare its report on the methods and ways likely to be most effective in preventing crime and improving the treatment of offenders, including recommendations on the measures most appropriate in such areas as law enforcement, judicial procedures and correctional practices (see General Assembly resolution 3021 (XXVII), para 8), commonly referred to as the international plan of action, which was intended to guide the crime prevention policies of the United Nations and of the States Members through the remainder of the twentieth century.

The Congress considered the scope of action to be undertaken at various levels, including the international, regional and national, and also, particularly under items 5, 6 and 9 of the agenda, raised issues and made recommendations cutting across the various aspects of criminal justice and having broader policy and planning implications. The following recommendations, listed under respective agenda items, merit the special attention of the Committee on Crime Prevention and Control for action.

CHANGES IN FORMS AND DIMENSIONS OF CRIMINALITY TRANSNATIONAL AND NATIONAL

Crime as business: organized crime, white-collar crime and corruption

In its recommendation on the issue or crime as business the Congress called, *inter alia*, for the provision of more information about economic criminality and for special studies on such issues as corruption and smuggling, in view of the extremely detrimental effect of such practices on national economic and international trade, particularly in developing countries; legislation against national and transnational abuses of economic power in the exercise of commercial activity by national and transational enterprises; greater participation of shareholders in the affairs of major corporations or of workers in public enterprises; the estblishment of national securities and exchange commissions or other administrative bodies and possibly the establishment of a similar body at the international level.

Offences Involving Works of Art and Other Cultural Property

The Congress stressed the need for better exchange of information concerning the protection of cultural objects, including particulars of national legislation designed to facilitate recovery of property which had been the object of illicit traffic and to deal effectively with those who engage in theft or destruction of cultural property. Such protection might be effected through the imposition of licensing requirements for auctioneers and dealers in antiques and the possible development of a code of ethics for professional art dealers. On the international level, the Congress called for wider ratification, acceptance or adherence to the 1970 Convention on the Means of Prohibiting and Preventing the Illicit Import, Export and Transfer of Ownership of Cultural Property.

Criminality Associated with Alcoholism and Drug Abuse

The Congress selected the following priority areas for consideration with a view to appropriate action:

(a) With respect to illicit traffic, (1) the drafting of an international convention on judicial assistance and the improvement of extradition procedures at both the bilateral and multilateral levels by reviewing and amending existing extradition treaties or the conclusion of new ones which would include drug offences as extraditable offences, and the possible elaboration of an international convention in that respect; (2) consideration of illicit traffic in drugs as a transnational crime, to be included in a list of transnational crimes to be drawn up by the United Nations; (3) ensuring, in conformity with national legislation, that drug offenders, having been convicted in one country but having escaped, served the sentence in the country in which they had taken refuge or were found, if extradition were not feasible; (4) the sharing of all knowledge in the law enforcement field and exchange of relevant information, in particular concerning new methods and routes used by illicit traffickers; (5) improvement of the mechanisms for expeditiously disseminating and receiving evidence concerning drug offenders; (6) strengthening of all forms of border control; (7) ensuring, by whatever possible means, that convicted traffickers might not take refuge in other countries; (8) the desirability of increasing penalties for illicit traffickers and of decreasing penalties of users or possessors of small quantities of drugs for personal use if a Government considered use and/or possession as punishable offences; (9) the possible destruction of seized drugs and relevant material connected with illicit activities and not needed for legitimate purposes under strict supervision; and (10) ensuring that any national drug policy—such as decriminalization of activities concerning *cannabis sativa*—did not adversely affect the drug control situation in neighbouring countries and at the international level;

(b) With respect to drug abuse, the Congress held that since it formed part of the general public health problem, preference should be given to measures of treatment and social reintegration of drug abusers and addicts, and that penal measures, if not excluded, should in no way prevent the application of these measures and should be restricted to ensuring their application, if appropriate;

(c) With regard to preventive measures, the Congress stressed that those were to be preferred, including the provision of meaningful and suitable information to those responsible for dealing with population groups most at risk. Such action should include the preparation and distribution of appropriate educational material and leisure-time programmes for juveniles.

Interpersonal Violence

The Congress adopted the following conclusions and recommendations in regard to interpersonal violence.

(a) The increase in violent behaviour should be analysed in the broader context of the social, economic and political problems facing contemporary communities in many parts of the world;

(b) Research should be initiated to ascertain whether there is a relation between development and violent crime. Special attention should be paid to such effects as might be produced by the rapid social change taking place in various countries, the disintergration of traditional community rules and values, the discrimination against particular ethnic groups, the decline in opportunities for constructive adjustment to the social environment and, in general, the shortcomings of economic and general structures;

(c) Special attention should be paid to the factors contributing to the violent behaviour of many young people in various parts of the world. In particular it would be well to consider how far violent behaviour in its myriad manifestations reflected a failure or absence of national youth policies. It was deemed particularly desirable to examine how far the interests and anxieties of young people were taken into consideration and met by the social policy in force and what real share they have had in the adoption of decisions designed to solve major national problems;

(d) The problem of violent behaviour, because of the damage and anxiety it causes, should receive priority consideration in the formulation and application of national policies of crime prevention. In particular, every effort should be made to prevent the development of social conditions conducive to violence. The family, the educational system, community organisations and the mass communication media should take a more effective part in that work of prevention.

Violence of Transnational and Comparative International Significance

It was suggested that acts currently described as "terrorism" or as "terrorist" in nature could be classified into three types: firstly, act committed by an individual in an international situation, for instance the unlawful interference with an aircraft in flight, whether intended for personal gain or because of psychopathology; secondly, acts similar to the first but committed by groups; thirdly, acts which appeared similar to the first two but which were committed to further not the private ends of the actors but some cause to which they felt committed. It was also suggested that acts of legitimate resistance against occupation should not be regarded as terrorism. The need for a clear-cut definition of terrorism was emphasized by those participants who wished to distinguish between transnational violence of an extended but essentially criminal type and the operation of national liberation organisations. In such a definition they wished to make the motivation of the actor the crucial distinguishing element. The concern of others were with the innocence of victims who often had no connexion with the parties in the struggle as the primary distinguishing factor.

The participants were agreed on the need for international and multilateral action to rid the world of all forms of international violence; but there was also agreement that politically inspired violence, committed for the sake of gaining national independence or ethnic recognition or security, could not be expected to recede until the underlying causes had been satisfactory dealt with.

In addition, there was agreement that measures should be studied with a view to strengthening the forces of criminal justice against the first two types of terrorism by: (a) extending universal jurisdiction to all such crimes (as already existed in the case of air piracy)—for example, the taking of innocent persons as hostages and attacks against public buildings with explosives—especially if those crimes endangered the lives of innocent persons; (b) stengthening extradition laws and observing them more completely; and (c) strengthening the technical co-operation of agencies such as the International Criminal Police Organization (INTERPOL) by increasing both the number of nations participating and the mutual exchange of information. It was proposed, furthermore, that the United Nations should arrange for a commentary on all relevant international conventions, which would ensure that all were fully understood and their scientific and legal validity clarified.

Criminality Related to Motorized Traffic

The discussion on criminality related to motorized traffic led to conclusions and recommendations in two main categories. With regard to the criminal justice system, it was recommended that—(a) minor traffic offences should be decriminalized or at least dealt with in a simplified manner; (b) the police should be relieved of the duty of controlling parking and of related tasks in order to enable them to concentrate their efforts on serious and dangerous offences, and that they should make greater use of technological aids; (c) traffic law enforcement should not be obstructed by national boundaries; (d) sentencing practices should be standardized to reflect the reality of international mass travel; (e) national criminal judgements should be valid in other countries whenever procedures might be transferred on the basis of treaties and conventions; and (f) short-term imprisonment should be avoided as far as possible and, in line with the urgent need for alternatives, unconventional methods should be developed.

Outside the criminal justice system, (a) diversified driver-education programmes should be organised; (b) manufacturers of motor vehicles should improve existing safety features and develop new ones, the use of safety devices should be encouraged and expanded, and legislation to make this compulsory might be considered, taking into account different experiences in various countries; (c) effective speed limits should be observed; (d) more complete examinations should be given in granting drivers' licenses, particularly with reference to psychological factors; and (e) periodic inspections of vehicles should be instituted.

Criminality Associated with Migration and Flight from Natural Disasters and Hostilities

It was recommended that (a) the United Nations consider offering migrants international travel documents for the period during which their status was being considered by national authorities, in order to allay the suspicions about political motivations, that sometimes attach to internationally active social welfare agencies; (b) consideration be given to the establishment of an international agency of world-wide competence to deal with immigrant workers and to the elaboration of a charter for such workers; (c) the labour legislation of countries with immigrant labour be revised whenever appropriate; (d) the international machinery to assist refugees and disaster victims should be strengthened; and (e) representatives of migrant worker groups be brought into the public administration, especially in the area of law enforcement, of the host communities in which they are employed, wherever feasible. There was a consensus that the best way to eradicate criminality associated with migrants and refugees was to develop social, educational and health services rather than stricter law enforcement, and it was suggested that in developing countries voluntary welfare agencies could supplement governmental resources in short supply.

Female Criminality

In order to remove the issue of female criminality from the realm of guesswork and to engage in successful social defence planning, the Congress agreed that all States should be invited to inform the United Nations, through the national correspondents, of developments pertaining to female criminality and of the success of failure of their counter-measures.

The Congress also considered it necessary that controlled scientifc studies be undertaken on the interelations among socio-economic development, the integration of women into national economic life and female criminality, noting that such studies should focus on comparisons of countries with different experiences and trends in female criminality and on the causes and extent of differential treatment of women by the criminal justice system, as well as on experiences in dealing with the pre-delinquent and delinquent behaviour of women and children outside the criminal justice system.

Forecasting of Crime and Crime Control Problems

The Congress deemed it essential to provide for the exchange of information among countries as to possible future conditions relating to crime and called upon the United Nations to provide leadership in setting up international collaborative machinery, which was to include the beginnings of a unified statistical data base. While recognizing that the technical, definitional and scientific problems involved were considerable, the Congress also recognized that since worthwhile forecasting was dependent upon the establishment of a scientifically sound research and data base, collaboration between national research bodies had to begin right away and immediate help made available to developing countries lacking the necessary resources.

CRIMINAL LEGISLATION, JUDICIAL PROCEDURES AND OTHER FORMS OF SOCIAL CONTROL IN THE PREVENTION OF CRIME

While the debate on the various forms of social control used in the prevention of crime revealed that while differences in traditions, economic and political structures, available resources and levels of development made it pointless to try to dictate a preventive policy applicable to all countries, certain common aspirations nevertheless emerged, which were embodied in the following conclusions and recommendations:

(a) Social justice being the best means of preventing crime, greater emphasis should be placed on social action than on criminal proceedings;

(b) Historically speaking, there had been an abuse of the principle of repression without according sufficient attention to forms on non-penal social control and means of primary prevention;

(c) All countries should strive constantly to re-evaluate their criminal justice systems in order to adapt them to current social needs.

That implied the replacement of laws and institutions which either were not indigenous or had become antiquated;

(d) Changes of penal systems and the practical application of their proceedings must always respect the human rights and fundamental freedoms of all persons involved;

(e) More frequent recourse should be had to the community for support of programmes of crime prevention and care of offenders;

(f) The many aspects of criminal policy should be co-ordinated and the whole should be integrated into the general social policy of each country;

(g) Criminological research providing the scientific basis for crime prevention policy should be extended to cover the interaction between delinquency and society, as well as the functioning of the judicial system and of community programmes of social control;

(h) Victim compensation schemes could serve as a useful substitute for retributive criminal justice;

(i) The training of judges in the art of sentencing was a prerequisite to the development of sentences that provided an alternative to imprisonment or fines;

(j) The United Nations had a special role to play in providing useful information and technical assistance to countries desirous of rationalizing and socializing their criminal policies, and in the promotion of the needed reforms.

EMERGING ROLES OF THE POLICE AND OTHER LAW ENFORCEMENT AGENCIES, WITH SPECIAL REFERENCES TO CHANGING EXPECTATIONS AND MINIMUM STANDARDS OF PERFORMANCE

In addition to calling for the elaboration of an international code of conduct for law enforcement officials, the Congress adopted a number of specific and more general conclusions and recommendations on the roles of the police and other law enforcement agencies. The participants agreed that:

(a) The United Nations should establish an international police academy, the facilities of which would be available to all nations, and which would concentrate on the preventive role of the police in crime control;

(b) Out-dated treaties relating to extradition and the gathering of evidence concerning criminal offences should be reviewed and new ones ratified to cope more effectively with contemporary criminality;

(c) International police co-operation should be strengthened and extended.

(d) Despite major differences in the structure and rationale of the world's police services there was common ground on which fruitful co-operation could be based;

(e) The police should be answerable to the laws of their respective countries;

(f) Integrity was the first quality required in police and other law enforcement officers;

(g) Police training should include the subjects of ethics, human rights and social science;

(h) Police were themselves part of the community whose support was indispensable to effective policing;

(i) Whenever possible, women should be employed as police officers on equal terms with men;

(j) Private security organizations should be subjected to a measure of public control;

(k) The police should participate in the preparation of legislation which would affect police functions.

TREATMENT OF OFFENDERS IN CUSTODY OR IN THE COMMUNITY, WITH SPECIAL REFERENCE TO THE IMPLEMENTATION OF THE STANDARD MINIMUM RULES FOR THE TREATMENT OF PRISONERS

In addition to the adoption of the anti-torture Declaration the following conclusions and recommendations were agreed upon:

(a) The use of imprisonment should be restricted to those offenders who needed to be neutralized in the interest of public safety and for the protection of society;

(b) A broad range of supporting after-care services and greater community involvement in facilitating the reintegration of the offender into the community should be provided for;

(c) A general reassessment of the purposes as well as the effectiveness of correctional systems was needed, along with special analytical studies under United Nations auspices to assess the effectiveness of various forms of imprisonment;

(d) The Standard Minimum Rules for the Treatment of Prisoners should not be subtantively revised, but consideration should be given to the need for revising specific rules to assure that they are not in conflict with correctional policies and practices;

(e) A suitable commentary on the Rules should be drafted with special attention to regional considerations and cultural factors, and an easily understandable brochure should also be prepared;

(f) More vigorous efforts should be undertaken to assure the dissemination of the Rules in line with the draft procedures outlined in Annex III of the working paper on the treatment of offenders.

(g) The United Nations, through appropriate bodies and agencies, should strongly encourage the full implementation of the Standard Minimum Rules throughout the world and offer assistance in this respect to countries requesting it;

(h) There was need to strengthen inmate grievance procedures through provisions for recourse to an independent authority such as an *ombudsman*;

(i) The United Nations should give serious consideration to the need for a continuing mechanism for the implementation of the rights of prisoners—for example, through the establishment of a sub-committee of the Committee on Crime Prevention and Control—but particularly through the continuation of the services of the Working Group of Experts on the Standard Minimum Rules or through the creation of a new committee on the treatment of prisoners;

(j) In order to facilitate the return to their domicile of persons serving sentences in foreign countries, policies and practices should be developed by utilizing regional co-operation and starting with bilateral arrangements;

(k) The United Nations should develop new rules for the treatment of offenders in the community, a task which could be undertaken in two phases—the first would concern itself with the articulation of principles and standards for programmes that are an alternative to imprisonment, while the second might address itself to guidelines concerning the content of the programmes.

ECONOMIC AND SOCIAL CONSEQUENCES OF CRIME; NEW CHALLENGES FOR RESEARCH AND PLANNING

The Congress recommended that, in the interest of promoting more equitable and effective systems of criminal justice, a wider range of economic and social factors must be considered. Planners, researchers and those concerned with criminal justice policies and administration should;

(a) Encourage cost-benefit thinking, if not cost-benefit research, with the understanding that economic costs were only a part of the measurable cost along the whole continuum of social cost and that cost-benefit thinking, supplemented by simple research and comparative analysis, could provide crucial information on directional changes, which for some purposes would be sufficient for policy-making;

(b) Promote the development of the indigenous criminal justice research capability to directly serve the needs of policy-makers, planners and administrators;

(c) Promote the use of extra-governmental institutions, including universities and their students, as a research resource, particularly in a developmental context, through collaboration, financial support and the articulation of research needs;

(d) Promote the development of interdisciplinary research

agencies for criminal justice and the organisation of interdisciplinary workshops at the national, regional and interregional levels;

(e) Promote the collection and analysis of data for policy-making purposes, using simple, cheap and effective techniques of assessment, particularly by building in an evaluation component in pilot or demonstration projects;

(f) Encourage simple research techniques for conducting problem-solving or action-research appropriate in particular national settings in order to avoid repeating the mistakes of some developed countries;

(g) Encourage the writing of research reports in clear, concise language and in a form easily understood by administrators;

(h) Encourage the use of victimization surveys and crime damage statistics to complement the development of comprehensive criminal justice statistics;

(i) Develop greater awareness of the significance of economic crimes, particularly of corruption and damage to the environment within a developmental context, and of the effects of such crimes on the development process;

(j) Develop the means to predict changes in the types of crimes resulting from the interplay of criminogenic factors which might appear in some stages or processes of development and as a result of actions or policies of agencies outside of the criminal justice system;

(k) While recognizing the development model as one of the possible means of identifying and analysing criminogenic factors, consider other models as a basis for interpreting criminogenic factors and initiating crime preventive activities.

(l) Promote research leading to a more equitable distribution of the costs and consequences of crime among different segments of society;

(m) Incorporate dynamic crime prevention planning of a comprehensive and special nature within the framework of national planning, with emphasis on the interdependence of crime and crime control activities with all other planning sectors;

(n) Further the co-ordination, as a smoothly working system, of the various agencies for preventing crime within countries, through the use of major structural reforms where necessary;

(o) Promote the maximization of individual freedom within the necessary constraints of effective crime control consistent with national policies;

(p) Promote the recognition of the fact that perhaps a substantial amount of crime was provoked by the nature of the social and economic structure and system of society itself, as well as by official action or negligence, and that effective crime control measures should be geared to changes in official actions as well as individual behaviour;

(q) Through the use of improved educational programmes and the mass communication media, promote a better understanding on the part of the public of the economic and social consequences of crime; narrow the gap between the perceptions of personnel working within criminal justice agencies and the general public, and further more active participation of the public in the prevention of criminality.

At the international level, the Congress called for:

(a) The inclusion of cost data in the reports on world crime trends, to the extent possible;

(b) The exchange of experts and experience between countries, with particular regard to regional and subregional needs;

(c) The convening of conferences, expert group meetings, seminars and workshops concerned with the assessment, minimization and redistribution of the costs of crime;

(d) The provision by the United Nations, within existing resources or from extra-budgetary funds, of technical assistance and training in order to encourage the use of cost-benefit analysis and systems analysis and other comprehensive comparative planning and evaluation techniques, as well as the collection and dissemination of information and reports using such techniques for crime control and prevention;

(e) The provision of United Nations assistance to national criminal justice programmes not only by specialized criminological services within the Organization but also by its regional planning institutes, public administration programmes, statistical services and the like;

(f) The Governments concerned and the United Nations to consider the early establishment of regional research facilities for crime prevention and the promotion of criminal justice in Africa, as well as in other areas where there was need, and the strengthening of the role of existing regional institutes in promoting research and training as a basis for policy-making and planning for crime prevention and criminal justice.

RULES OF PROCEDURE

The Congress, acting on a proposal by the representative of Czechoslovakia involving extensive amendments to provisional rules of procedure, decided to recommend that the Committee on Crime Prevention and Control review the rules of procedure of the Congress with a view to bringing them into conformity with current practice in other United Nations bodies.

COMMISSION FOR SOCIAL DEVELOPMENT

The conclusions and recommendations of the Congress will be submitted to the Commission for Social Development at its twenty-fifth session, in January 1977, together with the observations thereon and proposals of the Committee on Crime Prevention and Control.

THE COMMISSION ON NARCOTIC DRUGS AND THE INTERNATIONAL NARCOTICS CONTROL BOARD

In its resolution 1584 (L), the Economic and Social Council decided that the Committee on Crime Prevention and Control, in addition to reporting to the Commission for Social Development, should report as appropriate, on particular aspects, to the Commission on Narcotic Drugs. The attention of the Commission and of the International Narcotics Control Board (INCB) is drawn to the conclusions and recommendations of the Congress concerning criminality associated with alcoholism and drug abuse. In addition, the

Congress urged intensified international drug control, calling on Governments, if they had not yet done so, to adhere to the Single Convention on Narcotic Drugs of 1961 and the 1972 Protocol amending that convention, as well as the 1971 convention on Psychotropic Substances. They were also urged to coperate with the United Nations Fund for Drug Abuse Control in order to enable the United Nations to provide technical and financial assistance to Governments requiring it, in particular to Governments of those countries in which raw materials for narcotic drugs were produced, in order to enable them to carry out the provisions of international drug control treaties and to fight effectively against drug abuse problems and related criminality. The Commission on Narcotic Drugs and INCB may wish to consider the scope of co-operation of the Committee on Crime Prevention and Control in the areas emphasized.

THE STATISTICAL COMMISSION

The attention of the Statistical Commission is drawn to the recommendations of the Congress pertaining to the establishment of a viable statistical data base in the crime field to permit the development of more scientific policies based on the current situation and on forcasts; the use of techniques such as victimization studies and crime damage data to reveal the real extent and impact of crime; and the inclusion of cost data in crime reporting. The Commission may wish to indicate modalities for responding to the call for the establishment of collaborative arrangements to promote progress in that area and for the provision of immediate help to developing countries lacking the necessary resources in that respect.

THE COMMISSION ON HUMAN RIGHTS

Economic and Social Council resolution 1584 (L) also provided that the Committee on Crime Prevention and Control would report, as appropriate on particular aspects, to the Commission on Human Rights. The attention of the Commission is drawn, accordingly, to the conclusions and recommendations of the Congress relating to criminal legislation, judicial procedures and other forms of social control in the prevention of crime; the emerging roles of the police and other law enforcement agencies, with special reference to changing expectations and minimum standards of performance; and the treatment of offenders, in custody and in the community, with special reference to the implementation of the Standard Minimum Rules for the Treatment of Prisoners. More particularly, at the thirty-second session, in pursuance of General Assembly resolution 3453 (XXX), in considering the question of torture and other cruel, inhuman or degrading treatment or punishment, the Commission will be able to draw on the work of the Congress in this regard, as well as on the follow-up to its recommendations on the code of conduct for law enforcement officials. The Commission's attention is also drawn to the recommendations of the Congress concerning criminality associated with migration, in connexion with the implementation of General Assembly resolution 3449 (XXX) concerning measures to ensure the human rights and dignity of all migrant workers.

THE COMMISSION ON TRANSNATIONAL CORPORATION

The attention of the Commission on Transnational Corporations is drawn to the conclusions and recommendations of the Congress on the issue of crime as business: organised crime, white-collar crime and corruption. The Commission may wish to consider, in connexion with the implementation of General Assembly resolution 3514 (XXX) and the Declaration and Programme of Action on the Establishment of a New International Economic Order (General Assembly resolutions 3201 and 3202 (S-VI), the modalities of co-operation with the Committee on Crime Prevention and Control which would prove most useful.

THE COMMISSION ON THE STATUS OF WOMEN

The attention of the Commission on the Status of Women is drawn to the conclusions and recommendations of the Congress relating to female criminality, particularly in the context of the United Nations Decade for Women and the World Plan of Action for the

Implementation of the Objectives of the International Women's Year (General Assembly resolution 3250 (XXX)).

THE OFFICE OF THE UNITED NATIONS HIGH COMMISSION FOR REFUGEES AND THE OFFICE OF THE UNITED NATIONS DISASTER RELIEF CO-ORDINATOR

The recommendations of the Congress concerning criminality associated with migration and flight from natural disasters and hostilities are brought to the attention of the above-mentioned Offices.

THE UNITED NATIONS REGIONAL COMMISSIONS AND INSTITUTES

The attention of the regional commissions, the regional planning institutes and the crime prevention institutes is drawn to the conclusions and recommendations of the Congress, particularly to those contained in paragraphs and foregoing.

THE UNITED NATIONS DEVELOPMENT PROGRAMME

The Congress repeatedly stressed the need to strengthen United Nations technical assistance in the field of crime prevention and control, particularly in areas such as criminal legislation and judicial procedures, the implementation of the United Nations Standard Minimum Rules for the Treatment of Prisoners, the use of cost-benfit analysis and systems analysis and other comprehensive planning and evaluation techniques applied to crime prevention and criminal justice, and the like.

As noted above, the Congress also urged the exchange of experts and experience between countries in that field, with particular regard to regional and subregional needs, and called for the convening of conferences, expert group meetings, seminars and workshops concerned with the assessment, minimization and redistribution of the costs of crime. It also called for the strengthening of regional crime prevention training and research facilities and the establishment of new ones, as appropriate

THE INTERNATIONAL CIVIL AVIATION ORGANISATION

The conclusions and recommendations of the Congress on violence of transnational and comparative international significance, including the problem of air piracy are brought to the attention of the International Civil Aviation Organisation, particularly the recommendation that the United Nations arrange for a commentary on all relevant international conventions in order to ensure that all were fully understood and that their scientific and legal validity were clarified.

THE INTERNATIONAL LABOUR ORGANISATION

The conclusions of the Congress concerning criminality associated with migration, especially the recommendations concerning immigrant labour, are brought to the attention of the International Labour Organisation.

THE UNITED NATIONS EDUCATIONAL, SCIENTIFIC AND CULTURAL ORGANISATION

The attention of the United Nations Educational, Scientific and Cultural Organisation is drawn to the conclusions and recommendations of the Congress relating to offences involving works of art and other cultural property and to those concerning drug education. Furthermore, in its consideration of the problem of interpersonal violence and possible preventive measures, the Congress recommended that "the cultural organisations of the United Nations should explore proposals for an international convention providing minimum guidelines for the content of mass media intended for consumption by children or young persons, where needed, to avoid negative impact on behaviour patterns."

THE WORLD HEALTH ORGANISATION

The conclusions and recommendations of the Congress, concerning criminality associated with alcoholism and drug abuse, particularly those concerning the treatment of drug addicts and drug abusers are brought to the attention of the World Health Organisation. The attention of WHO is also drawn to the recommendations of the Congress concerning the treatment of offenders, in custody or in the community, with special reference to the implementation of the Standard Minimum Rules for the Treatment of Prisoners in pursuance of paragraph 4 of General Assembly resolution 3453 (XXX), in which the World Health Organisation was invited to give further attention to the study and elaboration of principles of medical ethics relevant to the protection of persons subjected to any form of detention or imprisonment against torture and other cruel, inhuman or degrading treatment or punishment.

5

CRIME AND POLICE ORGANISATION: AN OVERVIEW

In the past, police departments have been run by the rule-of-thumb method in which problems and issues were encountered and solved by a method which may accurately be referred to as "muddling through." Over the years, however, the law enforcement task has become too dynamic, complex, and essential to the very survival of an entire society to be administered by incompetent executives using hit-or-miss methods. Therefore, certain rules have been promulgated to insure that police departments will be organised and administered along lines consistent with principles of sound management. It must be stated initially that the most important factor in police administration is the selection of a chief administrator with the education, training, experience, competence, and courage to fulfil his role as top executive. Without a chief executive with talent and vision, little else will matter. It is the purpose of this chapter to give students of the discipline an insight into the administrative elements that go into the making of superior police departments.

Leadership in Law Enforcement

There are several categories of leadership in any sizable police agency, each requiring categories very specific talents. However, before examining these levels of leadership, one would do well to look at the general functions of police leadership. In any summary of the traits of leadership, the following should be possessed or acquired through a combination of education and experience before a person is allowed to ascend to a role of leadership in an agency:

1. Decisiveness—the knack of being able to make forthright decisions.
2. Judgment—the ability to weigh alternate courses of action.
3. Drive—vigor, enthusiam, and the ability to inspire action in others.
4. Vision—the faculty for long-range and broad perception.

In police departments, leadership is situational, i.e., its requirements vary in time and place due to the nature of the police task. Different leadership behaviour patterns are called for in differing situations, making it essential that men chosen for promotion are men who can adapt to a constantly fluid environment. Furthermore, the day of the old-line leader who rules by fiat is passing from the scene. In his place is appearing a "new breed" leader who places an emphasis on administrative skill and who believes in concepts such as shared decision-making, interpersonal relations, compromise, and persuasion. In this context the prime leadership strategy is manipulation rather than command.

Police leadership is divided into three broad categories: top management, middle management, and the first-line supervision. Each category requires different personal qualities.

Top Management

Top management in a police department consists of the chief and his immediate subordinates (generally deputy or assistant chiefs, inspectors, or majors). Top managers determine policy, direct programme execution, harmonize varying viewpoints, coordinate the processes of administration, and are responsible for the attainment of the department's goals. Probably no department head in government is delegated the authority and responsibility of top police managers, so it is absolutely essential that they possess qualities befitting their position. According to Professor Roscoe Martin, top managers must have the following qualities:

1. The faculty of generalising or abstracting general rules from analysis of large quantities of data.
2. High intelligence combined with imagination and willingness to accept new ideas.
3. Determination to operate at their own levels and to delegate performance of operational level to others.
4. Capacity of dealing with other men and judging them correctly.
5. Willingness to accept responsibility for important decisions.
6. Skill in communication and negotiation.
7. Orientation toward public service.

Top managers must delegate certain tasks to others; however, there are some functions that they cannot delegate. These are the fiscal function (deciding on what funds the agency needs to operate and how should be distributed), the personnel function (measuring the personnel needed by the department and assigning manpower on some logical basis), and the planning function (approving, modifying, or rejecting future programmes).

The environmental conditions of a large police agency require that top managers be generalists who can view their department and its programs as a whole, rather than specialists who see the institutional enterprise in the narrow perspective of particular functional duties. A police officer who is promoted to a top management position after long service in one assignment may not bring to his new job the generalist's view that is needed. To preclude this problem, many police departments regularly reassign their personnel to prepare them for future executive duties.

The essence of high-level leadership is influencing the actions of people. To influence people top managers must know and understand the general theories of human motivation, for men and women are not stamped from a single mold. An understanding of the needs of human personality can go a long way toward helping top managers bring their agencies closer to the citizenry, as well as lessing the chances of internal rank-and-file militancy.

Middle Management

Middle managers (usually captains and lieutenants) primarily function to activate the department's policies by adapting the organisation to particular tasks, by meshing personnel with methods and procedures, by maintaining operational control, and by setting standards and reviewing accomplishments. Simply stated, middle management directs the agency's operations. Although policy is made by top management, middle managers translate it into action.

Middle managers must possess great skill in devising specific work programmes that will blend with the total departmental programme. It is this level of management, more than any other, that will determine whether the police department operates as a functional system or as a group of semirelated divisions working at cross-purposes. It is essential that middle managers have a flair for organising and the capacity to inspire group loyalty.

First-line Supervision

First-line supervisors are those leaders who operate at the performance level. Usually uniformed sergeants, first-line supervisors are the ones who actually oversee the work of line officers. Their counterparts in industry are foremen. Their duties include devising work plans, laying out beat assignments, training and evaluating those they supervise, maintaining records, developing team spirit, presenting departmental policy to patrolmen, and cooperating with managers above them and with other supervisors. First-line supervisors must possess a good deal of technical competence and be thoroughly familiar with line tasks. In fact, a major portion of a promotional examination for sergeant is designed to measure technical ability. Only master patrolmen should be considered for promotion, and even then the final weeding out process, if undertaken properly, will eliminate most of them.

A recurring problem in police management, one that will never be completely resolved, is the failure of sergeants to view themselves as part of management's team, rather than just promoted patrolmen. Sergeants are so close to the action and emotions of everyday police work that they often find it difficult to identify with the administrative hierarchy, especially when they have worked for years with the partrolmen they are assigned to supervise. The protective instinct that results from supervising men who risk their lives daily often outweighs the tenets of sound management, however well-trained the sergeant may be. In this regard, one of the most valuable supervisory traits may be the capacity to switch roles, to "wear two hats" as some scholars have put it. As the most direct management link with uniformed patrolmen, sergeants have an incredibly important function, one which, if not propertly fulfilled, can mean failure for the department in eliminating goal impediments. Current research indicates that there is a direct correlation between small-group efficiency and the quality of supervision. Police squads have higher morale, greater effectiveness, and better production records when the first-line supervisor is liked and respected by his subordinates. As planner, coordinater, team leader, and management representative, the supervisor must possess more than the ordinary dynamic traits and should excel the average squad patrolman in intelligence, dependability, and intellectual integrity.

Some Organisational Principles

Contemporary police theorists have attempted to formulate organisational principles flexible enough to apply to all law enforcement agencies. The final test of whether or not organisational rules are correct is if they contribute in some way to the accomplishment of the police task. Apparently, no single "right" form of organisation has yet been devised, but in order to insure a healthy agency, certain administrative postulates should be adopted by chief executives desirous of professionalizing their departments. The following organisational principles reflect current scholarly thought on the subject of sound management:

1. Personnel performing similar duties should be grouped together to ensure more effective productivity.
2. The department's major divisions should be established according to the functions for which they will be

responsible, i.e., bureau of investigation, bureau of administration, bureau of operations, etc.

3. The responsibilities to be performed by each manager or unit should be defined in as clear an definite a manner as possible. Furthermore, two managers or two units should not be assigned the same duties, because such duplication produces confusion and makes it difficult to hold either fully responsible for performance.

4. No person should ordinarily have to task orders from more than one supervisor.

5. When responsibility for a task is assigned, corresponding authority should also be delegated. It is best not to accept responsibility for a mission unless it is coupled with the authority to act with some discretion.

6. Administrators should always have a means at their control whereby they can check on the quality of their agency's work.

7. A manager should have under him and reporting to him only that number of subordinates that he is capable of adequately supervising. His span of control should not be overextended.

8. The department's positions should be set up in accordance with the various classes of work to be accomplished, rather than being related to particular men and women. The demands of the work, rather than personal considerations, should determine the number and types of positions in the department.

9. The organisation of the department and its operating policies should be delineated in writing and disseminated to all members of the agency.

10. There should be a recognised chain of command, and the lines of authority should be as clear and direct as possible.

11. The department's enterprise should be fully coordinated.

Organisational Clarification

Internal conflicts often develop in police departments becasue personnel do not fully understand their duties and the assignments of others. Regardless of how well conceived the structure of an organisation is, if employees do not fully comprehend their roles in it, it will not work. Two administrative devices are used to see to it that personnel are informed of their functions in the agency: organisation charts and position descriptions.

Organisation Charts

There are a number of types of organisation charts, each serving a specific need; however, no purpose would be served by introducing them in this section, so only a brief, general explanation of the broad concept of charting will be given.

There can be no acceptable reason for a sizable department not to chart its organisation. Charts map lines of authority and point up organisational inconsistencies. They avoid conflict by clarification and serve as aids in orienting new employees to their jobs. According to the International City Management Association (ICMA), an organisation chart is a pictorial representation of personnel distributions. Manager— subordinate relations do not exist because of organisational charts, but they are strengthened because of charting, for uncertain decision-making often results when officers do not know how they tie into the entire structure. Yet, as invaluable as charts are, they have limitations: (1) They point out formal authority relationships, but they do not show how much authority exists at each point in the organisation; (2) they omit, by necessity, unofficial or informal relationships; and (3) charts often depict organisation as they are supposed to be, rather than as they are.

Position Descriptions

Each position in a police department, especially managerial positions, should be specifically defined in a position description, although not in minute detail. Basic job functions and the relationship to other officers are generally included in the description. A good position description will inform a new jobholder what he is supposed to do, to whom he reports, and who reports to him. There is no need for each uniformed patrolman in a police department to have a position description, but the general position of patrol officer should have one. In departments that have a civil service system, it is not generally necessary for an agency to have position descriptions as such, because jobs are classified into civil service classes to which descriptions are attached.

Duties of Identification Officers*

a. A member of the identification section shall become proficient in the science and techniques of fingerprinting and photography and the collection, preservation, and presentation in court of all physical evidence, including trace evidence.

b. The identification technician shall have the duty of searching crime scenes for physical evidence in conformity with the established and approved procedures set forth by recognised authorities.

c. He shall process all evidence brought to the section, classify fingerprints, search the files when necessary, and file all fingerprint records and photographs. He shall photograph and process persons taken into custody by the members of the department and shall take such other photographs as required by the commanding officer.

d. He shall preserve the chain of custody of evidence by issuing or receiving a receipt whenever evidence is received or transferred to another.

e. He shall assist investigating officers in identifying, marking, preserving, and packaging all physical evidence further processing or analysis by another laboratory and shall assist in any other way possible.

---

*A typical position description.

f. He shall conduct only authorized searches of the various files maintained by the section, and he is prohibited from divulging information to persons other than those authorised by the commanding officer.

g. A member of the section shall keep himself informed of all improved scientific methods and investigative techniques with regard to police identification and laboratory procedures.

h. He shall conduct such examinations and identification processes of all firearms involved in the commission of criminal acts as directed by the commanding officer.

The Administrative Processes

Probably the most clear-cut defintion of the term ''administrative process'' was given by the ICMA, which defined it is ''those interrelated means employed on a continuing basis by which an administrator achieves his organisational goals and objectives.'' The kinds of actions covered by this definition may number several score, or more. It is generally thought that there are five major processes that universally apply to police departments: planning, organising, staffing and assembling resources, direction, and control. Again, it should be emphasised that these processes are all interrelated.

Planning

Planning is the process of deciding on the objectives of a police department and then programming the efforts to accomplish those objectives. Planning is the first step which must be taken by an administrator in preparing for action because it is the process of formulating goals toward which the department's resources will be directed. Since the planning phase is such an important one, it is one element that the chief of police must personally spend a good deal of time thinking about. In his planning activities, the chief performs the significant function of applying foresight to his department's activities.

Planning may either be long- or short-ranged in nature, and it should relate to both policy and programming. Broad policy planning must be followed up with programme planning in which the more specific steps toward long-range goals are taken and actual work plans are laid out. Accordingly, there are three basic steps in planning: (1) formulation of objectives, (2) assessment of the means that can be assembled to achieve the objectives, and (3) the careful preparation of work programmes devised to accomplish the objectives.

Public administrator H.S. Person views planning as a continuing process concerned with dynamic situations and as a method for keeping to a minimum the frictions, confusions, and losses resulting from variability. Person has formulated eight postulates of planning:

1. The foundation of good planning is the laying out of the goals in as clear-cut and comprehensive a manner as possible by those possessing this authority.
2. The formulation of broad policies governing achievement of objectives must be undertaken.
3. It is essential that there be joint analysis by top management of alternative means and methods by which objectives can be accomplished.
4. A major step in planning is the setting up of an organisation within which administrators can divide up the different functions, all of which together will amount to a synthesis of effort by all organisational segments.
5. After the initial synthesis comes further detailed examinations of ways and means which will result in specifying the work flow.
6. Particular duties must be assigned to specific personnel and units in order to translate procedure into action.
7. A sense of responsibility for performing the various tasks must be infused into the organisation so that work is undertaken pursuant to prescribed procedure, not according to individual whim.

8. Work measurement should be provided for so that the operations of various subdivisions and the results of their efforts can be examined with some precision.

Organising

Organising (as a process) is the method by which group activity is structured and authority relationships are formalised. The logic behind organising is that departmental objectives will not be met unless the total resources of an agency are arranged and utilized in a way that is consistent with efficiency and economy. Police work is a fluid task with, for example, crime patterns constantly changing. Police administrators must look on organizing as an "action process" by which the dynamic internal and external environment with which they must grapple may be properly handled, even under constantly changing conditions.

Staffing and Assembling Resources

The assembling of men and materials to successfully complete the police task is high-priority process. A certain amount of money is allotted to police departments each year to perform rather specific functions. It is critical that these tax dollars be used in such a way that waste is minimized. Only those programmes that are necessary to the public safety should be created, and glamorous and frivolous equipment should not be purchased. In lean budget years essential programmes may have to be cut back, but even then some system of priorities must be established to ensure that the most-needed programs are kept alive. As far as manpower is concerned, the same principle applies. Personnel who have received specialized education or training (e.g., at Northwestern Traffic Institute or Southern Police Institute, or an advanced academic degree) should be assigned to those units where they can best put their knowledge to work.

Direction

The function of direction is to get employees to fulfil their duties. Direction involves working relationships at each departmental level, but it especially concerns commanding officers, whose job it is to guide the departmental on a true course. Orders are important in directing subordinates. A police department's orders may be either oral or written, although written orders are generally preferred. Written orders may be transmitted in a number of ways, including (1) training bulletins explaining departmental procedure in specific field situations (e.g., use of the long baton), (2) general orders describing permanent departmental policies (e.g., internal investigation procedures), (3) special orders appyling to ad hoc incidents (e.g., traffic assignments at a parade), (4) personnel orders notifying members in changes of status (e.g., transfers, promotions, disciplinary action), and (5) memos directing operational changes.

Control

Control is a managerial function which measures and corrects the performance of subordinates. According to Henri Fayol, the father of modern management theory, control "consists of verifying whether everything occurs in conformity with the plan adopted, the instructions issued, and principles established." There are certain systematic ways in which chief executives exert staff control over their departments. The most popular method, at least in large departments, is the creation of a special unit to inspect departmental operations on a continuing basis. Even similar departments often either assign one man to the job or place in the job description of a middle manager the authority and responsibility to perform that task.

Police Policymaking

In 1967 the Presidents's Commission on Law Enforcement took the nation's police chiefs to task for failing to assume the role of major policy-makers. From an administrative standpoint, no more serious charge can be made against a chief executive than that of shirking his decisions-making function, which is exactly what the Commission was referring to. There were reasons for this widespread failure, none of which is tenable; however, there is nothing to be gained here by a discussion of past neglect. Many, though not nearly all, departments have since corrected this weakness.

Sound policy has six essential characteristics:

1. It is based on clearly defined objectives.
2. It is as simple as possible.
3. It establishes standards.
4. It is flexible.
5. It is well-balanced.
6. It uses available resources before creating new authority and new resources.

Volumes have been written on the art of policy-making, so it is impossible to do little more than introduce some of the basic ideas relating to the subject. Accordingly, the following are some propositions regarding the making and expressing of policy:

1. Vagueness about general policy objectives renders administration almost ineffectual.
2. Basic policy statements should permit middle managers and field supervisors to act freely within broad limitations.
3. Policy-making is a continuous, cumulative, and collective process, widely diffused throughout a police department.
4. A police chief in his policy-making role is as dependent on middle managers and first-line supervisors as they are on him.
5. Sound policy can be made only on the basis of adequate information, detailed analysis, and careful research.
6. Nothing is more destructive of confidence in an agency and internal morale than policies which cannot be relied upon.
7. It is not enough for administrators to simply approve policy; they must also express it clearly and impart it throughout the police department.
8. Policies should generally be in writing.
9. Highly competent administrators will anticipate needed policy changes and keep policies up to date.

Communication in Police Administration

The element of communication, which may be defined as the functional process by which personnel from top to bottom of the administrative pyramid are kept informed, is inextricably bound up with every task in a police department. Communication brings understanding and dispels ignorance. When officers understand what they are doing and why, they are more productive. Conveying information from top management down is only part of the communication process; its essence is the will to listen and take in the interests and concern of personnel throughout the agency. This kind of reverse, or upward, communication is called feedback. Communication may be formal, i.e., a planned system of procedures and channels flowing along lines of formal authority with the object of transmitting information to all levels of the department, or it may be informal, i.e., a web of interpersonal contracts and personal relations which serves as a transmitting device for information. Police managers will never be able to eliminate the latter type, so they often learn to use it to the department's advantage.

One of the principal obstacles to communication is gobbledygook or "bureaucratic officialese"—language which becomes meaningless because of its officiousness, abstractness, and impersonalisation. The classic example of this problem, often quoted by public administrators, is the case of the San Francisco plumber who wrote the Bureau of Standards to ask if it was permissible to use hydrochloric acid to clean drains. Replied the Bureau: "The efficacy of hydrochloric acid is indisputable, but the chlorine residue is incompatible with metallic permanence." The plumber replied that he was happy the Bureau agreed the acid was a good drain cleaner. The Bureau wrote again: "We cannot assume responsibility for the production of toxic and noxious residues with hydrochloric acid, and we suggest you use an alternative." The plumber wrote back that he was happy the Bureau still agreed with him. Whereupon, the Bureau frantically replied: "Don't use hydrochloric acid: it eats hell out of the pipes!"

6

CRIMINAL REFORM AND SOCIAL DEFENCE

The non-responsible cannot be punished, but there must be some protective measures, e.g. segregation. While, as Saleilles of France says, responsibility is the basis of punishment, individualisation is the criterion of its application. In Italy, the Penal Code requires that the Court should exercise its discretion, in dealing with offenders; with the aid of knowledge of psychology and sociology there can be a determination of the mental condition and character of the accused at the time he committed the offence. The Spanish, the Roumanian, the Czechoslovakian, the Serb-Croat-Slovenian and the Polish Codes also combine measures of safety and prevention with those of punishment. Austria, Switzerland, Sweden and Denmark have also such Codes. As Saleilles observes: "The eyes of justice have too long been bandaged and prevented from seeing the position of her scales; and this has given rise to many an injustice. The bandage must be removed." The character of the offender must be carefully analysed, considered and valued, and the offender dealt with accordingly.

The Russian Code claims to have replaced punishment by measures of safety and security. The word 'penal' is abolished from the Code. Dr. Sen, however, considers that a linguistic accident. He considers the juridical guarantees against excessive application of measures of security as far from being substantial in the Soviet Code. The measures of social defence, under the Russian Code, are of three kinds; viz., Medico-pedegogic, Medical, and Judicial-correctional. The medico-pedagogic measures are applied to minors; the measures involve tutelage, internment in a medical educational institution. For the mentally deranged, there are medical measures. Judicial correctional measures are meant for adults (and not for young persons under 14 years of age, unless young person between 14 and 16 years of age are found unfit for the medico-pedagogic measures). The judicial-correctional measures include: warning, admonition, fine, payment of compensation to the aggrieved admonition, fine, payment of compensation to the aggrieved party (this indeed is a very worthy measure, for it recognises the importance of compensation), proclamation of the offender as an enemy of the proletarit, deprivation of citizenship, expulsion, hard labour without detention, imprisonment in a cell, loss of political and certain civil rights, and confiscation of property. Death penalty (by shooting) was used only for elimination of exceptionally dangerous persons. But in May 1947, the Supreme Soviet issued a decree abolishing death sentence in the Soviet Union during peace-time. For crimes for which death sentence had existed the penalty now is hard labour for 25 years.

In its application of measures of protection, the Russian Code empowers judges to take into consideration the character and antecedents of the offender.

Fellow-Workers' Courts, in Russia, were started in 1959, for maintaining labour discipline, trying minor offences and correcting anti-social behaviour such as drunkenness. These Courts are public bodies, elected at meetings in factories, offices, educational institutions, and collective farms. The object behind their establishment is that of correcting offenders through public influence.

Fellow-Workers' Courts hear cases concerning violation of labour discipline, unlawful use of materials, equipments and transport facilities, where there was not much damage to the State or to public organisations. Parasitic mode of life, evasion of socially useful labour, failure in dutifully bringing up children, petty speculation, property disputes where the amount involved does not exceed five hundred roubles, and other disputes upto one thousand roubles with the consent of both litigants, are also matters within the jurisdiction of these Courts.

Fellow-Workers' Courts may punish offenders by fining them upto one hundred roubles, or by public apology or public censure. The offender may merely be warned in a friendly way and let off.

Fellow-Workers' Courts are undoubtedly a worthy institution and deserve to be emulated by other countries. An offender finds himself judged, in the real sense, by fellow workers who hear the case very patiently and attempt to lead the offender away from crime by public influence.

In America the Massachusetts Reformatory System provides individualised treatment of offenders. Visits to the home, the place of work, and the school or schools attended by the offender, from part of the investigations into the antecedents of the offender. All available information is put before the official psychiatrist who then examines the individual offender. Since behviour the result of mental life, and since mental condition depends upon the development of personality traits, individualization for diagnosis and treatment are of the highest importance.

The American psychiatric-psychological examination at the Massachusetts Reformatory is followed by suggestions as to methods of mental and physical hygiene necessary for the offender's self-re-education. In the course of the psychiatric-psychological examination, specialised mental efficiency tests, ethical determination tests and an analysis of the offender's personality traits are hold.[1] And the American Elmira Reformatory is a monumental illustration of individualisation of treatment.

In England, today, individualization of treatment is the basic principle of prison management. And as persons skilled in psychology and sociology are appointed to offices in the prisons, good progress has been achieved. The judges, before sentencing offenders, inquire into their character and antecedents, as the law allows that and vests in them discretion in the matter.

In India, the taking into consideration the character and antecedents and age of the offender and releasing him on probation of good conduct are provided for by the Probation of Offenders Act.

Under the Probation of Offenders Act, 1958, the Court may release an offender after admonition or on probation of good conduct[2] and under the care of probation officers. Probation officers are brought on the scene even with regard to adult offenders, and that is a very desirable improvement. We suggest that, in proper cases, when released on probation, adult offenders should be kept under the supervision of probation officers, so as to guard against recidivism. It is not use merely releasing an offender without supervision; there must be some friend and guide to help him abstaining from crime.

We need a good development of the system of individualisation of offenders and punishment. There should be a wider exercise by the Courts of their powers to release on probation, and there should be investigation by probation officers or by police officers (who must be trained in social welfare work), as to the antecedents of every accused person brought before the Court, so that the information may be utilised while passing, sentence or orders. And there should be scientific methods employed in our prisons.

As Professor Vinogradoff, in his "Historical Jurisprudence", says, the judge "stands to the offender in the position of the physician who selects his remedy after diagnosing the disease and the resources of the patient's organisation."

HISTORY OF PUNISHMENT

From Primitive Times Onwards

In primitive society when a crime was committed, the aggreived party was the individual harmed and/or his relatives. There were blood-feuds. If a member of a tribe was harmed by a member of another tribe, there was a war, so to say, between the parties. But in course of time blood-feuds were found disastrous to the parties. To avoid blood-feuds between the offender's group or tribe and the aggrieved person's group, what is known as 'wergild' was made payable to the aggrieved party, or his relatives, as compensation for the injury suffered. Generally speaking, there was a traditional tariff schedule, describing the different payments to be made for different kinds of offences. There was a complicated scheme of fines for the adjustment of all sorts of difficulties. The practice of the Chukchi was that of more readily accepting wergild in lieu of inflicting personal chastisement for minor transgressions than in cases of murder. In many places even felonies were compounded in the interests of the public peace.[3] A murderer could atone for his crime by giving feasts and articles for the deceased victims's relatives. According to the Samoan treatment of murder and adultery, the wrongdoer atoned for his crime by giving articles and gifts to the aggrieved party or his relatives and throwing himself at their mercy; generally, that succeeded well.

In ancient times, in Europe as also in India, punishments were very severe. It was Beccaria, who, in Europe, by his "Crimes and Punishments," advocated that by justice was meant nothing more than the bond necessary for keeping the interests of individuals united, and that punishments which exceeded the necessity of preserving that bond were in their nature unjust. Till the advent of the Neo-Classical School, the Penal Codes were based mainly on the doctrine of deterrence and repression of crime. Punishment was proportionate to the gravity of the offence, and no regard was entertained for the offender himself. At times the offender met his fate in the same way as his victim. In ancient systems of punishment, elimination of the offender from society by exile or outlawry was not uncommon. According to Aschaffenburg, it is the stigmatising of certain acts and/or omissions as offences the commission of which would be met with severe punishment that deters people who would otherwise be inclined to commit such acts or omissions. General prevention is educative and deterrent.

Among the punishments of the past rank the following:

The rack, the wheel, strangulation, burning alive, boiling in oil, flogging with the cat-o'-nine, mutilation, branding, pillory, galley, torturing in heavy irons and maddening shackles, incarceration in dungeons.

In their much illuminating works, Dr. Fredrick Wines and Dr. Theodor Hampe, give complete accounts of the various punishments of the past. Dr. Wines[4] and Dr. Hampe[5] very well describe the various cruel punishments, of old times, inflicted on men and women alike-even children often left unspared. The various illustrations, given by Dr. Hampe, especially the one of his book, showing the most terrible and cruel methods of execution, and showing the pains of the Stocks, are sufficient to tear one's heart out. One wonders today, how the society then tolerated such cruel punishments of a useless type. And in a work entitled: Chinese Punishments: A Collection of 24 Chinese Drawings depicting various Chinese punishments, the various forms of Chinese punishments, are depicted. Those punishments (as are depicted by those drawings) are savage, harmful and useless indeed. Beheading by the axe, execution by strangulation, putting the prisoner in tormenting instruments, chaining him in the neck and in the legs also—these are some of the punishments of the past.

The death penalty was imposed for several kinds of robberies, and thefts, and in spite of such severity, crime showed no decline—thus showing how crime cannot be repressed by desperate punishments.

Among those who had the honour of advocating and working for penal reform were: Tarde and La Crasserie in France; Liszt in Germany; Lucchini, Lombroso, Ferri, Garofalo in Italy; Van Hamel in Holland; John Howard and Elizabeth Fry in England; Stoos in Switzerland; Prins in Belgium; Drill in Russia; Basia in Greece; Mendes Martins in Portugal; Pope Clement XI in Rome; Obermaier in Bavaria; Montesinos in Spain; Maconochie in Australia; and Sir Walter Crofton in Ireland.

About 1875, Colonel Montesinos, of the Valencia prison, had established his semi-reformatory regime with good results upon the 1500 men under his care; reports of his system reached. America also. The success of Obermaier, Governor of the Kaiserslautern prison in Bavaria, and of the remarkable Irish prison system inaugurated by Sir Walter Crofton, greatly influenced America and England.

The Declaration of the Rights of Man, and the Decree of January 21, 1790, marked a new era. Only acts causing substantial injury were considered crimes. The law revised the inflicting of punishments, and only such punishments as were then considered necessary were allowed or recognised by the State. Mutilation became illegal. The individual was no longer left sacrificed to the injured party or his relatives but was dealt with by the State alone. The principle of reformation came to the recognised. Even before the birth of modern criminology, Karl Roder (1806-1879) had first voiced the idea of aiming at the reform of the criminal as a part of the tutelary function of the State.

The German School of Reformers headed by Professor Von Liszt devised a 'double entry' system whereby the traditional methods were kept for habituals, and the preventive methods for occasional offenders. The views of this School of Reform have been expressed in the resolutions arrived at by the International Union of Criminal Law which assembled in 1889. Since 1846, there have been numerous conferences of prison officials in America and in Europe. The first International Congress for prison reform was held in Frankfort, and has, since 1872, been held every five years. In Cincinnati, in 1870, a conference was held under the leadership of Dr. Wines, Theodore Dwight, Rutherford B. Hayes, F. B. Sanborn and Zenos R. Brockway. And this group formed utlimately the American Prison Association, at New York, and affirmed the Declaration of Principles as relavant to modern criminology.

The Declaration of Principles lays down the following, among other, essential principles of criminology:

(1) Crime involves an intentional breach of duty imposed by the law, so as to render injury to some person or persons. And a criminal is a person who is convicted of crime by a Court having the necessary jurisdiction. For the crime committed, society inflicts punishments on the criminal, with a view that such treatment may reform him.

(2) The treatment of criminals by society should be directed more to the criminal than to the crime, and its great object is the moral regeneration, not degeneration, of the criminal. Such treatment of criminals protects society and restores criminals.

(3) There must be progressive classification of prisoners, based on character and some properly adjusted mark system.

(4) Since hope is effective and fear useless and harmful as the instrument of correction, prisoners should not be coerced but should be treated properly, so as not to deprive them of their spirit of hope; for this reason there should be a good system of rewards given to prisoners for good conduct, industry and attention. Rewards, more than punishment, are needed for the efficiency of a prison system.

(5) Prison environment should be such as enables the prisoner to improve his lot, through his own exertions. He must be taught the value of self-help and the blessings of work.

(6) The prison or reformatory officers must be persons who are worthy of handling criminals in a proper and humanitarian manner. They must be well-versed in social sevice, work, and must have good qualities of head and heart. There must be special courses of study and training for persons desiring to become prison officials.

(7) Instead of peremptory sentences there should be indeterminate sentences.

(8) Of all reformatory agencies, religion is first in importance, because it is most potent in its effect upon the human heart and life.

(9) Education is a vital force in the reformation of persons who have gone astray. It develops the intellect, moulds and enriches the sentiments and raises the moral attitude of the offender.

(10) If reformation of the prisoner is to be successfully atttained, the prison system should be such as enables the gaining of the prisoner's co-operation and goodwill.

(11) The interests of society ought not to conflict with the legitimate interests of the prisoner; the criminal must be won over.

(12) Greatest care must be taken to ensure the cultivation of the prisoner's self-respect.

(13) Instead of coercion there should be organised persuasion, the object being to train the prisoners to be honest and independent freemen rather than to make them remain and behave as orderly and obedient prisoners doing everything only under the repressive force of an artificially stubborn or meaningless prison discipline. Moral training and persuasion should take the place of all coercive punishments.

(14) There should be classification of prisoners and prisons also.

(15) Repeated be short-term sentences for persons guilty of minor offences are worse than useless, for they rather stimulate crime, insofar as they can have no reformative value, nor any deterrent value. Reformation requires time; sometimes much time. So the sentence must be long enough to enable the prison authorities to bring about reformation of prisoners in their care.

(16) For children, treatment should be in preventive institutions

and industrial or other certified schools.

(17) There should be systematic and comprehensive methods for aiding released prisoners.

(18) Whenever injustice has been done by imprisonment of an innocent person, it is the duty of the State, on proof of his mistake, to award reasonable compensation for such wrongful imprisonment and not to take cover under the cloak of an official act.

(19) Society should do everything substantial to prevent crime.

The abovementioned conclusions, arrived at the Conference of 1870, are of paramount importance in our appreciation of the fundamental principles of criminology; these should be adopted in every country.

We have also the School of Penology, known as the Radical School, which advocated humanitarian principles to be applied to criminals, in an extreme form. That School is against all sorts of reaction against criminals and advocates cure by persuasion. Solveiff, a leader of the Radical School, advocates brotherly treatment of the criminal, who is as much to be pitied as the victim of the offence.

Crime and Punishment in India from Pre-Buddhist Time Till the Nineteenth Century

In Pre-Buddhist India, administration of justice was one of the primary functions of the State. Justice was administered with due deliberation. Punishment was awarded with careful measure (nisamma) in proportion to the nature of the offence. But on the whole, the judicial arrangements were not quite sound.

The King was the head of justice. As a rule, he heard cases, each morning, at the Court House. In his absence a minister heard the cases. Some of the judgments—the judgments which were considered righteous and meritorious—were inscribed on golden plates; and the rest of the judgments were published. Precedents or judge-made law thus grew up, though cases were often decided according to the personal views of the judges.

Theft and robbery were very common. Methods of torture were employed with a view to eliciting confessions. Some of the punishments were meaningless, but a desirable factor going with punishment was that of compensation of the aggrieved party so as to bring him to status quo.

Trial by ordeal does not, in the Pre-Buddhist period, appear to be a prevalent system, though there appears to have been the ordeal by fire by which a woman could prove her chastity. For offences generally, the State did not support the system of trials by ordeal. Drunkenness was punished with heavy fines. Slander was punished with a fine of eight Kahapanas. Adultery in woman was punished very heavily; even death of mutilation was imposed. The main types of punishment were: fines, whipping, imprisonment, mutilation, confiscation and banishment. Thieves and robbers were whipped very severely. Executions were terrible.

The idea behind the severe punishments that prevailed in early times and in the middle ages was that of preventing crime.

In ancient India, during the Epic Age, there were the Dharma Castras (law books) and Dharma-pathakas (law professors). Manu was, as shown by Brehaspati, the greatest law giver of ancient India, and his Manava Dharma Castra is the most important law book in ancient India. The Dharma Sutras emanated from Vedic Schools, and, therefore, on the whole, the law books at first represented certain schools of Brahmanical teaching. The law-books of Vishnu and of Yajnavalkya are exponents of Yajurveda school; and the works of this class lose all connexion with any one school and become unviersally authroitative. Later legal works were Dharma Nibandhas, of the eleventh century and later, and the learned commentaries, like the Mitakshara.[6] The Manava Dharma Castra was followed by the work of Vishnu in the third century, A.D., and the law code of Yajnavalkya in the 4th century and the Code of Narada in the 5th century.

Distinction between civil and criminal law then came to be made. The first enumeration of legal titles is found in Manu and is as follows: (1) Recovery of debts; (2) Deposit and pledges; (3) Sale; (4) Partnership; (5) Resumption of gifts; (6) Non-payment of wages; (7) Breach of contract; (8) Annulling of sale and purchase; (9) Disputes regarding cattle; (10) Disputes regarding boundaries; (11) Assault; (12) Defamation; (13) Theft; (14) Robbery; (15) Adultery; (16) Duties of man and wife; (17) Partition; (18) Gambling and betting. In this category, criminal law is shown in the titles eleven to fifteen and eighteen. Probably theft ws the first crime to be recognised legally.[7]

The Sutras show that the judge originally was the King. The thief, or the criminal, was brought before the King for being dealt with. Theft, especially, theft of cattle, and robbery are regarded, in the Vedas, as the chief crimes. According to Brehaspati, there were different kinds of theft. He treats theft as a form of violence. Violence according to him is of four kinds—homicide, theft, assault on another's wife, and injury (either assault or abuse). Thieves are also classified into different kinds, viz., 'open thieves' and 'concealed thieves'; and according to their skill and methods they are further classified. Trials were by ordeal. Manu recognised only two types of ordeals. Later writers introduced additional types. Ordeal by oath was given effect to. A farmer could swear by his cattle. One could swear and say that a thing was truly as he deposed; if his house then was burnt up within a week, it could mean that he had perjured himself. The two earliest ordeals recognised by Manu are fire and water. Then came elaborate trials with the use of the balance, etc. till eventually there were nine formal ordeals. Those nine ordeals were: (1) by fire, (2) by water, (3) the balance, (4) the sacred libation, (5) ploughshare, (6) the ordeal by dharma, (7) by grains of rice, (8) by hot gold piece, and (9) by poison. The heated gold is reserved for cases of theft; the ploughshare for those accused of theft of cattle. Originally ordeal by fire meant walking through fire; and ordeal by water meant that the accused was thrown into water, and if he was not drowned he was held innocent. In the ordeal by fire one had to carry a hot iron ball, and if he remained unburned he was held innocent. In the ordeal by water the accused had to plunge under water and had to remain in as long as it took for a dart; if he could do that, he was found innocent. The ordeal by balance lay in weighing the accused twice. If he weighted more the second time, then he was found guilty, because the weight of sin went against him. And the ordeal by Dharma and Adharma lay in painting pictures of Justice (Right) and Injustice (Wrong) upon two leaves (one picture painted white and the other black). The leaves were then, unobserved by the accused, rolled in balls of earth and set in a jar. The accused was then asked to draw one of these balls. If he drew Dharma he was held innocent; if he drew Adharma he was found guilty and punished.[8]

For murder, the offender had to render compensation to the relatives of the deceased or to the King or to both. Later this compensation was made in favour of the priests; a hundred cows had to be handed over. In the Sutra period, compensation was treated as a 'royal right.' In the time of Manu, compensation was regarded as a penance; hence it was renderable in favour of the priests. Treason was punishable with death. Punishing a person by making him an outcast (thereby causing him loss of social right) was also resorted to, especially in the case of the priests.

Excepting cases of treason, differential treatment existed. The social condition of the victim of the offence was also considered while considering the question of punishment. Slaves, however, were punished with undue severity. When a priest was defamed by a warrior, the latter was fined one hundred panas; if a non-warrior (of the people-caste) did so, the penalty was one hundred and fifty panas; but for a slave there was corporal punishment for defamation of a priest. Adultery was, in legal theory, punishable by death, but in practice, male offenders were fined, and female offenders were liable to have their hair cut off and treated with contempt; but a slave guilty of adultery with a high-caste lady could be slain. If a Vaisya man committed adultery with a high-caste lady, his property could be forfeited.

The King tried cases personally or by a priest. He was the source of pardon also. Even a murderer could, except under the later law, expiate his crime by fighting in a battle and risking his life for the sake of the King; if he fought thrice and remained unslain in battle he was freed. The pardon awarded, or the punishment inflicted by the King, was supposed to purify the offender. Punishment was meant for the purpose of religious expiation; it was intended to be reformatory and deterrent.

When punishment is properly prescribed, it procures good results; but if inflicted unreasonably, its effect are ruinous not only on the offender but on the community.

Punishment, in early codes, is a law of righteousness emanating from the divine right of kings, but its leading principles are intimidation and deterrence. The ruler is the fountain of divine authority, and is looked upon as the dispenser of punishment. Punishment acts as a means of public defense and social safety also. It shows the social disapproval of the offender's act or omission. It is meant for the protection of society, but then, as Manu declared, it is good only if justly and properly inflicted.

In the Mughal period, the judges thought it fit and best to follow Koranic precepts;......Punishment was discretionary with the officer who tried the case, and might assume any form. In the reign of Akbar, instructions were issued to the provincial governor asking him "to pursue what the witnesses deposed by manifold inquiries, by study of physiognomy and the exercise of foresight."[9] Superior executive officers had the authority to try criminal cases. Shayesta Khan, during his administration of Bengal, held open durbar daily for administering of justice and redressing of wrongs.[10] The Kazi attended the hearing of cases by the trying officers and assisted them to arrive at decisions according to the precepts of Koran. Where the Koran was silent on a point in issue in a case, the trying officer applied his own discretion in arriving at decision. There was a right of appeal to the Emperor. The criminal law of the Mughal period was originated in precepts of the Holy Koran; and the professed idea in punishing the wrongdoer was that of teaching him righteousness.

The highest Court in Mughal India was that of the Emperor himself. The Emperor was the fountain of justice. Akbar was noted for devoting several hours in the day hearing cases and appeals. Shah Jahan had his Court every Wednesday in the Diwan-i-Khass; and justice was administered by Aurangzeb daily in his private chamber.

The Maratha system of administration of justice was simple and suited to the needs of the time. The law was not codified, but was based on old customs and treaties like the Mitakshara and the Code of Manu. Ordeals and oaths were allowed in determining the guilt or innocence of the accused. The Judiciary and the Executive were not separate. The Peshwas personally also went out on tour every year for trial of cases and punishment of offenders. Capital punishment seems to have been unknown in the days of Shahu Chhatrapati and Balaji Baji Rao. For murder the penalties were fine, confiscation of property and imprisonment. Punishment was meant for being used as a corrective only. Fines were imposed according to the financial capacity of the offender; payment by instalments was also allowed. The offender was not needlessly sent to jail for non-payment of fine. Witchcraft was punished with fine, imprisonment and ex-communication. For adultery, the punishment for female offenders was slavery and penal servitude; but such persons were released if some relation stood surety for their future good behaviour. Sometimes mutilation was ordered in place of slavery. For the male offender the punishment generally was fine, and sometimes imprisonment. The condition of the slaves was, in spite of hard labour they were put to, relatively good. Penalties for forcible marriage were confiscation of property and ex-communication. Sometimes the offender was let off with a fine. But robbers and thieves were mutilated.

In the Mughal period, the legal precedents by Mahapinnyakyaw, placing the interpretations of Manu on a definitely Buddhist basis, were compiled; that became the most valuable work of its kinds throughout Burma.[11]

The nineteenth century witnessed the introduction of English Law in India. The Indian Penal Code, drafted by Lord Macaulay, was introduced in India. In 1833, Lord Macaulay persuaded the House of Commons that the ideal moment had come for codification of Indian laws. He prepared the draft of the Indian Penal Code which became law in 1860. The same was followed by the Criminal Procedure Code in 1861. Female infanticide was declared to be an offence of murder. In 1870 a Central Act was passed to combat infanticide. In 1829 and 1830, regulations were passed in Bengal, Madras and Bombay to put at end to Sati. India Act V of 1843 prohibited slavery, and in 1860, under the Indian Penal Code, dealing in slaves became a criminal offence.[12]

In 1853, a special police department was organised in India, under Captain (afterwards Sir) William Sleeman, to fight crimes committed by the thugs who committed murders in the acts of robbery. In 1836, a special Act was passed by which of a gang of thugs was made liable to imprisonment for life. Lord Minto launched a vigorous campaign against dacoity.[13]

In 1816, district munsiffs were appointed; and they proved popular. Soon afterwards "auxiliary" and "native" civil and criminal Courts were established. The Torture Commission of 1855 rendered change of the police system imperative. Police administration was vested in an Inspector-General. The jails were in strong buildings utilised for the purpose.[14] Prisons were very unhealthy places. For breaches of discipline, the prisoners were flogged very severely and frequently. Prisoners were, however, paid daily subsistence allowances. This allowance system, however, was abused by the jailors who got all the advantage they could out of it. Had it not been for the unscrupulousness of some of the jailors in making all they could out of the prisoners' catering arrangements, better results would have been attained.[15]

In 1855, an Inspector-General of Prisons was appointed in each Presidency. Ten years later civil surgeons were appointed. In 1857, the work of building central jails were commenced. Fixed diet-scales and the system of remission of sentences were introduced in 1867.[16]

Law and Punishment in Ancient Iran

In the Avesta language, law is known as data, da meaning 'to establish'. The origin of the Iranian law lies in religious precepts. The law of the land had the divine law at substratum. Religion, being "the fountain-head of all law, is especially called Data Vidaeva, i.e., the law against the demons. No less than seven books, that is, fully one-third of the entire Zoroastrian cannon are devoted to law. The third line of Ahuna Vairya, the primeval Word of Ahura Mazda, is declared to be the quintessence of this legal section of Zoroastrianism."[17] Only one of these even legal work, i.e., Vidaeva Data, or Vendidad, has reached us rather in complete form. This work has formed a part of the Zoroastrian ritual and furnishes considerable material regarding laws prevailing among the Avestan people.[18] The Vendidad is "the codification of religious, ethical, ecclesiastical, ritual, social, penal and hygienic laws." The Iranian State punished even some of the wrongs which were purely of a theological nature.[19] The temples were the centres of both religious and judicial activities.

To determine the innocence or guilt of an accused person, the ordeal and the oath were often resorted to.[5] "Above all an ordeal was an appeal to divine powers, when human resources had failed.......the celestial beings were invoked, by means of religious formulas and elaborate ceremonials, to come down to the Court to help the human officers of the ordeal court."[20] The *judicium Dei*, that is to say, the judgment of God as to the merits of the case, was invoked and pronounced through the ordeal.

The raison d'etre of punishment was deterrence and reformation. Theoretically punishments were very severe, but, in practice, the judges inflicted moderate punishments, a formation, for the first offence. There is evidence to show that women also were appointed judges to try cases.[21]

TYPES OF PUNISHMENTS

Introductory—Uselessness of Brutal Punishments

Bertrand Russell points out the lack of usefulness in the system of punishments based on the infliction of useless and brutal pain. He says: "...the object of the prison adminstration is to save trouble, not to study the individual case. He (meaning prisoner) is kept in captivity in a cell from which all sight of the earth is shut out :.......He is solemnly denounced as an enemy to society. He is compelled to perform mechanical tasks, chosen for their wearisomeness. He is given no education, and no incentive to self-improvement. Is it to be wondered at, if at the end of such course of treatment, his feelings towards the community are no more friendly than they were at the beginning?"[22] The treatment of offenders to-day is much different from what it used to beat the time Bertrand Russell made the above-mentioned statement. Nevertheless, in certain matters the prison system needs improvement.

Capital Punishment

In ancient times, and even in the middle ages, it was thought that the best way of protecting society from serious or dangerous types of offenders was that of sentencing them to death. About 1800, the death penalty existed for as many as 200 felonies. In the reign of Henry VIII, many thieves and vagabonds were hanged. And in the reign of Queen Elizabeth (in 1562), the punishment for forgery and coining was torture, maiming and forfeiture. In 1634, forgery was punishable with death.

Sir Samuel Romilly, a distinguished lawyer, became opposed to the infliction of capital punishment for offences other than the most serious ones. Bentham and Bright supported the movement for reform. Since then there have been commissions appointed and Bills passed by Parliament, as the result of which capital punishment has been limited in its application, in practice, to cases of wilful murder.

In India, in the Pre-Buddhist times the death sentence was carried out in a terrible manner. The offender was dragged a long distance and chained and whipped, arrayed in such a way that the public could have a grasp of him, and ultimately put to death. Even to-day the death penalty has been retained in many of the civilized countries of the world, though in some of the States of the United States of America where it has been abolished, statistics have shown lesser number of homicides than where it has been retained.

Hackel regarded capital punishment as a process of artificial selection. And Garofalo even went to the extent of saying that elimination of criminals was a sort of moral war for the good of society. According to Lombroso capital punishment should be good as a threat to habituals and incorrigibles. Even George Ives is of the opinion that the incorrigible or hopeless criminal should be painlessly removed rather than that the State should have to maintain him unnecessarily.

Baccaria denounced capital punishment. The State, according to him, has no right to put an individual to death, because the life of the individual was not surrendered to it as part of the consideration for the social contract; he believed in the theory of the social contract. In England, Copinger opposed capital punishment. Stutsman, with considerable experience as an able prison officer, definitely is against it and suggests its abolition.[24] Modern writers reiterate views of Bentham who advocated its abolition, agreeing with the opinion of Beccaria. ''By disusing the death penalty, we will prevent it as a crime.''

Capital punishment has a demoralising effect upon society. If a person, not quite normal or cultured, takes life in a state of quasi-insanity or in a state or moral imbecility, should the law ordain the imposing of a penalty which is tantamount to taking life for life taken? Professor Hentig has said: "...the State can only put real life into the principle of the inviolability of life, which it continually and rightly advocates in its reasons for condemning murders, and in its laws, it it sticks to its own principle, through thick and thin. The State is paramount. If it, the unbriddled despot, bows down to the holiness of life, then it has found and brought into use the strongest of all suggestions." He continues, "Thus I see in capital punishment a means of punishment whose advantages can be obtained by other means and whose disadvantages can be prevented in no other way than by abolishing it. It is a socially insufficient means of punishment, to which must be added the possibility of a judicial error, which one cannot exclude."[25] Instead of taking revenge on the offender, is it not advisable that Nemesis may play her part, and the offender be brought home to repentance and to atonement, through the detention while under a sentence of transportation or imprisonment? Death penalty should be abolished; imprisonment for a long term of years would be effective in not only bringing about deterrence but also penitence and reformation. Retribution will work better through Nemesis, and not vengeance. Making the offender realise that his being in prison for a long period of time has been necessitated by his own conduct serves a very useful purpose. The prisoner then gets time and opportunity for deliberation over his wrongful act; he is a human being and not a stone; penitence would soon come to him, and he may become a reformed man. He would probably atone for his crime by proper behaviour both in prison and after he comes out. If while he is in prison, the magnetic personality of some zealous and devout preacher touches his heart right, the fire of truth within him would soon burn within him, and would bring him to sincere repentance and a desire to atone for the wrong done by him. Reformation, deterrence and retribution would, if punishments are properly prescribed under the law, go together, because these are the necessary elements in the one great purpose, viz., making the prisoner realise that nothing but good is good or desirable, and that crime leads to one's own deterioration. The splendid example of the working of Nemesis is superbly demonstrated in Shakespeare's

"Macbeth". What happens to Macbeth and Lady Macbeth is not punishment imposed by any legal authority but by the working of Nemesis, the working of the great force within the man or woman so as to bring him or her to repentance, and often to the neurosis that has been deserved. Different are the types of murderers, but it should be remembered that all of them are human beings, with a human heart, and that treatment and detention would be much more beneficial than the rope or the electric chair.

Statistics show that there is not deterrent value in capital punishment. By its very nature it cannot be reformative; but whereas its value according to advocates for its retention, can be deterrence, there is not even such value in it.[26] In places where the death penalty has been abolished, statistics do not show any rise in homicides; on the contrary those States of America in which the penalty has been abolished show a lesser number of homicides than the States where it has been retained; its abolition has not caused a rise in the number of homicides. What, then, may it be asked, is the value or social utility of capital punishment? We advocate its abolition. We appeal to the legislators to move in the matter. If they succeed, it would not only be good for India, and for humanity, but it would also show the advanced spirit of the age. Portugal, the Cantons of Switzerland, Holland, Norway, Denmark, Finland, Belgium, Latvia, Sweden, Queensland, Lithuania, Uruguay and several States of America have abolished the death punishment, with beneficial results. In May 1947 Russia abolished capital punishment in the Soviet Union during peace-time, and in January 1948, Italy abandoned it. In 1948, England suspended as an experimental measure the death sentence, for a period of five years; the death sentence was, however, not suspended for cases of premeditated murders where the offender had the deliberate intention of causing death, or where death was caused by poisoning or by the use of an explosive or in the course of violent robbery or for prevention of a lawful arrest or where the murder was of a police officer. India should follow the example of those countries, and undoubtedly benefit will result.

In India, even in the Buddhist age when Ahimsa was the rule of conduct, that principle was not applied in the realm of penology. King Ashoka did not have capital punishment disallowed. A respite of three days, however, was allowed, during which a friend, relative, or any other person, on behalf of the condemned prisoner could apply for getting the death sentence annulled. But in Sukracharya, it was stated: "One should not kill living beings—this is the truth of Sruti. So the King should carefully avoid capital punishment and restrain by detention and imprisonment. But drawing from the Sukranti and the Sruti, the opposite view also could be arrived at. In the Mahabharata there is a very interesting and excellent discussion between King Dyumatsena and his son Prince Satyavan, as regards the justification or otherwise of capital punishment. The arguments of the Prince are strong against capital punishment. The Prince asks: "Why penalise the unfortunate wife and children, parents and relatives of the offender by killing him? Why put an end to all chances of reformation by destroying the prisoner? Again it is seen that good children sometimes spring from wicked persons; so why deprive the world of that advantage?"

One of the arguments in favour of the death penalty is that it is a very effective deterrent (though it cannot be reformative), because death is most dreaded by the intending murderer. But the question is: Does death penalty really deter? What do facts the figures show? Facts and figures show that death penalty does not deter. In India, the death penalty has not yet been abolished, but we believe that with its abolition homicides will not increase in this century. What do we find in the United States of America? The States, *viz.*, Kansas, Maine, Michigan, Minnesota, North Dakota, Rhode Island, South Dakota, and Wisconsin, where capital punishment has been abolished do not show any increase in the number of homicides.

In his Reports for the years 1905-24, the Chief of the Norwegian Prisons declared that the number of homicides had declined considerably, in spite of the fact that the death penalty was abolished, in Norway, in 1905. Similarly did the Chief of Prison Administration is Sweden report a notable decrease in crime, with reduction in the number of death sentences and the final abolition of capital punishment. Such a report was also made by the Representative of the Danish Government.[27] We may expect similar results in India.

An important fact to be remembered is that only 26.28 per cent. of the homicides are premeditated; even assuming that the fear of death deters a prospective murderer, such deterrence would be limited only to cases of deliberate murder. In other cases, however, murder not having been premeditated, the assaulter could not be said to have had the time to think of the consequences of his act. He may have even repented later for the horrible act; but at the time he did it, the thought of punishment could hardly have entered his mind. So many of the homicides are caused in the course in quarrel; as the result of anger deteriorating into harsh words and blows. Very often, then, in the heat of the moment the knife is whipped out, or a blow given, which causes the death of one of the disputants. Out of 507 cases of homicides investigated by me (by personal observations at the Criminal Sessions of the Bombay High Court, and by going through facts mentioned in various briefs and records), I found that the percentage of cases of premeditated murder was 26.28 and that of unpremeditated cases was 73.72.

Homicide, in India, has been found to be due mainly to rage degenerating into the vengeful emotion. Most of the homicides are without premeditation. Horrible malice asserts itself in an homicidal act. "Murder committed because of rage," says Dr. Anita Muhl "may be due to rage associated with (1) merely an uncontrolled temper; (2) the epileptic furor; (3) the manic excitement in manic-depressive psychosis; (4) the catatonic excitement in schizophrenia; (5) the outbursts of the low grade moron, as well as to other causes associated with organic disease."[28] That is so. Where is the question of deterrence then? Whether capital punishment existed or not, the offender would have committed the act.[29] Both deduction and induction show that it has no deterrent value. If that argument, then, in favour of capital punishment is eliminated and nullified, there remains no further argument in its favour.

Concluding our arguments regarding capital punishment, we saw that it is useless; it is not capable of a deterrent value; it is not reformative; it is inhuman. Punishment should not be destructive of the offender. It is not the severity of the punishment, but the certainty of the punishment that deters. If the offender can escape, or think or believe that he can remain undetected, he may plan a murder. Sometimes even in the case of predetermined and cold-blooded murders of the most brutal types, the true offenders have remained undetected;

or, if arrested, then for want of sufficient evidence given the benefit of the doubt and acquitted. When so many persons go free, what deterrence, even in the case of cold-blooded murders, can the death penalty bring about? Hardly any.

Deportation

Next to capital punishment, a method of elimination of incorrigible or dangerous offenders is the punishment of deportation. The punishment in old times was that of outlawry and ex-communication. Sometimes the deported prisoner was made a galley slave. In India, the Indian Penal Settlements at Port Blair and the Andaman Islands were places for confining incorrigibles. According to the French School, change of environment for the prisoner is desirable. But Lombroso was against change of environment. According to Lombroso for habitual criminals deportation can hardly have any effect but for offenders by passion it may have good results.

Corporal Punishments: Mutilation, Flogging and Torture

Mutilation was very common in ancient times. Sometimes it was followed by death, burning or boiling alive. In ancient India, and even in the Mughal and Maratha periods, mutilation was resorted to. The idea, however, behind this type of punishment was one of deterrence.

Flogging prevailed from the earliest times. It was a hard punishment. The punishment of flogging was not inflicted when the offender was found medically unfit to bear it. In times of old and even in the middle ages, whipping was the commonest of punishments. Whipping in public was resorted to. For forcing out confessions from prisoners, they were put to the rack and severely totured. Many of the prisoners chained and whipped, bled to death, and the whipping went on mercilessly even after the prisoner fainted.[30] Slaves were flogged with three-thronged whips. Till 1917, even women were not spared. Lombroso was against flogging, and preferred the substitutes of fasting and hard labour.

In ancient Iran, and in ancient India, and even in the times of the Mughal rulers and the Marathas, whipping was much resorted to; it was very severe indeed, and many of the prisoners bled to death as the result of the wounds received through the lashes.

In 1838, Dr. Barnes, giving his opinion before the English Prison Commission of 1838, said: "I never knew a convict benefited by flagellation. The beaten man becomes a more desperate character."

In the Criminal Sessions of the Bombay High Court, in 1944, four persons involved in a rape case were sentenced to imprisonment ranging from 2 to 3 years and to whipping ranging from 20 to 30 strokes each. One wonders whether such punishment does any good or serves any useful purpose by way of deterrence or reformation. We vote against it, insofar as we are convinced that whipping either breaks and degrades the prisoner or makes him accustomed to pain and hardship, making him more inclined to crime in the future. It is possible, if not quite probable, that whipping may arouse in the person whipped even a sadistic tendency, and thus produce grosser perversity than before. In the case mentioned above, the victim was a young girl under 18 years of age, and the crime was committed by threats as also false inducements; the learned judge desired passing an exemplary sentence. But we would say that whipping was not necessary or desirable, and that imprisonment even for a longer period, i.e., even for five or six years, would have been effective.

Flogging might be resorted to, when the conditions are such that there is no other adequate way left. Veronica King shows how in an American prison, a riot was successfully dealt with by a warden, on hiw own responsibility, flogging the rioters.[31]

In March, 1944, Mr. M.A. Kazmi introduced in the Legislative Assembly a Bill for the abolition of whipping as punishment for offenders. It was, however, rejected, on the ground that Government was not in favour of the demand for the total abolition of whipping, but would consider the question of abolition of whipping in the case of certain offences. The State Governments were not in favour of complete abolition of whipping. In 1955, the Union Government of India had their Bill for the abolition of whipping passed in Parliament. The Government of India deserves congratulations for having abolished the punishment of whipping.

We purpose the abolition of whipping as a punishment; whipping should not be inflicted, except to control or otherwise uncontrollable offender. Not even in cases of brutal offences should whipping be allowed, for by whipping a man, whom society may call a brute, society is making him either a misanthrope, an enemy, or a coward. Whipping produces the rougher kind of criminal, the more maladjusted being, the braver desperado, or else the broken-down man. And whipping in a mild form is ineffective. So either way whipping is of no use. Our conclusion then is that whipping should be abolished subject, however, to using it only for bringing an otherwise uncontrollable prisoner to check.

It is gratifying to note, in 1948, England abolished whipping as a punishment. The Indian legislature in 1955, emulated the English Parliament, in this respect.

Fine as Deterrent

Garofalo declared that the levying of fine is supported by the necessity for maintaining prisoners and of providing expenses for their prosecution and for compensating the aggrieved party. It is a form of punishment which may be resorted to in dealing with casual offenders and first offenders whose crimes are not grave enough for institutional dealing. As far as possible, probation should be resorted to, and fines even should be avoided, if a fine can serve no useful purpose in a case at hand. Probation and suspension of sentences are more effective ways of dealing with criminals than fines and imprisonment, and in all fit cases, even fines should be avoided.

An important thing to be remembered with regard to the infliction of fines is that imprisonment should not be inflicted in cases where default is made in payment of the fine, so as to send a poor person to prison. It would not be fair or just to send a poor person to prison when he does not deserve going there. Poverty should not mean imprisonment. Time should be given to poor persons for payment of fines and the amount of the fines inflicted should be proportionate not merely to the injury but should vary with the pecuniary power of the offender. Fines may also be made payable by small convenient instalments, i.e., as the offender earns.

Imprisonment—Its Purpose and Value

Originally imprisonment was a mode of custody of under-trial persosn. Under-trial persons were locked up sometimes for years together before they were put up for trial. As early as 1597, jails were established. These jails were miserable places where prisoners were hurled up together. The inspiring of fear or terror was at the substratum of the old systems of social defense and control. It ws in the 18th century that due to the agitation set up by prison reformers, prisons were built of the cellular type. But as prisoners could not stand the tortures of solitary confinement, they were put in communal confinement, and thus an important change in the prison system took place.

Solitary confinement which was at one time the ordinary mode of confinement had to be given up, and confinement on the principle of communal living was substituted. Fetters and dietary punishment are resorted to in our prisons even to-day, as penalties for breach of prison discipline or rules ror for insubordination. Fetters should not be used except to bring an otherwise uncontrollable prisoner to control.

The main purposes of imprisonment are those of (a) disabling the offender from being a danger to society, by locking him up, (b) preventing prospective offenders by the threat of long-term lock- up, and (c) reforming the offender under healthy and transforming conditions (provided, of course, the prison is an ideal one).

Imprisonment, in order to be an effective reformative method of dealing with offenders, must be *long-term* imprisonment, or imprisonment for at least a sufficient time, so as to give the prison officials sufficient opportunities of successfully dealing with the offender for his re-education and rehabilitation. Short-term sentences are worse than useless, as such sentences have no reformative value and may lead to congestion in prison and thus expose the offender to the danger of contamination in prison by letting him come into contact with hard and rough offenders. As Garofalo says, "As for its reformatory, effect it is not worth wasting words on". Our conclusion then is that short-term imprisonment should be substituted by fine, or better still, by release of the offender on probation under the care of a probation officer.

Imprisonment is a good substitute for the death sentence. Having studied the arguments for and against capital punishment, we should suggest its abolition and have instead fourteen years' rigorous imprisonment. At present, in India, the alternative for capital punishment is transportation for life which really means imprisonment for 14 years. Whereas capital punishment has neither a deterrent nor a reformative value, imprisonment has reformative value, if the system of imprisonment is a healthy system.

Imprisonment should not be inflicted for genuine inability to pay a fine, when the offender is a poor person and has not the money to pay the fine. The Courts should, after a due consideration, allow the payment of fine even in petty instalments.

Habitual offenders should not be unduly harassed by preventive detention. Under our law, whenever, the police suspect the probability of the commission of some crime by a habitual offender, the police can put him up before a magistrate who may order the suspect to provide security, if he finds that the suspect is likely to commit a crime again. If the suspect fails to provide security, he may be sent to prison under the provisions of the Criminal Procedure Code. At times, habitual offenders are harassed by the police. On any frail suspicion and without any good cause or justification, the police arrest such persons and put them before a magistrate. Even upon their genuine inability to furnish the bond, they are unnecessarily sent to prison. Such offenders thus become enemies to society. Instead of sending them to prison for non-satisfaction of the security, they should be made to report to the police at regular intervals; that would be quite satisfactory.

Solitary Confinement

Regarding solitary confinement, Dr. Havelock Ellis says: "Regarded as a rational method of treatment, cellular confinement is a curious monument of human perversity. That it should have been established shows the ignorance of criminal nature which existed at the time; that it should still persist shows the present necessity for a widespread popular knowledge of these matters. It may be possible to learn to ride on a wooden horse, or to swim on a table, but the solitary cell does not provide even a wooden substitute for the harmonising influences of honest society. To suppose that cellular confinement will tend to make the criminal a reasonable human being is as rational as to suppose that it will tend to make him a soldier or a sailor, a doctor or a celergyman. The mistake here is the old one that has vitiated so much of human action where the criminal is concerned— the mistake, that is, of supposing that at all points he is an average human being. Solitary confinement on a refined and cultured human being may produce a deep and lasting impression; a period of solitude, indeed, is for every intellectual person of immense value in helping him to know himself; though even here, if compulsory and unbroken, it can scarcely be without demoralising effect. But the case is quite different when we turn to the vacuous-minded, erratic, and animal person who is usually the criminal. Solitude produces in him, as Professor Prins remarks, no intellectual activity, and no searching of conscience; it serves merely to deepen his mental vacuity and to deliver him over to unnatural indulgence in the one animal appetite of which he cannot be deprived. Professor Prins points out, as does Prince Krapotkine, that the cell excludes all the bracing influences of struggle; the morality of the cell is submission, punctuality, quietness, politeness to warders. A human life shut up in such a frame has nothing in common with social morality. Beltrani-Scalia, formerly Inspector General of Prisons in Italy, is of the same opinion, and remarks that "the cellular system looks upon man as a brother of 'La Trappe'."[32]

Our conclusion, in this respect, should be that it all depends on the type of person confined whether solitary confinement would work well or produce evil results on body and mind. If imposed, it should be noted well whether the person would be capable of bearing the same. On the whole, it may be said that, except in some suitable cases (certified as such by medical or psychological expert), the punishment of solitary confinement should not be imposed.

Solitary confinement does not exist in Russia.[33] The prisoner is allowed association with his fellows.

Indefinite Imprisonment

Indefinite term of imprisonment means that the Court prescribes the minimum and maximum terms. The prisoner cannot be released by the jail authorities till the minimum period of sentence is served; nor can he be kept in prison beyond the maximum allowed by the Court. A parole board, or some such other administrative body, decides when the prisoner is to be released in between these terms.

The '*indefinite* sentence' is sometimes described also as the '*indeterminate*' or '*relatively indeterminate*' sentence. But it should be distinguished from the 'indeterminate sentence' which is really based on a different principle. We should rather adhere to strict terminology, and call it 'the indefinite sentence', and not the 'indeterminate sentence', for in the 'indeterminate sentence' there is no maximum or minimum term laid down by the Court which leaves the determination of the term to the prison body. On the other hand, the 'indefinite sentence' is one in which the Court fixes the maximum and the minimum terms, but does not lay down any definite period of imprisonment, that being left to the jail body, subject to the minimum and maximum periods.

The '*indefinite system*' is the outcome of the provisions in the French Penal Code of 1810. The system was developed by the French law provisions of 1824 and 1832. Later in U.S.A., Dr. Benjamin Rush, a Philadelphia physician and humanitarian, said: "Let the various kinds of punishment be defined and fixed by law. But let no notice be taken in the law of the punishment that awaits any particular crime. Punishments should be varied in degree according to the temper of criminals or the progress of their reformation. Let the duration of punishments be limited *but let this limitation be unknown.*"[34] Later in Great Britain, similar arguments were advanced and proposals put forward by persons such as Archbishop Whately of Dublin, Fredric Hill, Mathew Davenport Hill.[35] So from the indefinite sentence, proposals came for a shifting to the *indeterminate* sentence.

Indeterminate Sentence

As early as 1781, James Hanway, in his "Distributive Justice and

Mercy," suggested the institution of the indeterminate sentence. And in 1853, in his book on Crime, Matthew Davenport Hill advocated the indeterminate sentence. In 1880, Garofalo advocated indefinite imprisonment, in his work called "Criterio Positiva della Penalita," published at Naples. In 1880 Dr. Kraepelin advocated the abolition of fixed term imprisonment. And the principle of indeterminate sentence was approved and adopted by the International Association of Criminal Law.

Imprisonment is indeterminate when the discharge of the prisoner depends upon his behaviour in prison and the progress made by him towards reformation. If reformation be an essential factor in dealing with offenders, there can be no doubt that the sentence should be an indeterminate one, as it is then that the prison officers can bring about a proper transformation of the offender. Why should the prisoner be kept in prison after he has been reformed? Likewise, how could the prisoner be released before his transformation! It is dangerous to release him before he is reformed, for he may commit a crime again. Where the sentence prescribes a fixed period internment, the prison authorities cannot detain a prisoner after expiry of that period; whether the prisoner has been reformed or not, he must be released, as soon as the period of detention inflicted by the Court gets over. It is for this reason that reformative treatment requires an indeterminate sentence, as is the case in some of the States of the United States of America.

Colonel Montesinos of Spain who, in 1835, was Governor of the Valencia prison, established the system of dividing the population of the prison in companies (on the military basis), and he introduced an element of self-government among prisoners by selecting prisoners as company officers. He offered the prisoners remission of their sentences on the ground of good behaviour and work. Prisoners could thus get their sentences reduced by one-third. This sytem proved successful. The law, however, intervened and provided that prisoners must serve their full terms; Montesinos resigned in 1846, and wrote that personal interest by the prison officials in the prisoners under their care secured results which severity or constancy of punishments could not procure. The prisoner who goes to prison, already degraded by his crime, should not be further degraded. Self-respect (he wrote) is one of the most powerful sentiments, since it is the most personal, and the effect of ill-treatment could only be irritation rather than correction or sublimation. And so also did Obermaler, the Governor of the Prison at Kaiserslautern in Bavaria, in 1830, work well on the sentiments of the prisoners under his care because the law did not disallow indeterminate treatment. M. Bonneville de Marsangy, discoursing at the opening of the Civil Tribunal of Rheims, in 1846, said that society should release the prisoner on a ticket-of-leave, whenever he gives satisfactory evidence of his genuine reformation.

In 1876, in America, the Elmira Reformatory was opened, with indeterminate imprisonment as its object. First-offenders being males (between the ages of 16 and 30) were kept there. At the Elmira Reformatory the primary business is the reformation of the offender, and the inmate's stay in made dependent upon the progress shown by him.

Different Types of Indefinite Sentence

In New York, there are three different types of the indefinite sentence. The first type of the indefinite system is, as is the case in the Elmira, where the prisoner can be detained for any period of time as the authorities at the prison think necessary for his reformation, but subject, however, to the maximum period prescribed under the Code for the offence. There is no minimum period prescribed. In practice, before a prisoner is released on parole a year's training is given. In 1889, the system of indefinite sentence became, in the State prisons in New York, a permissive measure. The second type of the indefinite sentence involves that the law fixes a maximum and a minimum period of detention. The minimum period of detention (under this type of sentence) is a year for each offence under the Code; the maximum period is prescribed by the Code for the offence concerned. Subject to the minimum of a year's imprisonment and the maximum prescribed under the Code, it is for the prison authorities to determine when the prisoner is fit for being discharged. Later it was provided that the minimum period of detention should not exceed half the maximum. So that if 10 years be the maximum for an offence the Code, the minimum prescribed by the Court cannot be more than 5 years. The third type of the indefinite sentence in New York involves that the maximum period of detention, for all offences, is three years in the case of detention in a penitentiary of reformatory, while in the case of the detention in a workhouse the general maximum is two years. The Parole Commission has, with the approval of the judge who sentenced the offender, discretion to release a prisoner on parole.

In one form or the other, the system of indefinite sentence has been adopted in several States of the U.S.A., e.g., Ohio, Michigan, Illinois, Massachusetts, Pennsylvania, Minnesota, Kansas, California, Indiana, South Dakota.

In the first type of indefinite sentence, the minimum period of detention is not fixed by the Court, but is determined by the prison authorities; that is a very proper thing. But as regards the maximum period of detention the prison authorities are rendered helpless if and when the same as fixed by the Code is not sufficient for reformation of the prisoner concerned. It may be argued that if there is no maximum laid down, the interests of the prisoner may be at stake. Should we leave it arbitrarily in the hands of the prison officials? Would that not be a hazardous affair? Where prison officers are fit and proper persons to guide, help and educate the prisoners under their care, society can well trust them to treat the prisoners and detain them as they think fit. But where they are not (as it might happen) quite capable of determining the period of imprisonment for the prisoner, the latter may suffer. It may be suggested that maximum periods of detention may be fixed by the Code, with liberty to the prison authorities to cut the same down to any short period they may think fit looking to the individual offender and his reformation. And legislators should not forget that the maximum periods of detention fixed by our Codes for different offences *should be long enough to enable the prison authorities of officers to work satisfactorily the methods of reformation for the individual offender*. If the maximum periods for different offences, fixed by the Codes, are not sufficiently long to enable the prison officers to reform the inmates under their care, then how can they be held responsible if our prison, systems fail in the achievement of their purpose, viz. of rehabilitating the prisoners? The law, then, and not the prison officials, should be blamed. A short-term of imprisonment is worse than useless, for it is harmful to the offender and may expose him to the risk of contamination. Why send anybody for a short-term to prison when that serves no useful purpose? Offenders guilty of petty offences should not be sent to prison, but may be fined, or ordered to compensate the aggrieved party and released on probation. Short-term imprisonment, by its very nature, has no reformative value, for the prison cannot be the place for education within a time too short for the achievement of that purpose. Short-term imprisonment can have no deterrent, preventive or intimidating value, for it is for a short time only that the prisoner has to endure confinement.

Imprisonment in Default of Payment of Fine

Under our law, the Court can order imprisonment in default of payment of fine. We suggest that persons who are genuinely unable to pay the fine should not be sent to prison sufficient time should be allowed for the payment of the fine, say, by instalments, if necessary.

Preventive Detention

In England, under the Prevention of Crime Act, 1908, provision is made for preventive detention. For the protection of society, habitual offenders can be kept in detention even after the expiry of their penal servitude. In India, where a habitual offender is suspected by the police and found by the Court to be likely to commit crime again he can be asked to give security; for failure to provide security, he may be sent to prison.

It is sometimes found that old offenders are unnecessairly put to hardship; on some doubt in the mind of a police officer, a habitual offender may be unnecessarily apprehended, and if he cannot furnish the amount of the bond or a surety when required to do so, he may be sent back to prison. He feels then a disgust and hatred for the law which leaves him no rest; he may, because of the injustice done to him, go against society and contract a thorough conflict with civilised society and its ways. He may thus become an enemy to the Community. A relieving feature, however, may be the clemancy and the patience and goodness of some sympathetic magistrates who would refuse to make any harsh order of a harassing type, and instead would pass a more useful order, e.g., that the habitual should report to the police.

Under an Act, such as the Bombay Habitual Offenders Restriction Act, 1947, the Court can restrict the movements of habitual offenders; such offenders can be made to report themselves, and can be placed in special settlements. Under such Act the State Government can establish industrial, agricultural or reformatory settlements.

The law relating to habitual offenders needs considerable amendment. Surveillance over the habitual offender is desirable; but that surveillance must be actually carried out with sympathy, so that the offender may be won over, and not feel that he is harassed. Surveillance may even well be accommodated with rehabilitation.[38]

Effects of Imprisonment

In the case of a short-term imprisonment the offender gets the idea that imprisonment is not so bad after all. Short-term detention is devoid of any deterrent effect; and it can have no reformative benefit. Garofalo says: ''As for its reformatory effect, it is not worth wasting words on.'' The remedy lies in making greater use of the system of releasing offenders on probation, and abstaining from passing short-term sentences.

A drawback of imprisonment is contamintation likely to result in the absence of proper segregation. Another drawback is that of deprivation of sexual like for a long time, sometimes resulting in unnatural sexual practices. The remedy lies in granting holidays to prisoners, for example, once every quarter, provided the prisoner has been found to be of such good character and conduct as would not leave reasons for suspecting that he would abscond; such a system would create the impetus for good conduct.

The physiognomy of the offender is also liable to undergo changes after imprisonment.[39] In Dr. William Healy's monumental work ''The Individual Delinquent,'' In the same work, show how the features of the offender become, due to imprisonment, rough, hard, with marks and bear the ''prison look''.

Alternatives to Imprisonment

Punishment by fine and releasing of casual offenders on probation are good alternatives to imprisonment. If, however, imprisonment has to be inflicted, it should be detention under healthy and ameliorating conditions. And short-term sentences should be avoided. As Lieutenant Colonel F. A. Barker says, "large numbers of convictions to simple imprisonment continue to be, with the short sentences of one month or less, which represent 19 per cent. of total admissions, a most regrettable feature of Indian Penal Administration and the two combined are real obstacles to prison reform."[40]

INQUIRING INTO ANTECEDENTS OF ACCUSED PERSONS

Probation officers now allowed to visit the homes of accused persons with a view of investigating into their antecedents, so that, in case the accused is found guilty, the Court can, without any further delay, prescribe proper treatment for the offender. Though an accused person is presumed to be innocent unless proved guilty to the satisfaction of the Court, and though it may be an affront to the accused's sense of self-respect if a probation officer is allowed to visit his home before he is proved guilty, yet it is worthwhile allowing the same, because trouble and delay would be avoided at the time of sentence if the accused is found guilty. In the interests of the accused himself, such a system has been introduced.[41]

DEALING WITH ABLE-BODIED BEGGARS AND DRUNKARDS

By virtue of legislation in some of the States, able-bodied beggars are dealt with by being kept to work to work-houses and poor-houses. Disabled beggars, of course, must be protected and dealt with sympathetically.

Criminals who are habitual drunkards should be detained in special asylums for special treatment.[42]

INDIVIDUALIZATION OF TREATMENT

Individualization of treatment should be followed in prisons. Every prison should have a clinic for psychological and pschiatrical determination of the prisoner's mental condition. Treatment in prison and work and diet should be afforded according to what is medically and morally best for each individual prisoner. To ensure safe treatment in prison, it is of the highest importance that prison officials are all fit and proper persons. Where able and sympathetic persons, skilled in social welfare work, are appointed as prison officers, prisoners get good treatment, and reformation is made more probable.

Mentally abnormal prisoners require being kept in special institutions or special prisons. The jail administration of the Madras Presidency has really attempted to deal efficiently with mental defectives; and a special jail has been set apart for such classes of prisoners at Cuddalore.[43] The Superintendent of that prison is a medical man skilled in cases of mental abnormality. The population of that jail is about 300. Individual attention is devoted.[44] Other States should emulate Madras.

CONCLUSION

Useless punishments should be abolished. It is not true to say the punishment necessarily involves degradation; degradation or useless pain need not be inflicted. Punishment (if it to be a good) must be elevating. It should seek to bring about a transformation of the offender, making him realize the wrongfulness of his act or omission, and making him feel sincerely penitent and prepared for compensation. The two great concomitants of punishment are, or ought to be, *compensation* and *reformation.*

REFERENCES

1. Glueck, S. and Glueck, E.: 500 *Criminal Careers*, pp. 43, 44.
2. Sections 3 and 4 of the Probation of Offenders Act, 1958.
3. Lowie, R.: *Primitive Society*, p. 388.

4. Wines, F.: *Punishment and Reformation*; A Study of the Penitentiary System, p. 105.

5. Hampe, T.: *Crime and Punishment in Germany*, pp. 53, 62, 68, 99.

6. *The Cambridge History of India*, Vol. I, p. 277; (Ancient India) edited by Rapson, E. J. (Ch. XXI on the Growth of Law and Legal Institutions by Prof. E. Washburn Hopkins).

7. *Cambridge History of India*, Vol. I, pp. 281, 282.

8. *The Cambridge History of India*, Vol. I. pp. 283, 284.

9. Edwards, S. M. and Garrett, H. L. *Mughal Rule in India*, p. 190.

10. Sarkar, J.N.: Studies in Mughal India, p. 160.

11. *Cambridge History of India*, Vol. IV, *The Mughal Period*, edited by Sir Richard Burn, Chap. XVII, p. 478.

12. *Cambridge History of India*, Vol. VI, p. 127.

13. *Cambridge History of India*, Vol. VI, p. 127.

14. *Ibid.*, p. 56.

15. Cambridge History of India, Vol. VI, p. 56.

16. *Ibid.*, p. 57.

17. Dhalla, M. N.: *Zoroastrian Civilization* p. 95.

18. *Ibid.*, p. 96.

19. *Ibid.*, p. 106.

20. Dhalla, M.: Zoroastrian Civilization, pp. 96, 97.

21. *Ibid.*, p. 111.

22. Russell, B.: *Roads to Freedom*, p. 135.

24. Stustman, J.: *Curing the Criminal*, pp. 335, 336.

25. Hentig, H.: Punishment—*Its Origin, Purpose and Psychology.*, p. 169.

26. The hopelessness of capital punishment as a deterrent can well be realized when we note what David Abrahamsen has to say in this connection. During the eighteenth and even the earlier part of the nineteenth centuries, pick-pocketing was punishable with death. Even when the offender was being hanged, there were sharpers ready to pick pockets of those who delighted themselves as spectators at the scene of the execution. The clearly shows how "effective a deterrent", the punishment of death is. If spectators had their pockets successfully picked at the very scene of the hanging, how does the punishment deter? (See Abrahamsen D.: The Psychology of Crime, p. 246).

27. Pamphlet published by the National Council for the Abolition of the Death Penalty; cited by Dr. P. K. Sen in his "*Penology Old and New*", at p. 225.

28. Muhl, A. M.: *Criminology*, p. 123.

29. Stutsman, with his experience as prison Governor, says, "Many many times I have heard the condemned criminal remorsefully say, "I didn't know what I was doing—seem to have been beside myself." (Stutsman, J.: *Curing the Criminal*), p. 338.

30. Scott, G.R.: *The History of Corporal Punishment*, pp. 38, 39, 64.

31. King, V.: *Problems of Modern American Crime*, pp. 276-278.

32. Ellis. H.: *The Criminal*, pp. 327, 328.

33. Koerber, L.: *Soviet Russian Fights Crime*, p. 12.

34. Rush B.: An Inquiry into the Effects of Public Punishments upon Criminals and upon Society, Philadelphia, 1787; Cited by Tappan, P. W. in his excellent Work: Crime, Justice Correction, 1960, p. 433.

35. Tappen, P. W.: Crime, Justice and Correction, p. 433.

36. Sen, P. K.: *Penology Old and New*. p. 174.

37. *Ibid.*, pp. 174, 175.

38. At the Second All India Police Science Congress, held in September, 1961, in Bombay, Shri K.P. Venkatesha Murthy, Deputy Central Intelligence Officer, Central Detective Training School, Calcutta, in his Paper entitled: "*Control over Criminals and Crime through Domiciliary Visits, Habitual Offenders Act, and section 565 of the Criminal Procedure Code*" declared the deep need for Habitual Offenders Acts in *all* the States in India. He pleaded that such Acts may be so amended as to remove fears of unnecessary harassment and at the same time empower the police to exercise sufficient sureillence over habitual offendes so that crime may be efficiently prevented and minimised. At the same meeting of this Police Science Congress, another delegate, Shri S. B. Sahai, Superintendent of Police. Monghyr (Bihar), in his Paper entitled: "*Crime Prevention through Rehabilitation of Criminals,*" strongly pleaded for rehabilitation of offenders. He expressed his opinion that surveillance by the Police is not required, and that prevention of crime and of recidivism can well be attained through rehabilitation. It should be our view that rehabilitation is, no doubt, desirable and even necessary, but, at the same time, the police may also be given adequate powers of surveillance over habitual offenders, that surveillance being of a *sympathetic, useful and constructive type*. Mere negative surveillance is not of use; it should be *positive and constructive*. Surveillance may well be associated with rehabilitation. Professor J. J. Panekal, Head of the Department of Criminology at the Tata Institute of Social Sciences, Bombay, advocated that police officers should be empowered to inquire into the antecedents of the offenders, to as to enable the Court not only to pass proper orders but also to classify offenders as habituals.

39. Healy, W.: *The Indivdual Delinquent*, p. 311.

40. Barker, F.A.: *The Modern Prison System of India*, p. 24.

41. Sec. 14 (a) of the Probation of Offenders Act, 1958.
42. Ellis, H.: *The Criminal*, p. 348.
43. Barker, F.A.: *The Modern Prison System of India*, p. 59.
44. *Ibid*, pp. 59, 60, 61.

7

CRIME, VIOLENCE AND EDUCATION

Wrong education is at the root of criminal behaviour. The human mind records by using Amidha. Byanjana and Lakshna capacity, and such a recording is always influenced by the situation, atmosphere and conditions. It is Just like a video camera which records the scene and voice within the reach of the camera lenses. Due to the developments of the physical sciences, television, video, radio, tape recorder etc. available as ordinary, common appliances. Human mind is inclined more towards fall rather than solvation just like it is easier to spend than earn. There have been growing use of goods to see, listen, eat, touch and smell that have a bad effect. The news full of terrorism, weapons and cinemas using weapons, naked pictures to arouse the senses, perfumes that destroy the human glands, drinks and food that destroy the health of the people, cosmetics that destroy the beauty and the body, all combine everday to incline to bad education rather than education in the proper sense of the term. There are neither schools nor workshops to promote and develop good qualities such as kindness, love, affection, cordiality and humanity. A pistol in the hands of children becomes a toy but it encourages the fighting instinct among them. It is not the seed of love that is planted in the fertile minds of the children but the seed of hatred. Thus, better results call for better education. The goal of education should be the development of a human personality. According to a study done by John Huber-man: although punishment seemed to stop the inappropriate behaviour for the moment, it had little long term effect. When top management finally analyzed the system during the preparation for the doubling of its capacity, they analyzed that...not a single desirable result could be detected."

(Management of Organization Behaviour, Paul Hersey and K.H. Blanchared, Prantice-Hell Inc., New Jersey 07632).

It proves that man's sentiment should be reformed but not by terrorizing. suppressing and ordering. Suppression and punishment are actions and bound to produce reactions. Terror is also a reaction. In order to uproot terror, its main causes such as hate, selfishness, jealousy against humanity should be dealt with first. An educational system designed to help solve these problems as well as promoting cordiality is the need of the day. The greatest weapon against terror and violence is loving behaviour among the human beings.

Role of Religion

No religion advocates violence. Buddhism, of all emphasises ideals of peace and compassion. In popular understanding, Himsa is associated with killing—a physical act. Buddhism, going deeper, connects it with the realm of mind. Defining hatred from Buddhist stand point, Samtani goes to show that mental sin is vaster— volition itself in an act". Against this Buddhism upholds loving kindness and equates it with non-violence. As such the much advertised recent concept of "Just War" fades out, being alien to Buddhist thinking. Once unwholesome violence in its entirety is given up, the vacuum is filled by joy and happiness which in its turn, helps meditative concentration, Purna-Buddha dialogue illuminates this point. Buddhism does not go as far as Jainism, which preaches self-mortification. Gandhiji took it up but made a distinction between cowardice and violence, prefering, given a choice, the latter. Similarly Satyagraha, to him, was a moral substitute for war. One of the greatest threats to the world at present is growing violence. which is appearing in various forms viz. terrorism, internecine clashes communal riots, wars between neighbouring countries threatening the global peace. Development of Nuclear weaponary is the culmination of this growing violence leading to mutual distrust among nations of the world.

No founder of any religion advocated violence. Love, mercy and fellowship have been cardinal principles of religion. Yet in the name of religion, violence destruction, mutual acrimony are frequently reported in the world news. The speakers in this Conference will present their views on "Violence: Roots and Resolution" from their different perspectives. I would like to share my views on the basis of my study of Budhist texts and try to find whether we can find some guidelines in rooting out the growing cancer of violence. In this year of Nehru centenery, let me quote Jawaharlal, who was greately influenced by the personality of Buddha and for whom Buddhism had an answer not only to personal problems but also to national and international problems as well. He says:

> In these great times I see a ray of hope in the path shown by the Buddha. My mind gets a little relief and confidence not from what is happening in the world but from the message of Buddha.
>
> His message was one of universal benevolence, of love for all. For never in the world does hatred cease by hatred: hatred ceases by love. And let a man overcome anger by kindness, evil by good.

History of Buddhism has been history of deals of peace, benevolence, compassion in action. Wherever Buddhism went, it spread the message of kindness, love and renunciation. The practical results of this development of compassion have been seen in the way Buddhism has softened the rough warrior races of Tibet and Mangolia, nearly effecting all traces of their original brutality.

For Violence, the term used in Indian languages is himsa which is generally associated with its physical aspects, like killing or injuring a living being. Thus popular meaning of himsa is killing a living being, that which causes the separation to life (prana) from the body of other. The Buddhist term is pranatipata. However, if we analyse the concept of 'violence' deeply it is associated with the realm of mind. The violence or war first begins in the mind of man. It surfaces in its physical form only after the mental agitation has reached its culmination.

Now, before we discuss the causes of violence, let us analyse the violent mind. The words come up before us for violence and violent measure: rancoax, contempt, malice, antagonism, quarrel, prejudice. revenge, aggression, murder, assassination. We shall discuss now how Buddhist texts define a violent mind. The synonymous words for violent mind in Buddhist terminology are 'hatred' (*dvesa*) repugnence (*pratigha*) and ill-will (*vyapada*).

In the early Buddhist texts there are two definitions of "hatred" (dvesah):

> What is hatred? The hate hating, hatred, which on that occasion is a distorted temper, the getting upset, opposition, hostility, churlishness, aburptness, disgust of heart. This is called hatred.

Another definition of hatred is somewhat elaborate which is as follows:

> Therein what is hatred? He has done me harm thus vexation arises: He is doing me harm, thus vexation arises; He will do me harm, thus vexation arises; He has done harm to one that is dear and pleasant to me, he is doing harm, he will do harm, thus vexation arises: He has done good to one not dear and not pleasant to me, he is doing good, he will do good why not plesant to me, thus vexation arises, or vexation arises unreasonably. That which is similar, vexation or consciousness, resentment, repulsion, hostility, irritation, exasperation, incensement hatred, antipathy, abhorrence, mental disorder, detestation, anger, being angry, state of being angry, hatred, being hateful, state of bang hateful, disorder, disorderly, antagonism, hostility, ferocity, abruptness, absence of delight of consciousness. This is called hatred.

Buddhism stresses that mind is the main factor in the personality of man: The first two verses of Dahammapada state that:—

> Mind is the forenumer of all evil and good in the world. If one speak of acts with wicked mind, pain pursues him as the wheel follows the hoof of the draught-ox. Similarly is one speaks and acts with pure thought, happiness follows him like a shadown that never leaves.

In the discussion with a Jain devotee, the Buddha contradicts the view that physical action is more significant. He explains to him that mental aspect in life is more important that a physical one. committing a mental offence brings more sin than the physical one because it object is vast. Physically you can attack one or two persons at a time but mentally you can think ill of or curse many and also spread violent thoughts among others resulting in more physical violence. The communal riots that occur frequently in some countries are the result of spread of thoughts of violence. Thus Buddhism lays great emphasis on mental culture. Violition (cetana) is called the act itself. Hence in the Buddhist textsmind (citta) and mental factors (cetesika) are analysed in details.

Maitre (loning kindness) Karuna (compassion) are the sheet-anchor of Buddhism. Maitri is another name of *ahimsa* (non-violence). Non-violence and peace are the cardinal virtues which Buddhism preaches. There is no place of any kind of violence and destruction in Buddhism. There is no place of war, even the so-called 'just war' in the reigion of the Buddha. Waipola Rahula in What the Buddha taught rightly remarks:

> "According to Buddhism there is nothing that can be called a just war'—which is only a false term coined and put into circulation to justify excuse hatred, cruelty, violence and massacre. Who decides what is just or unjust? The mighty and the victorious are 'just' and the weak and the defeated are 'unjust'. Our war is always 'just' and your war is always 'just' and your war is always (unjust). Buddhism does not accept this position.

The Buddha not only taught virtues of non-violence and peace but prevented a war between two opposing warrior groups, Sakya and Koliya when they were poised to attack each other.

It may, however, be noted that for the non-violence the word often used in Buddhist texts is not shimsa, but avihimsa. A monk is required to inculcate thought without any kind of rancour (*abyapada-samkappa*) and not to give place to the thought of violence (*avihimsa-samkappa*) along with the thought of renunciation (*nekkhamma samkappa*). In fact this is the explanation of one of the factors of the Noble Eightfold Path called "Right Thought" or "Right Resolution" (Incidentally this Conference also) discusses the theme. "Violence: Roots and Resolutions'). Thus cultivation of thoughts of non-violence of non-harming is the "Right Resolution" or "Right Thought" according to Buddha.

Buddhist texts tell us that those who give up unwholesome

thoughts of hatred, violence and cruelty, in them happiness spontaneously springs up and the joy wells up. One is at ease and the peaceful happiness follows him which leads to concentrated mind (*samahita citta*). And we know how concentration plays a role in the life of a man. Some of the great achievements of great persons are made because they could concentrate on their subject of then study. A violent and agitated mind therefore can not concentrate in a peaceful way and therefore cannot be creative.

The Buddha was a personification of loving kindness and compassion. In the Buddhist canon is found the story of one of the greatest terrorists of ancient India. Angulimala who wore a garland of one thousand fingers around his neck. He was tamed not by stones, swords of any other weapon but by the Maitri of the Blessed one. He was a changed personality after he met Buddha. As students of Indian history we know how Ashoka after being converted to Buddhism realised the futility of war as a state policy. His heart was full of remorse after the Kalinga war. The Ashokan edicts speak of the tremandous agony of the Beloved of Gods, Emperor Ashoka feels very much for the destruction of human beings, causing great suffering to families of victims of war. That Buddhism taught the virtues of forbearance and tolerance in the trying circumstances and in the face of violent people in best illustrated by a famous story of a monk named Purna. Monk Purna resolves to go as a missionary to a country which was inhabited by wild barbarous tribes. He asked permission from the Buddha. But the Buddha at first discouraged him to take the tisk. The Buddha told him that people of Sronaparant (name of country where barbarous tribes lived) were fierce, violent and cruel. They were given to abusing, reviling and would be annoying him with evil, harm and falsehood.

The rest of the dialogue between Purna and Buddha is reproduced below:

"*Buddha* : What would you do, Purna, if they abuse you with harsh and false words?

Purna : In that case Lord, I would think that people of Sronaparant are really good and gentle folk, as they do not strike me with the hands or with stones.

Buddha :"But if they strike you Purna, with their hands of with clods, what would you think?".

Purna : "In that case, Lord, I would think that they are good and gentle folk, as they do not strike me with a cudgel or a weapon".

Buddha: "But if they strike you Purna, with a cudgel or a weapon, what would you think?

Purna: In that case, Lord, I would think that they are good and gentle folk, as they do not take my life.

Buddha: "But it they kill you, Purna, what would think?

Purna: "In that case, Lord, I would still think that they are good and gentle folk, as they release me from this rotten carcass of the body without much difficulty. I know that there are monks, who are ashamed of the body and distressed and disgusted with it, and who slay themselves with ropes or throw themselves down from precipice. So I shall thank those people for rendering me a service".

Buddha: You are, Purna, endowed with the greatest gentleness and forbearence. You can live and stay in that country of the Sronaparent. Go. Purna and teach them how to be free, as you yourself are free.

The above story of Purna, is an illustration of non-violent approach. Such stories extolling virtues of non-violence, loving kindness, commpassion, are found in abundance in Buddhist texts.

Jainism like Buddhism also stresses the mental aspects of non-violence but emphasis of the physical aspects is also found. Violence (*himsa*) in any form, even to material thing (*draya*) is deprecated. The physical mortification finds an important place in Jainism. But non-violence is a sheet-anchor or forte of the Jain teaching. Whether jains were successful in creating a mass awareness against the violence, it is difficult to say. But vegetarianism which we find in India owes much to the teaching of Jain monks in our country.

However, it was Mahatma Gandhi who popularised the concept of nonviolence of a mass scale. He was more influenced by Jain teachings but Buddha's gospel influenced him no less. Gandhiji had a courage to give his own interpretation of violence preached in Gita during the Kurukshetra war when armies of Kauravas and Pandavas were arrayed fora war and Arjun asked Krishna as to how he could fight against his who kith and kin.

Gandhiji does not approve of non-violence of the sense of mere nonkilling. Like Buddhist teachers, he says that violence is wrong at any time. According to him fear stimulates structural violence and exploitation. Gandhiji has shown that a coward in need of protection can never be non-violent. However, when there is choice between cowardice and violence, Gandhiji would even advice violence.

Evil. according to Gandhiji cannot be cured by evel, nor hated is conqured by hale, echoing the famous Dhammapada quotation.

> na hi verena veranis samanti idha Kadacina i.e. hatred never ceases by cultivating eratred)

Satan according to Gandhiji cannot be exercised by Satan, Gandhiji further says:

> "It is no non-violence if we merely love those that come to us. I know how difficult it is to follow the grand law of love. But are not all great and good things difficult to do. Love of hater is the most difficult of all. But by the grace of God even this most difficult thing becomes easy to accomplish if we want to do it. Humanity must therefore, find some other way than crooked diplomacy, violence and war for the solution of political and international problems involving injustice, tyranny and cruelties.

Gandhiji's Satyagraha showed the way. It is a moral substituted for war.

Thus we can see that violence does not solve problems that we face. Hence Buddha and Gandhi emphasised the non-violent approach in personal, social as well in other spheres of human life. Hatred will never cease by hatred. The path of love compassion and friendless is the only path for uprooting the cancer of violence.

LAW AS SOCIAL FORCE

Profusely punctuated with quotations and instances and illustrations, this very 'novel' paper impliedly states: King can do no wrong. Amidst the clash of arms, if the law is silent, it is undenially a bad law. Under the conditions of insurrection and clamping of marshal law, though marshal law is no law at all, becomes a law on the basis of the principle of necessity, Mr. Selvaratnam has dwelt on the Doctrine of Necessity at length clarifying that in view of the safety of the people (fundamental right) even unlawful becomes 'lawful' provided it is proportionate to the harm sought to be prevented. Safety of the people is indeed a supreme law, and when annuled constitution fails to do that, illegal regimes passing laws or decrees become valid on the basis of necessity. Thus, Doctrine of Necessity can 'twist' law anyway it likes. Rightly, therefore, Court is said to be the least dangerous branch of government. If the usurper is ruthless, Courts are helpless. The Law of Indemnity protects the law-breaker. Mandamus is a feeble remedy.

In the matter of government when nothing else is turned up, 'Clubs are Trump.' Hobbes, Dialogue between a Philosopher and a Student, of the Common Laws of England Punishments, p. 140.

In a famous case decided by the house of Lords during the Second World War one of the judges Lord Atkin, dissenting from the majority of the court, said in his speech:

"In view of the apprehension the attitude of judges who, on mere question of construction, when face to face with claims involving the liberty of the subject, show themselves more executive minded than the executive. Their function is to give words their natural meaning, not, perhaps in war time, leaning towards liberty, but following the dictum of Pollock C.B. who said in a case in which the liberty of the subject is concerned, we cannot go beyond the natural construction of the statute.

In England amidst the clash of arms the laws are not silent. They may be changed, but they speak the same language in war as in peace. It has always been one of the pillars of freedom, one of the principles of liberty for which, on recent authority, we are now fighting, that the judges are no respecters of persons, and stand between the subject and any attempted encroachments on his liberty by the executive, alert to see that any coercive action is justified in law. In this case, I have listened to arguments which might have been addressed acceptable to the Court of King's Bench in the time of Charles I.

In protest, even if I do it alone, against a strained construction put upon words with the effect of giving an uncontrolled power of imprisonment to the Minister. To recapitulate, the words have only one meaning. They are used with that meaning in statements of the common law and in statutes. They have never been used in the sense now imputed to them. They are used in the Defence Regulations in the natural meaning, and, when it is intended to express the meaning now imputed to them, different and apt words are used in the Defence Regulations generally and in this regulation in particular.

In the *Pro Milone*, Marcus Tullius Cicero said '*Silent leges inter arma.*' Amidst the clash of arms the laws are silent. He meant that in times of war, legal procedures come to a standstill. When the very security of the state is in peril, it is futile to insist on the due observance of legal forms. These same words are inscribed in the war memorial in Lincoln's Inn in London— '*Inter arma silent leges.*' The maxim was used in the famous case of Shipmoney (Rv Hampden 1637). Leqal proceedings were taken against John Hampden, a Buckinghamshire gentleman for refusing to pay the amount of £1 assessed on him.

Charles I levied a tax in order to furnish ships in time of national danger. Counsel for Hampden conceded the point that sometimes the existence of danger would justify the taking of goods belonging to a subject without his consent, but only in actual as opposed to threatened emergency. The Crown conceded that the subject could not be taxed in normal circumstances without the consent of Parliament but contended that the King was the sole judge of whether an emergency justified the exercise of his prerogative power to impose taxes to meet a national danger. The Court by a majority decided in favour of the King. The royal prerogative means the inherent legal attributes which are unique to the Crown. The decision in the Shipmoney case was, declared by Parliament to be wrong and five of the judges were imprisoned. The maxim *inter arma silent leges*' is bad law. Though in time of war the Queen has wider powers than in peacetime, the laws are not silent. It is the law which determines the scope and limits of her powers. If her powers are exceeded, her subjects can take legal proceedings.

So though the Crown and its officials do have vast powers, these powers have their limits defined by law. This is so even in time of emergency.

In the 13th century Henry of Bratton, generally known as Bracton wrote. The King shall not be subject to men, but to God and the law: since law makes the King.

A government official must show legal authority for his actions. In *Entickv Carrington* 1765, a very famous case, two King's messengers sent by Lord Halifax, the Secretary of State were sued for having unlawfully broken and entered the plaintiff's house and ransacked his papers. In an ordinary action, £300 were awarded to Entick as damages. The particular servants who did the deed were sued just as it they were private individuals. Lord Camden said "...And with respect to the argument of State necessity, or a distinction that has been aimed at between State offences and others, the common law does not understand that kind of reasoning, nor do our books take notice of any such distinction. The general warrant issued by the Secretary of State to enter and seize the plaintiff's papers was illegal and state necessity did not justify it. I referred to a famous case at the beginning of this paper. This was *Liversidge* v. *Anderson* 1942. The House of Lords had to interpret a wartime regulation—Regulation 18β—which empowered the Home Secretary to detain without trial persons whom he had reasonable cause to believe were of hostile origin or association. The House of Lords by a majority held that the power to detain could not be controlled by the courts. The courts could not enquire into the grounds for the belief which led to the making of a detention order. It was a matter for executive discretion. The statement of his belief by the Home Secretary was conclusive.

However, in *Liversidge v. Anderson*, Lord Atkin dissented. He held that the Home Secretary's powers were the Home Secretary's powers were conditional on his having reasonable cause to believe that the man was of hostile origin. If the matter was disputed, it must be decided by the courts and the Home Secretary's order could only be legal if a court of law found that the condition was fulfilled. Lord Atkin held that it was not enough to show that the Home Secretary reasonably believed in his own mind. The Home Secretary had to show objectively, to the satisfaction of an independent judge, that he had grounds for his belief which were reasonable in the judgement of the court, He said:

I know of only one authority which might justify the suggested method of construction, "When I use a word' Humpty Dumpty said in rather a scornful tone, it means just what I choose it to mean and neither more not less., 'The question is, said Alice, 'whether you can mean so, many different things'. 'The question is, said Humpty Dumpty, 'which is to be master—that's all.'' (Through the Looking Glass, Chap. VI).

Liversidge v. *Anderson*, of course, was a wartime case. Indeed, the decision has been described as the House of Lord's contribution to the war effort. Fortunately, the highest tribunal in England, the House of Lords later recognized the justice of Lord Atkin's insistence that reasonable cause' must be interpreted objectively. There must in fact, be reasonable cause for the Home Secretary to take the steps provided for in the regulation. Indeed, in an important later case in 1964 an eminent Law Lord, Lord Reid described the majority decision in *Liversidge* v. ***Anderson*** as a very peculiar decision of the House. So Lord Atkin's dissenting view has been accepted as right. I mentioned *Liversidge* v. ***Anderson*** to show that in times of crisis even the highest tribunal in a democratic country might seem to have abandoned established canons of statutory interpretation.

The principle of legality is a vital legal principle in constitutional systems of government. The principle is often stated in its Latin dress 'Nulla poena sine lege'. There must be no punishment except in accordance with fixed, predetermined law. As the famous constitutional lawyer, Albert Venn Dicey said, "A man may with us be punished for a breach of law, but he can be punished for nothing else". The Universal Declaration of Human Rights states. "No one shall be held guilty of any penal offence on account of any act or omission which did not constitute a penal offence at the time when it was committed." However, In *Joyce* 1946, William Joyce was convicted of treason under an Act of 1351. He had broadcast as Lord Haw-Haw from Germany on behalf of the Germans. Joyce was a U.S. citizen. But he obtained a British passport by falsely declaring himself to be a British citizen.

The House of Lords held that even though he was an alien, he was guilty of treason. His possession of a British passport extended to him the protection of the Crown outside the realm. Protection was the counterpart of the duty of allegiance. Since he had availed himself of the protection of the Crown, he owned allegiance to the Crown. By broadcasting for Germany he had committed treason. This decision of the highest tribunal in Britain is quite indefensible. The Crown owed no duty to protect him by the *fact* of his having the passport. So why did Joyce own allegiance to the Crown while Germany? In the end, Joyce hanged. The decision was not base on the existing law and is an ilitimate extension of the crime law. It seems that the judges want somehow to convict William Joy of treason. Perhaps, during or just after a war, fundamental principle of law are easily overturned for other reasons such as the desire for revenge. The decision is indefensible.

In times of civil was or disturbance the officers of the government may have to take action which is illegal. Their action may bc a violation of the law, laying them open to prosecution or court actions. That is why an Act of Indemnity may have to be passed by Parliament in order to make legal, transactions which were illegal at the time they took place or to free individuals from liability for having broken the law. The Act of Indemnity protects the law-breaker from the consequences of his acts. A.V. Dicey states: The protection of military men and others against actions or prosecutions in respect of unlawful acts done during a time of war, *bone fide*, and in the service of the country, is an Act of Indemnity. So an Act of Indemnity legalises past illegalities.

This brings us to martial law. After a state of martial law an Act of Indemnity may be passed to give retrospective protection to the armed forces. When martial law ends, the courts may review the legality of acts committed when martial law was in force. An Act of Indemnity will give protection to the armed forces for such acts. But since the decision if a 1798 case Wright v Fitzgerald it has been thought that in interpreting an Indemnity Act the courts presume that Parliament does not intend to protect persons who have committed want-on or cruel acts which the situation did not call for. The person should have acted in good faith: However, the working of the Indemnity Act may be very wide. Martial law is the situation which arises when the civil authorities cannot govern an insurrection having prevented this. It is the military authorities take charge and during the time this state of affairs prevails, their acts cannot be questioned in the courts. It has, therefore, been said that martial law is no law at all. The actions of the military authorities in restoring order are legally unchallengeable. The principle of necessity, which I refer to below, is the basis of martial law.

There is another sense in which the term martial law is often used. As has happened, in certain countries, the military may seize the government and proclaim martial law. So there is an usurpation of power. That do the judges do? The Pakistani Constitution of 1956 was over thrown in a coup by Aybu Khan against President Iskander Mirza and in The *State* v *Dosso* 1958 (later overruled but only after the regime was no onger in power) this is what the Supreme Court said :

"A charge is, in law, a revolution it annuals the Constitution and the annulment is effective. If the attempt of break the Constitution fails, those who sponsor of organise it are adjudged by the existing Constitution as guilty of the crime of treason. But, if the revolution is victorious in the sense that the persons assuming power can successfully require the inhabitants of the state to conform to the new regime, then the revolution itself has become a law-creating fact because, thereafter, its own legality is judged not by reference to the annulled Constitution but by reference to its own success." The court recognized the supersession in 1958 of the old order by Ayub Khan as valid. The new regime was held to have established a new legal order. The revolutionary regime, which was effectively in power, was legal and had overthrown the previous Constitution. So the usurpers are entitled to judicial recognition as being legitimate and they are, in consequence, legally immune in respect of their revolutionary acts. In Uganda the court applied the decision in *Dosso* and held that the overthrow of the Constitution by Obote was valid (ex parte Matovu 1966). After the Unilateral Declaration of Independence in Rhodesia in 1965, the courts in Rhodesia and the Privy Council followed this approach. Reliance was placed on the theory of the eminent jurist, Hans Kelsen, based on effectiveness. The Court said in *Dosso*:

If the revolution is victorious in the sense that the persons assuming power under the change can successfully require the inhabitants of the country to conform to the new regime, then the revolution itself becomes a law creating fact because thereafter its own legality is judged not by reference to the annulled constitution but by reference to its own success. Persuasion, coercion, oppression may all be reasons for the effectiveness of the new regime. It there is approval for the unsurping regime or if there is no resistance to it, then there is effectiveness.

There is also another way in which the courts can decide in favour of the unsurpet. Even if the old order is valid, it may be impossible to act in accordance with it because an emergency has arisen.

This is the principle of necessity, which renders lawful what would otherwise be unlawful. Martial law during a state of civil disorder is an application of this principle. It has been said that the law *includes* the doctrine of necessity; the defence of necessity is an implied exception to particular rules of law. However, the concept of necessity does not involve the consequence that the courts give up their power of review. Acts will be justified under the doctrine only if they are proportionate to the harm sought to be prevented. State necessity has been recognised by the courts as justifying unconstitutional action. For instance, in Pakistan, the principle was accepted in 1955 in a case in which the court held that the powers and responsibilities of the Head of a State in preserving the State and Society during an extraordinary emergency and preventing from disruption the constitution and government of the country are analouges to the powers which an army commander has during martial law. When the legislature is not in existence, the head of the state may temporarily assume to himself legislative powers to prevent the state and society from dissolution. The relevant branch of the law was the law of civil or state necessity. That which otherwise is not lawful necessity makes lawful. Salus *popil suprema lex.* The safety of the pupil is the supreme law. Salus *reipublicanest suprema lex.* The safety of the state is the supreme law. The court said that the best statement of the reason underlying the law of necessity waṣ Cromwell's famous utterance. "If nothing should be done but what is according to law, the throat of the nation might be cut while, we send for someonẹ to make a law. The maxim sited above *Salus populi suprema lex* was based on the implied agreement of every member of society that his own individual welfare shall, in cases of necessity, yield to that of the community; and that his property, liberty and life shall, in certain circumstanes, be placed in jeopardy or even sacrificed for the public good.

The court held that the principle *salus populi suprema lex* must apply not only in respect of the acquisition of a citizen's property in time of war but also in the situation where the State was in danger of collapse owing to other factors. *Special Reference No. 1 of 1955.* The court in Pakistan upheld the acts of the Governor-General even though they were inconsistent with the Constutution.

In a Cyprus case *A.G.* v *Mustafa Ibrahim* 1964, legislation inconsistent with the Constitution was held to be valid on the principle of necessity. The communal problem was so severe that the doctrine had to be invoked to justify the inconsistency. Necessity render validly applicable what would otherwise be illegal and invalid. The State and the people cannot perish for the sake of the Constitution, said the court.

In a Nigerian case *Lakanni* 1970 the Suprerpe Court held that the justification for the military take-over in January 1966 was the doctrine of state necessity. So, unless the doctrine necessitated the restriction of a fundamental right, the fundamental right was in force. The Government's arguments that the fundamental rights no longer operated were rejected. A decree authorising the forfeiture of assets was held to the invalid on the grounds that the principle of necessity did not cover the restriction of a fundamental right when there was no emergency situation.

The necessity doctrine has been a way by which the courts, while not accepting the claim of the new regime to legitimacy, do recognise the acts of the regime as valid. So in the case of Rhodesia where on 11 November 1965, the Rhodesian government unilaterally declared its independence, scrapped the Constitution and substituted a new one, the Rhodesian court decided that the new regime was illegal. At the same time, the court accepted the orders of a Minister as valid on the basis of the necessity principle. An appeal court later reversed the decision on a technical point while maintaining that the regime had not acquired legitimacy though it was the *de facto* government later, the Privy Council on appeal also held that the regime was illegal. It rejected the adoption of the necessity principle by the courts in Rhodesia. Lord Pearce, however, dissented from the majority on this point. *Madzimbamuto* v. *Lardner Burke* 1969.

Another interesting point in Rhodesian situation. Though the new regime was illegal in the opinion of the court, some of its decrees may be valid laws if they were in accordance with the overthrown Constitution. This was the view of the two Rhodesian courts and also of the dessenting judge in the Privy Council, Lord Pearce. This means that even an illegal regime can pass valid laws. The old order is the legal one, though not effective *de facto*. Nevertheless, the enactments of the new regime are valid if they conform to the overthrown Constitution. So the validity of a law and the law creating source are quite separate matters.

The court may have to decide on the validity of an order of the new regime. It may be that the court does not want to accept the legality or legitimacy of the usurper. The court can maintain that the new regime has no legitimacy. Nevertheless, the court may not be ready to face open conflict with the usurper. After all, even in a established constitutional system such as that of the United States, the courts have been called the least dangerous branch of government. If an usurper is ruthless, the courts are helpless. So the court, basing itself on the concept of necessity, while holding that the new regime is illegal, accepts its acts as valid if they can be shown to be justified on the basis of necessity. This happened in Pakistan where, though Yahya Khan's regime was held to be illegal, its acts were accepted as valid by the court on "grounds of necessity, *Jilani* v *Government of Punjab* 1972. Again, in 1977, the court, while declaring that General Zia-ul-Haq's regime was illegal, accepted, the regime's acts as valid. *Begum Bhutto* 1977.

In theory, at any rate the necessity approach to the acts of an usurping regime enables a court to retain a certain control over the acts of the usurper. Under the doctrine the acts must be proportionate to the evil to be averted. It is the court which decides this. So it may be that, at least in theory this approach enables a court to uphold constitutionalism in a situation where the usurper is in control. Perhaps, the courts, maintaining their independent stance can contribute in some way, to the return of normalcy. We are seeing this happen in Pakistan where an elected government is now in control.

Insurrection and internal civil commotion obviously raise severe law and order problems. The ordinary procedures of constitutional government may have to be suspended if the situation is to be brought under control. Civil rights may have to be curtailed, the rules regarding arrest and custody may have to be adapted to the abnormal situation.

In such situations, the usual way of dealing with them is the proclamation of an emergency and the passing of regulations by the executive. Some measure of control is retained by Parliament, which may have to approve the extension of the emergency at prescribed intervals. The Special Presidential Commission of Inquiry reported that the Prime Minister during the 1970-1977 government and kept the state of emergency in operation, even when the situation no longer demanded its retention.

The exercise of the discretionary power vested in the government to declare a state of emergency is unreviewable by the courts. It is the government which is vested with the power to decide whether the situation calls for a declaration of a state of emergency. However, in a very interesting 1980 decision of the Privy Council in a Malaysian appeal, it was held that is was an abuse of discretion for the head of state not to revoke a proclamation of emergency, once he considered it to be no longer necessary for the purpose for which it was issued. So his power to revoke it is not entirely unfettered. The ruler himself was not subject to court proceedings. However, an order of *mandamus* could be tought against the members of his cabinet requiring them to advise the ruler to revoke the proclamation.

Under the Constitution of Malaysia, Article 40 the King, the Yang di-Pertuan. Agong acts in accordance with ministerial advice in most matters.

Perhaps, I may end this paper on the law in turbulent times with a reference to England. We usually think of the government of England as a model of constitutional government where the rule of law is respected.

Anyway, if we go by the law, it may be that every law passed by Parliament since 1688 is a nullity and that: Queen Elizabeth II is not England's lawful sovereign. In July 1688 James II dissolved his Parliament. In December, of the same year he fied from London dropping the Great Seal into the Thamas. William, Prince of Orange met a Convention of peers, former MPs and other leading citizens who advised him that elections be held. The Convention 'Parliament' met in January 1689 and offered the Crown to William and May jointly on conditions stated in a Declaration of Right. This offer was accepted.

The Convention Parliament passed an Act in which it stated that it was Parliament. The great legal historian, F. W. Maitland refers to this crucial event in England history as follows:

''Now certainly it was very difficult for any lawyer to argue that there had not been a revolution. Those who conducted the revolution sought, and we may well say where wise in seeking, to make the revolution look as small as possible, to make it is like a legal proceeding, as by any stretch of ingenuity it could be made. But to make it out to be a perfectly legal act seems impossible. Had it failed, those who attempted it would have suffered as traitors, and I do not think that any lawyer can maintain that their execution would have been unlawful... it is difficult for a lawyer to regard the Convention as a lawfully constituted assembly. By whom was it summoned? Not by a King of England, but by a Prince of Orange.''

REFERENCES

1. Quoted in *Buddhism seen by Great Minds, ed. by Nemisiri Mutukumara, Allceylon Buddhist Congress Diamond Jubilee Volume, Colombo, 1980. p.14.

2. J. Nehru, discovery of India Meridian Books Ltd., London, 1960, p.117.

3. H. Dumoulin (ed.) Buddhism in the Modern World. Collier Books, London 1976, p. 30.

4. C.A.F. Rhys Davids: A Buddhist Manual of Psychological Ethics, Oriental Books Reprint Corporation 1975, p. 111.

5. Cf. P.A. Thittla (tr.) The Book of Analysis (Vibhanga) London, 1969, p. 471.

6. Dhammapada Verses I. 1-2 (Nalanda ed.), p. 120.

7. Anguttaranikaya, Vol. III (Nalanda, ed.), p. 120.

8. W. Rahula: What the Buddha Taught. New York, 1974, p. 84.

9. *Ibid.*

10. For the story of Angulimala, see Majjhima Nikaya, Vol. II (Nalanda ed.), pp. 344ff.
11. Har Dayal : Bodhisatva Doctrine in Buddhist Literature, Delhi, 1970, pp. 213-14.
12. Bhagavadgita I. 31ff.
13. Cf. J.B. Kriplani, Gandhi : His Life and Thought pp. 347-48
14. Dhammapada I. 5.
15. J. B Kripalani, *op. cit.*, pp. 347.

8

COMBATING CRIME: SOME COUNTRY EXPERIENCES

Introduction

A number of disciplines, such as law and sociology, have found it fruitful to study the institution of foreign countries. Observing the operation of a different legal system of foreign police agency may at times suggest improvement in our own procedures.

In view of our current crime problem, which is certainly serious if not critical, it would appear that we can use all the help we can get.

Our crime rate has been soaring almost without check since 1950, and all components of the criminal justice system (police, courts, and corrections) have been subjected to severe criticism.

Crime rates are also rising elsewhere but they are still considerably less than ours.

A comparison, for example, or crime figures in Japan and England with New York City (Table 8.1) is striking. Their figures are an argument for comparative police studies. They indicate that a study of policing in countries with low crime rates may yield insights which will enable us to cope more successfully with our own crime situation.

Up to now very little has been done in the field of comparative policing. The literature available on foreign police systems is quite limited, although there has been some increase in recent years.

If we accept that police work is carried out under the influence of a political culture, it follows that comparative police studies involve more than a simple overview of an agency's organisation, training, and operational methods Some attempt must be made to understand cultural patterns, historical factors, and sociological processes. The interrelationship among police, courts, corrections, and population must also be studied.

For example, it is of interest to speculate why policing in almost every country in the world is at the national level, while in a few countries like Brazil and Australia it is primarily at the state level, and in the United States and England it is primarily at the local level. Even in England the trend has been toward centralization, and there are currently no city police agencies outside of London.

In the United States we still have some 17,000 police departments. Although there have been many recommendations for consolidation, there has been little movement in that direction. Perhaps a look abroad would encourage further progress toward that goal.

Comparative studies are not easy even in countries where English is the national language. In other countries the lingual barrier makes the task difficult, and in countries like Japan or Yugoslavia the task becomes formidable.

In spite of the difficulties and the paucity of information, I believe there are certain aspects of policing in other countries that can be usefully considered by American police agencies to improve their effectiveness.

Table 8.1
Crime Figures

	New York City[1]	*England*[2]	*Japan*[3]
Population	7,605,000[4]	49,000,000[5]	112,000,000[6]
Homicides	1,600	420	2,111
Rate per 100,000	21	0.9	1.9
Robberies	86,000	6,000	2,095
Rate per 100,000	1,131	12	1.9

Burglaries	200,000	407,000	328,000
Rate per 100,000	2,632	831	293

UNITED KINGDOM

English policing resembles military service much more closely than does American policing. Where our police officers are likely to consider policing as a job, their English counterparts are more likely to consider it as a career.

An English police officer, at least outside London, is likely to find not only his working time but also his recreation time spent within the service. Especially in ranks above constable, he will eat meals in the police mess: he is apt to do his socializing with his family at the police club, or attend sporting events played by a team of his own force against the team of another force; or simply spend his off-duty time with fellow officers.

Policing in England, as in the United States, is basically at the local level. But where our federal government has no supervision whatsoever over local police departments (except on a very limited basis when a department is the recipient of a federal grant), in England the national government, through the home secretary, has considerable influence over English policing. The home secretary has direct control over the Metropolitan Police by virtue of the statute that created the force. In addition, he exercises indirect control over the other forces by virtue of an exchequer grant of 50 per cent of expenditures available to all "efficient" police agencies, since he can withold the entire grant if dissatisfied with the efficiency of a force.

Under pressure from the home secretary, there has been an accelerated programme of consolidation (amalgamation is the English term) resulting in a reduction from almost 200 forces to 43 at present. Each force, except within London, now has jurisdiction over one or more counties and the only city forces left are within that city. A constable has jurisdiction to exercise his powers throughout England and Wales, regardless of the force to which he is assigned.

The Police Act of 1964 vests control over each force outside London in a Local Police Committee (LPC). The LPCs have their roots in an Act of 1361, which assigned responsibility for preserving the King's Peace to the local justices. To this day, one-third of each LPC must consist of a justice, while the remaining two thirds must consist of county councillors. The LPCs are responsible for appointing chief constables, subject to approval by the home secretary. The LPC must also support their respective forces with the 50 per cent of the cost of operations not provided by the exchequer.

At one time, the chief constable was almost always a civilian, likely to be a retired Army Officer. Today, he is almost always someone who has come up from the ranks. One of the questions that has never been clearly answered is how much control the LPC has over the chief constable. It is clear that he has complete operational authority, including promotions and assignments. He cannot be removed by the LPC unless he can be shown to be corrupt or inefficient. What is not clear is what power the LPC has with respect to policy. Another area that is not settled in the allocation of funds, although the county treasurer helps prepare the annual budget.

Perhaps the greatest difference in control is the manner in which supervision is actually exercised by local authorities. In the United States the chief is generally appointed by the mayor of city manager as an employee of the city and is removable at the pleasure of the appointing authority. On the other hand, in England the courts have held that there is no relationship of master and servant between constables and the local authorities; they are therefore independent of the authorities in the performance of their duties, and this has been confirmed by the home secretary.[9]

With the exception of complaints made by civilians against any of his subordinates and the need to pass inspection by the inspector of constabulary, the chief constable is practically autonomous once appointed. He therefore is not subject to the type of political pressure which are commonplace in the United States.

Basic Training

Recruits in England receive a ten-week training programme, except for the Metroplitan Police who have a 13-week program. At one time each force determined its own training needs, but training is now a national requirement and the syllabus has been standardized since 1971.

Recruit training is conducted in the nine Regional Training Centers established in England and Wales. The ten-week recruit training is considerably less than is generally considered necessary in this country. For example, in the United States, the National Advisory Commission on Criminal Justice Standards and Goals recommends a minimum of 400 hours.

The briefness of the ten-week program is justified as being sufficient for the needs of a new constable. Much material has been eliminated (coinage violation etc.) and other subjects have been abbreviated, such as homicide, procedures (rarely experienced by the new constable). Courses in sociology, psychology, etc., are not regarded as essential for recruits.

A Regional Training Center's efficiency is helped by reason of resident instruction. Students have definite study periods and are encouraged to study. Exams are given frequently, and a student failing and exam is given supplementary instruction at night. They also have access to cassettes as an additional aid.

The students do not use textbooks. Instead, each one is issued a large looseleaf book entitled "Training of Probationary Constables: Initial Course,'' prepared by the Central Planning Unit in the office of the Home Secretary, and issued by the home secretary. This book contains outlines of each subject to be covered during the ten-week course.

Each instructor receives a companion notebook which additionally contains the equipment or training aids needed for each subject. The instruction stresses practical situations rather than lecture. I was privileged to spend a day at the #1 District Training Center at Bruche, near Manchester. During my visit, I attended one class in a mock bedroom to test the actions of a student upon being informed that someone was seriously ill and alone at his home. It was interesting to follow his questioning of the informant, his immediate action in calling for assistance, and the comments of class and instructor.

Each student wears the uniform of the force to which he is assigned, and the faculty consists of superior officers drawn from the various forces within the training district.

The six-week programme just prior to the completion of the two-year probationary period in carried out in a similar manner.

Courtesy to the public is constantly stressed, although only one hour is devoted to formal instruction. Rudeness to the public is regarded as a serious offense.

Midmanagement Training

There is also a course of training for sergeants and inspectors. A newly promoted sergeant, prior to assuming his new duties, receives a three-week course. Inspectors are given a three-month resident course at the National Police College, designed to broaden their outlooks and to train them for higher responsibilities. This course includes history, sociology, economics, public relations and communication. A briefer ten-week course is given locally to inspectors for whom there are no spaces available at the college. It is rare that midmanagers in the United States receive equivalent courses.

Command Training

The English emphasize training for high command to a degree unknown in this country. Those regarded as possessing the necessary potential for the higher ranks are sent to the National Police College for intensive instruction and assessment.

Command Course, Part I, is a six-month course for officers of middle rank such as superintendens (roughly equivalent to our captain), which is designed to qualify them for executive responsibilities. Command Course, Part II, is a six-month course designed to train candidates for the top jubs in the police service. A prerequisite to Command Course, Part II, is completion of Part I.

Both Parts I and II emphasize leadership and management. The courses include technology, especially computerization, as well as current police and social problems. Outside lecturers are utilized.

Scholarships

In addition to the training programmes within the police system, there is a scholarship program for individuals under 34. A scholarship includes tuition, books, travel, food, lodging, etc. The LPC must approve and agree to pay the necessary expenses, and the chief constable must agree to release to individual for a full-time course of study, not to exceed three years.

Patrol

The English have gradually supplanted the traditional beat with the Unit Beat System. It combines three or more beats into an "area " corresponding to our term "zone" or "sector." Each area is assigned a car, popularly called a panda, and a small number of constables on foot, preferably working from their homes. Constables set their own hours of duty, subject to approval by their supervisor. Each constable carries a personal radio, and contact is maintained regularly.

The primary mission of the resident bear officer is to "liais" with the public. He visits factories, places of business, schools, churches, social clubs, and similar places—his objective being to convince the people on his beat that he is their officer. He tries to gain their confidence so that they will be encouraged to give him information and to cooperate with him in matters of law enforcement.

In order that information received from the public should be as useful as possible, each officer turns in any item he receives, or anything he observes which he believes is important, to the central office, where it is "collated."

The collator is responsible for recording the items and connecting related information. A card is made for each item and an index is kept of all residents with criminal records, as well as known or suspected criminals checked or sighted within any of the areas.

The collator turns the collected information into criminal intelligence by evaluating what is received and disseminating the relevant items in a biweekly bulletin which is distributed to officers or patrolmen. Supplemental bulletins are issued, as required. There have been instances where the collator was able to pinpoint the presence of a suspect at the scene of a crime, thus leading to his arrest.

Investigations

In 1878, the first Criminal Investigation Department (CID) was created at Scotland Yard. Today, each Metropolitan Division and local police forces has a CID of its own.

In the Metropolitan Police, assignment to, or removal from, the CID is at the pleasure of the commissioner. Elsewhere, it is at the pleasure of the chief constable.

Officers who demonstrate special investigative aptitude are assigned initially for a three-month period to their department's CID. If their performance is satisfactory, they are continued for another three months.

At the end of the six-month trial period, those deemed sufficiently qualified are given a ten-week training course at one of the detective training schools. Those completing the course satisfactorily are assigned to their agency's CID, as vacancies occur.

There is no national CID, but the local CIDs are supplemented by nine Regional Crime Squads. These are mobile units assigned to the investigation of serious offenses with arrangements for national coordination. They concentrate on the investgation of target criminals, as giving assistance to local CIDs.

Finally, the CID of Scotland Yard, by far the most prestigious CID in England, is available to assist in important investigations.

Interrogation[10]

There are interesting differences between the English system and our own with respect to interrogation. In the United States, the case of

Miranda v *Arizona*[11] specified that prior to a custodial interrogation, a suspect must be warned that he may remain silent, that if he does say anything it may be used against him, that he is entitled to counsel, and that if he cannot afford counsel, counself will be supplied. A custodial interrogation is defined as one in which the suspect is in custody or deprived of his freedom in any significant way.

In England, police interrogation is regulated by what is known as the Judge's Rules, formulated by the Judges of the Kings Bench Division in 1912 and 1918. These Rules were not imposed on the police, but rather issued at the request of the police for guidance.

There are no judicial restraints on interrogation during what we would call "the investigative stage." In fact, Rule I provides that when an officer is endeavouring to ascertain the "author of a crime" there is no objection to his putting questions to anyone, whether suspected or not, as long as he believes "useful information" can be obtained. Until the suspect has been charged, he may be questioned.

Rule 2 provides that as soon as an officer has evidence which would afford "reasonable grounds" to "suspect" that a person has committed an offense, he shall "caution" such person before questioning him. The word "suspect" in this context is the equivalent of "believe." The English "caution" is similar to the Miranda warnings except that there is no requirement concerning the right to counsel. However, there is no doubt that if the suspect or prisoner requests counsel it would have to be granted.

In the United States, failure to give the required warning is grounds for suppressing the confession, regardless of the officer's good faith. In England, on the other hand, where there is a breach of the judge's Rules by a police officer, the trial judge has discretion whether or not to admit the confession.

If there is only a technical or an excusable breach, the confession will probably be admitted. But a serious violation would make the confession inadmissible. For example, if an officer should unduly prolong the questioning of a suspect without giving the required caution, claiming he did not as yet have "reasonable grounds" within Rule 2 to believe that the suspect had committed the offense, he would do so at his peril. If the trial judge regarded his conduct as a pretext to evade the Judge's Rules, the confession would not be admitted.

In both countries, psychological pressure will make a confession involuntary. Threats or promises of reward or benefit are taboo there as well as here. Whereas our courts have not regarded an admonition to tell the truth as undue psychological pressure, in England the opposite view is taken.

Searches

One of the sharp differences between English and American police procedures is in the area of search warrants. In our system the Fourth Amendment provides that no warrant may issue except on oath, particularly describing the items sought, and the premises where the items are believed to be. Our courts require an affidavit in support of the application setting forth the specific facts on which the application is based. If the source of information is an informant, fact must be furnished giving the grounds for believing the informant's information is reliable.

The English system, by comparison, is rather informal. No affidavit is required. The officer simply furnishes the information orally, and if the magistrate is satisfied, he takes the officer's oath and issues the warrant.

Prosecutions by Police

The English police, for historical reasons, play a greater role in the criminal justice system than American police. The English police carry out investigations and also perform prosecutorial duties.

The right to decide whether proceedings shall be instituted, against whom, and for what offense, rests with the chief constable, although there are a number of offenses which cannot be prosecuted, except with the approval of the director of public prosecutions.

The jub of presenting evidence of the Magistrate's Court is in many forces still delegated to police officers, usually above the rank of sergeant, but generally without legal training. However, the trend in recent years has been to hire a solicitor to act as police prosecutor.

Complaints Against Policemen

Until 1964, the handling of a complaint against a police officer was almost completely within the discretion of the chief constable. He could completely ignore it if he believed it unwarranted; he could send a letter of apology on behalf of the officer involved; or he could hold an inquiry. If he held an inquiry and found the officer not guilty, the civilian had no further recourse.

Section 49 of the Police Act of 1964 required for the first time that all such complaints be recorded and investigated. The section authorized the chief constable concerned to request the chief constable of any other area to provide an officer from such other force to carry out the investigation. Where a complaint alleged the commission of a criminal offense by an officer, the chief constable had to refer the matter directly to the director of public prosecutions.

Section 50 of the Police Act of 1964 provided that the local police authority and the inspector of constabulary, in determining the efficiency of a force, must take into account the manner in which complaints were dealt with by the chief constable.

The Police Act of 1976, effective June 1, 1977, has limited further the powers of the chief constable in handling complaints. Section 1 establishes a Police Complaints Board (PCB) of at least nine members, none of whom can ever have been a constable.

Section 2(1) requires that a copy of every complaint be sent to the PCB, together with a memo from the chief constable concerning the merits of the complaint, whether he has filed charges, and, if so, the nature of the charges. This procedure does not apply if disciplinary charges are preferred and the accused admits the charge, or if the complaint is withdrawn and the complainant indicates he does not wish further steps taken. In such event, however, the chief constable must forward to the PCB a copy of the complaint, a report of the investigation, particulars of the charges preferred, and the punishment imposed (Section 2 ([3]).

Section 3 (2) is almost starting in its effect on the chief constable. It provides that if the chief constable has not preferred charges and the PCB disagrees with his decision, they may make recommendations as to the charges they consider should be preferred. If the chief constable disagrees, the PCB may then *direct* him to prefer such charges as it specifies, giving reasons in writing for such direction.

Where a disciplinary hearing is held as the result of such direction, the officer will now be tried by a tribunal consisting of the chief constable as chairman and two members of the PCB. If the accused is a member of the Metropolitan Police, the Commissioner may designate an assistant commissioner or a high- ranking officer to sit as chairman. Obviously, under the new arrangement, an officer may be found guilty by the vote of the two civilians. However, the punishment to be imposed, if any, is still the prerogative of the chief constable (Section 4 [(1]).

Research

The English are considerably ahead of us in the field of research. The home office includes a Research and Development Board operating actively to develop improved procedures and equipment. Senior officers are assigned from their various agencies to work full-time with scientists in anticipating the needs of police service and formulating operational requirements.

Among the important innovations developed by this branch have been the Unit Beat System, the Regional Crime Squads, and consolidation of forces.[15]

JAPAN

In order to understand the Japanese police organisation, a note must be made of the Japanese governmental structure. Japan is divided into seven regions, each containing a number of prefectures. A prefecture is roughly equivalent to our state and is the basic unit of government. A region can be visualized if we imagine a governmental office for our southeast states, located in Jacksonville, Mississippi, with supervisory powers over Florida, Georgia, Mississippi and Alabama.

The Japanese police system has gone through a number of transformations. Prior to 1874, law enforcement was the responsibility of officials appointed by the emperor, somewhat similar to English justices of the peace. In 1874, the first police agency, including the Metropolitan Police of Tokyo, was established in the Ministry of Home Affairs, modelled on the German and French systems, and thus highly centralized. The police exercised wide powers, often in an authoritarian fashion.

In 1947, during the U.S. occupation, Police Law was enacted, imposing on the police the duty to defend democracy and placing limitations on their powers of arrest and interrogation. The police courts were eliminated, and thc policc could no longer issue any regulations, except for traffic control. The police were decentralized, and policing was carried out primarily at the local level, somewhat as in this country. For the first time, every police force was placed under the jurisdiction of a Public Safety Commission, composed of civilians, somewhat like the English system of local police authorities. No one was eligible to serve on any Public Safety Commission who had served as a policeman of prosecutor within five years prior to the proposed appointment.

Local policing, however, was found to cause problems of financing, coordination, training, and overall efficiency. Accordingly, in 1954. Police Law 162 was enacted, recentralizing the police but maintaining Public Safety Commissions. In fact, the chairman of the National Public Safety Commission was given the status of a minister of state.

In the revised system there are two major police organisations, the National Police Agency (NPA) and the Metropolitan Police Department of Tokyo (MPDT).

The NPA is under the jurisdiction of the National Public Safety Commission (NPSC). This commission is composed of five members appointed by the Prime Minister, subject to approval by the Diet (Congress), plus the chairman, who as I have indicated, has the status of a minister and maintains liaison with the cabinet. He cannot vote except in case of a tie.

The MPDT is under the Tokyo Metropolitan Police Public Safety

Commission, consisting of five members appointed by the governor of Tokyo, with the approval of the Tokyo Metropolitan Assembly.

There are also Public Safety Commissions for each prefecture, selected by the prefectural governor with the consent of the prefectural assembly, consisting of five members for the larger prefectures and three members for the smaller prefectures.

The Public Safety Commissions are responsible for supervising their respective agencies, to see that they operate within democratic principles, and to assist the heads of the police on such problems as planning, budget and overall policy. They do not attempt to regulate everyday operations of the agency. Some Commissions actively supervise their agencies. Others tend to routinely approve actions taken by their police departments.

National Police Agency

There are approximately 1950,000 sworn officers and 35,000 civilians in the NPA. Females are increasingly entering the Japanese police. Currently there are approximately 3,700 female sworn officers, 2,800 traffic wardens, and 700 guidance personnel. The NPA is commanded by commissioner general, appointed by the National Public Safety Commission, subject to the approval of the Prime Minister.

The NPA has: a secretariat which deals with public information, equipment and fiscal matters; an Administration Bureau for personnel, education and internal affairs; a Criminal Investigations Bureau which contains indentification, statistics, and investigative units, as well as the Interpol section; a Traffic Bureau; a Security Bureau which contains riot control units and carries out countermeasures against terrorism, etc.; and a Communications Bureau. In addition the NPA conducts the National Police Academy and the National Research Institute of Police Science.

Under the NPA are seven regional offices, one for each of the seven regions. Under each regional office are a number of prefectures, generally commanded by a chief superintendent (deputy chief inspector) or a superintendent supervisor (assistant chief inspector). The actual command authority of a region over its prefectures is limited to emergencies such as large-scale disasters and serious civil disturbances. The region does coordinate activities of its prefectural forces and conducts the regional school for training sergeants and assistant inspectors. However, the prefectural forces are quite autonomous.

Each prefecture has a number of police stations (we commonly call them precincts). For example, the prefecture of Kyoto has 29 precincts; the prefecture of Osaka has 56 precincts; Metroplitan Tokyo, which is an autonomous organisation, has 94 percincts.

A precinct in Japan has patrol personnel plus complements of criminal investigations, traffic officers, juvenile specialists and so on. All are under the supervision and control of thc precinct chief, generally a senior superintendent (roughly equivalent to our inspector).

In the urban areas the precincts are broken down into sectors or zones, each sector under an assistant inpector, containing a number of substations knows as "kobans," under sergeants. The kobans are distinguished by red light globes which are maintained around the clock, and serve a number of functions.

First and most important, they maintain close contact with the community—one of their tasks being a personal contact at least once a year with every resident within the koban, during which the officer emphasizes "at your service."

Second, foot patrol, which is still the basic type of patrol in Japan, is carried out primarily from the kobans. Motorized units operate directly from the precinct station house, although they are required to check at the kobans periodically. Actually, a considerable amount of an officer's time is spent just outside the koban where the public can see him, rather than on actual patrol.

Patrol is normally solo during the daytime, in pairs at night. While on patrol, the officers wear sidearms and carry pocket radios, but do not wear badges or other means of identification. Japanese police do not carry sidearms when not on duty.

The tours of duty by koban officers vary drastically from our own system. In this country the normal tour is eight hours performed consecutively, either midnight to 8 a.m., 8 a.m. to 4 p.m., or 4 p.m. to midnight. In most departments, officers work different shifts periodically, although in many departments an officer is assigned to a particular shift and works that shift indefinitely.

In the kobans, on the other hand, officers work a chart involving two tours of over 20 hours, each one followed by a day off, plus two tours of eight or ten hours. During the two long tours there are, of course, rest periods but none over four hours. It is estimated that koban officers work a 44-hour week.

The number of officers on duty at a koban varies, depending on the need for police services, but there is always someone stationed at the koban itself, ready to give information, to act as a referral service, or generally to assist citizens with their problems. Some kobans issue their own newspapers, financed by the police. They have been asked to serve as mediators and have been consulted frequently on problems ranging from family disputes to choice of career. They also give special attention to the elderly. It appears to be a permanent "Officer Friendly" programme.[13]

The koban system seems to be the pride of Japanese policing. The system was introduced about 1890 and is given a large part of the credit for the excellent crime clearance rate of the Japanese police. This is because the personnel of the koban, by reason of their closeness to the community, receive information concerning crime on a scale unknown in the United States. In fact, one writer cites a survey which indicated that 60 per cent of Japanese with knowledge of crimes will report the information to the police, and 25 per cent more would report if asked.[14] This certainly explains in part their extraordinary clearance rates; for example, 60 per cent for burglaries[15] contrasted to 27 per cent here.[16]

The koban system has received praise from many sources, including one of Australia's most prestigious weekly journals.[17]

In the new suburban areas, pending the installation of regular kobans, mobile units are being utilized to serve as temporary kobans.

In the rural areas the prefectures have residential officers quite similar to the English system. The officers try to establish close links with the community from their homes, and in their absence their wives receive the necessary information concerning crimes and complaints. The wives receive a modest stipend for this extra duty.

The residential officers have some leeway with respect to their working hours but must respond at any time required by their duties.

Japan has a uniform telephone dial system called 110, corresponding to our 911 system, whereby individuals can communicate directly with the police without needing to know the police telephone number. Over 2 million calls are received annually by such direct dialing.

Although policing is said to be centralized in japan, it is a limited centralization. The National Public Safety Commission does have authority over all officers above the rank of superintendent and does assign them around the country to be directors of prefectures, heads of large precincts, or major division chiefs. In fact the current commissioner general of NPA was formerly the Chief of the Osaka Prefectural Police.

Furthermore, the commissioner general, through the regional chiefs, does have authority over the prefectures in the event of national emergencies such as serious disasters or riots. But the Japanese police cannot be said to be as centralized as the French police, where the director has complete authority to assign any of his personnel to any part of France, or the New Zealand police, where the commissioner has similar authority. Each prefecture selects, trains, and pays its own personnel, and promotes up to and including the rank of superintendent (roughly equivalent to deputy inspector). No one under the rank of senior superintendent (roughly equivalent to inspector) is subject to the control of the NPA.

I believe it is more accurate to say that the Japanese police system resembles the present English system. It will be recalled that there are 43 forces in England (including Wales); there are 47 prefectural forces in Japan. England has police regions which conduct recruit and specialized training, and extend investigative support as needed; Japan has police regions which conduct specialized and midmanagement training, and coordinate activities of the prefectures. In neither case do the regional offices have command authority over the police agencies within their regions. In both England and Japan, police organisations are subject to the control of civilian authorities.

It is true that England does not have a national police agency, but practically speaking, the home secretary has the same influence over selection, training, promotion, and pay as the head of NPA. The Home Secretary also conducts the British Police College as the NPA conducts the National Police Academy. In addition both provide support in communication and identification.

Metropolitan Police Department of Tokyo (MPDT)

The MPDT is the largest police agency in Japan, except for the NPS. It has over 40,000 sworn officers and about 3,000 civilians, under a superintendent general (chief of police) who is appointed by the National Public Safety Commission with the consent of the Tokyo Metropolitan Public Safety Commission with the consent of the Tokyo Metropolitan Public Safety Commission and the Prime Minister. About 1,500 of the sworn officers were women as of September 1977.

The MPDT has eight bureaus, including Personnel and Training, Patrol, Traffic, Criminal Investigation, Public Security, and Crime Prevention. Juvenile delinquency activities are directed from the Crime Prevention Bureau.

The Public Security Bureau contains the famed "Kidotai" mobile units used to cope with civil disturbances. They are specially trained and equipped to handle situations without the use of firearms. They are also utilized in the event of disasters, for crowd and traffic control, and for group patrolling, somewhat like Tactical Patrol Forces in this country.

The MPDT also operates the Metropolitan Police School which trains recruits, gives midmanagement training to sergeants and Assistant inspectors, and also give some refresher courses and specialized training.

For purposes of operations there are 94 stations (usually called precincts in the United States) organized into eight districts (more likely to be called divisions here). As with prefectural precincts, each police station has a complement of personnel for patrol, traffic, criminal investigations and crime prevention.

Likewise, the MPDT has both kobans and residential boxes. At present there are over 1,200 of these boxes in Tokyo.

Recruitment

Applicants for police officer must have a high school education or the equivalent. Strong efforts are made, however, to recruit university graduates, and approximately 13 per cent of Japanese police officers are in that category.

The first stage of testing is a mental and preliminary physical exam. The mental exam consists of multiple-choice questions to test the knowledge expected of a high school graduate, plus an essay on an assigned subject.

The second stage involves an aptitude test, a more thorough physical and an interview with a representative of the Police and of the Civil Service Commission sitting jointly.

Only about 10 per cent of male applicants and 5 per cent of female applicants are hired.

Training

Training in Japan is extensive and well-organised. Each prefecture has its own school for recruits, but the instruction is standardized. Above the prefectural schools are the regional schools offering midmanagement and specialized instruction. Finally, the National Police Academy trains senior officers.

The obectives of training not only include improving skills in police practices and fostering good judgment, but imparing a correct understanding of the essence of democratic police behaviour.[18]

Recruit Training. High school graduates receive a year of schooling University graduates receive six month.

Japanese training at all levels includes physical exercises, but in the recruit schools there is intensive instruction and practice in the martial arts such as judo, kendo and aikido. In fact no one can graduate from the recruit school until he has qualified for the white belt in judo.

The emphasis on martial arts is justified on the grounds that it reduces the need for a police officer to use a nightstick or firearm.

The importance of the martial arts in Japanese police training can be better understood by the fact that assistant inspectors (roughly equivalent to our lieutenant) designated to teach these subjects must attend a six-month course of special training at the National Police Academy. In addition. NPA sponsors a national tournament each year for prefectural teams.

Command Training. Newly appointed inspectors (roughly equivalent to captain) are sent to the National Police Academy at Tokyo. This course is similar to the first six-month command course given at National Police College in England, teaching management techniques, budgeting personnel practice, and so on.

There is also a six-month course to train top leaders in the investigations branch. This course in limited to specially selected inspectors and superintendents under the age of 45 who have completed the regular course and have appropriate field experience.

Juvenile Delinquency

Although the Japanese police pride themselves on their low crime rate, they are worried about a problem that seems to be common almost everywhere—the increase in juvenile delinquency. This worry is expreseed not only at the national and metropolitan levels, but also at the prefectural and precinct levels. For example, in 1976, there was a nationwide increase of ten per cent. There is increasing delinquency by high school students and females.

A Japanese authority attributes the increase, in part, to the migration of young people to the cities and changing life-styles. For example, today it is common in the cities for both parents to work, creating a class of "key" children left to fend for themselves.[19]

In dealing with juveniles, some quirks of Japanese law create more difficulties for the Japanese police than we would encounter. For example, in Japan a juvenile is anyone under 20, whereas with us the usual age is 18, although some states set the age at 16 or 17. This means, of course, that offenders of 18 or 19 still must be treated as juveniles. The police have some hope, albeit a faint one, that the age will be reduced to 18.

Another problem arises in riot situations. The Japanese Penal Code requires proof of two essential elements for riot. One is "common criminal intent" of an assembly of persons resorting to violence or intimidation. The other element is that the action disturbs the "public peace of a particular locality or area." This makes a conviction difficult.

For example, in 1968, a group of some 7,000 students, in order to stop a rail shipment of jet fuel for U.S. military aircraft, paralyzed the operation of a railroad station by stoning trains, destroying signal facilities, and attacking the police assigned to protect the station. It was necessary to cease operations on the rail line from 9 p.m. until 10 a.m. the next day, and destruction amounted to about $125,000. It took until 1977 to get a conviction of 15 ringleaders in the Tokyo District Court.

However, there is a good possibility of reversal by the Tokyo High Court based on one of their prior decisions, in which the court ruled that a hotel does not contain inhabitants as such, and so the riot did not directly menace the safety or property of ordinary citizens. Defense counsel in the current case argues that a railroad station likewise does not contain inhabitants.[20]

In attempting to cope with delinquency, the Japanese "first line of defense" is in the precincts, where as I have indicated, a complement of juvenile officers are assigned. These officers are assisted in their tasks by a corps of volunteers. For example, there are, 'Juvenile Guidance Officers'' (MPDT calls them ''agents'') who work in the steets in cooperation with the police. Tokyo has about 1,100 such individuals, including teachers, junior probation officers, and parents, and four offices have been established from which they operate.[21]

There are also police-liaison councils affiliated with some 40,000 private firms to counsel youthful employees.

Japanese programmes include athletics, taking youngsters camping, trying to identify potential delinquents at an early age, cracking down on pornography shops and other premises having an unowholesome influence on the young, and encouraging the efforts of citizen groups in this concern.

An interesting aspect of NPA in connection with delinquency is the creation of a Crime Prevention and Juvenile Division within the National Research Institute of Police Science. This division includes a Juvenile Guidance Section which has carried out some research on the personalities of delinquents and has made some studies to determine reasons for engaging in delinquency. In 1974, it conducted a nationwide survey of juvenile runaways to ascertain the reasons for their running away. However, the Japanese are the first to admit that they have not as yet discovered the solution to the juvenile delinquency problem.

Discipline

Like all major police forces, the Japanese police system has provisions for dealing with dereliction of duty or breaches of discipline. the proper conduct of subordinates is a serious responsibility of all commanding officers, not merely the immediate supervisor. For example, in February 1978, the chief of the Metropolitan Tokyo Police, second highest officer in the entire Japanese police hierarchy, resigned after one of his officers raped and murdered a college student. Eleven of his ranking officers were reprimanded.[22]

Narcotics

The Japanese drug situation is minor compared with our own problem, although apparently increasing in every category. The almost incredible figures for persons charged with drug offenses are illustrative (Table 8.2).

As these figures indicate, Japan is hardly troubled by hard drugs. However, there was a period from 1957 to 1963 when heroin did cause considerable concern, and it was estimated that there were 40,000 heroin addicts.[24] In 1963, there were 2,135 cases reported to public prosecutors offices on narcotics charges.

A programme of enforcement and education drastically reduced the number of addicts and narcotics offenses. The Narcotics Control Law was amended to increase the maximum penalty for drug trafficking from ten years to life and to require compulsory hospitalization of addicts.

In addition, it was made compulsory for doctors and law enforcement officers to report to the prefectural governor all cases of addicts or suspected addicts. The governor orders an examination of each individual reported by a medical examiner of mental health, and can order hospitalization for a month on the medical examiner's recommendation. Further hospitalization can be ordered, up to six months, only if approved by a Narcotics Addiction Examination Committee, consisting of five members who are medical and legal experts in the field of narcotic addiction.

An interesting aspect of treatment is the elimination of methadone. The Japanese believe that dependence on narcotic drugs is basically physical and psychological and that substituting one drug for another does not solve the problem. Patients must quit cold turkey, and if the withdrawal symptoms are too acute, a tranquilizer will be administered.

After discharge from the hospital, addicts report for aftercare to special counsellors. If five years pass without the further use of drugs, and it is believed there will not be a relapse, they are deemed to be rehabilitated and their names are dropped from the list of addicts.

That the Japanese programme for narcotic addicts has been effective is indicated by the sharp drop in narcotics cases reported to the public prosecutor.

For some unexplained reason cannabis and opium have never been serious problems in Japan. The highest number of cases reported for opium offenses was 1,136 in 1968. The very next year the figure dropped to 377, and the number of opium cases reported has remained under 300 since that time.

The use of cannabis has been gradually increasing but is still minor compared to us. In 1963, only 147 persons were involved in cannabis violations. From 1970 through 1974, the number of known cannabis violators varied from 717 to 761. In 1975 and 1976, as indicated above, the figures have been ober 900.

Stimulants are the only from of drug abuse that has been a real problem in Japan. For ten years following the end of World War II, when living conditions were desperate, stimulants that were advertised to slake off sleep and provide energy gained general acceptance among night workers, students, etc. The use of such stimulants became so widespread that it bacame necessary for the government to enact the Stimulants Control Law, with stiff penalties for violations, and to amend the Mental Health Law to provide for compulsory hospitalization of stimulant addicts. By 1958, the problem seemed to be over.

Since 1970, there has again been a substantial increase in the use of stimulant druge. In that year, 1,618 violations were reported. In 1973, the figure had climbed to 8,510, and after a drop in 1974, climbed again to a record 10,919 in 1976.

The Japanese have instituted various countermeasures designed to cope with the situation, including more intensive inspections by customs agents, closer supervision of legitimate drug sources, stepped up activity against traffickers, enforced medical treatment, and a publicity campaign concerning the evils of drugs. Similar measures proved effective in 1963, and it is to be hoped that current measures will have the same degree of success.

Of course, the tremendous disparity in crime rates, clearance tates, and drug abuse cannot be attributed solefy to the superiority of the Japanese police. The homogeneity of the Japanese people and their cultural traditions undoubtedly account in large measure for the low crime rate. Nevertheless, the Japanese police must be credited with an excellent relationship with the Japanese people which helped make possible its outstanding record.

Table 8.2
Number of Persons Charged with Drug Offenses in Japan

	1975	1976
Narcotics	232	175
Opium	140	185
Cannabis	909	960
Stimulants	8,422	10,919
	9,703	12,229

NEW ZEALAND

The area of New Zealand is approximately 100,000 square miles, comprising two major islands, North Island and South Island, and a number of smaller islands such as Steward Island, Chatham Island, and the Cook Island Group.

The population is some 3 million, over 90 per cent of British descent. About 8 per cent are descended form the Maoris who inhabited New Zealand when the white man arrived. There are also small minorities of Islanders (from Tongo, etc.), Geeks, Poles, Chinese and Hollanders.

Almost 50 per cent of all New Zealanders live in the four cities of over 100,000: Auckland, Christchurch, Wellington and Dunedir. Approximately another third live in smaller cities and villages, leaving large areas of New Zealand, especially in the South Island, very sparsely populated.

For operational purposes New Zealand is organised into 16 districts. The organisation of districts varies according to area, population, and crime conditions, but each district has a complement of detectives, and personnel assigned for patrol, youth aid, recruitment, in-service training, and crime prevention. The detectives at the district level may include a drug squad, a fraud squad, a regional crime squad, and a criminal intelligence section.

Recruitment

Every district in New Zealand has a recruitment officer. In the busy districts he is a full-time recruiter, in other districts his recruitment tasks are in addition to his other duties. This officer does the initial screening of those obviously unsuitable because of age, wearing glasses, etc. There is no educational requirement, but before a candidate is given an application form he must undergo the Otis test of mental ability and a number of written tests conducted by the recruitment officer. The written tests involve vocabulary, memory for details presented in a photograph, listening comprehension, reading comprehension and a written report based on information provided about some event.

The objective of these tests is to evaluate the ability of the applicant to keep abreast of the educational demands of recruit training and police work in the field. In order to prepare the candidate for the test, he is issued a handbook of instructions with sample questions. A manual is also issued to test administrators on how to give the tests and mark the papers.

Recruit Training

Recruit training lasts 14-1/2 weeks. An interesting aspect of the instruction is 12 periods of "protest training," having as its objective the ability to tolerate stress under conditions of mob behaviour, or verbal and physical abuse from demonstrators, without over-reaction. It considers the rights and duties of individuals in connection with freedom of speech and assembly and police responsibilities concerning demonstrations, strikes, and public meetings.

There is also a block of 66 hours of social science taught by professional educators at the New Zealand Police College. The rationale for this portion of the senior studies is the need to promote community-oriented policemen who are skilled communicators and who understand their role in social and humanitarian terms. Therefore, the instruction includes 13 hours of communication, 33 hours in human behaviour, generally, and in the New Zealand social setting specifically, with discussion of New Zealand society and its social and cultural problems, and race/community relations, especially with respect to Polynesians.

The syllabus emphasizes that the end of the senior studies course is an opportune time to consider the dilemma of "college idealism versus the reality of front-line situations." It is pointed out that new recruits are particularly vulnerable to detraining influences in field situations. This situation is by no means limited to New Zealand. It is probably universal that much of what is taught in the police school is ignored in the field.

Recruits, upon graduation from the New Zealand Police College, must continue their education based on a series of "Extension Studies Notes." These" Notes" consist of handout materials on 20 subjects, which the recruit obtains one at a time from the district instructor.

(Every district has an instructor either full-time or part-time depending on the type of district.) When the recruit feels he has mastered the material (an average time would be about three weeks), he asks the district instructor for a test consisting of 25 multiple-choice questions on which he must score 80 per cent. If the recruit fails, he is permitted a second, or even third chance, each time on a different set of questions. If he fails after the third try, the department will consider whether to terminate him. The probationary officer is not given a permanent appointment unless the extension studies have been completed.

Patrol

As in this country, patrol is primarily by auto. However, the cars are not assigned to sectors, zones, or other areas with fixed perimeters. Instead the New Zealand Police have instituted a rather unique system called "pivot patrol," based on a patrol work load study carried out by their management services section.

Their computerized statistics indicate where and when the greatest need for police services occurs. Cars on patrol are directed to patrol the immediate areas around such "pivot points" at the times indicated. As the day progresses, and the greatest need for police services shifts to other locations, the pivot points or patrols are shifted accordingly. For example, statistics may show that on Monday at 8 a.m. the greatest call for police services is at the intersection of A and B Streets, hence this is the pivot point at that time. However, by 10 a.m. the greatest need may shift to X and Y Streets, nearer the suburbs. Hence, X and Y Streets would be the new pivot point. Each car must drive through the pivot point a certain number of times per shift.

In the larger cities, such as Auckland, routine patrol is performed by two man "Incident" cars (I cars), who normally are the first to respond to an incident and carry out the preliminary investigation. If further investigation is needed, the I car notifies the Criminal Investigation Bureau if the matter is serious or the Enquiries car (E car) if it is comparatively minor.

The E car is assigned to uniformed officers who perform patrol solo from 7 a.m. to 3 p.m. and from 3 p.m. to 11 p.m. The theory of the E car was to take the place of the suburban constable and carry out liaison with the community. In practice the E car is used more frequently to relieve the I car in the supplemental investigation of minor matters, thereby permitting the I car to resume patrol.

Protection of the crime scene is stressed. Recruits are instructed how to mark out boundaries, recognize physical evidence, and prevent intrusion by unauthorized persons. When assigned to patrol, the importance of guarding the crime scene continues to be emphsized.

In the small one-to-four man stations, of which there are about 200 in New Zealand, the hours of duty vary according to the needs of the particular community. There may only be one car, and the constable or constables assigned to such stations not only perform patrol but conduct most of their own investigations. In serious cases, they can request detective assistance from the subarea headquarters.

Detective Division

The Criminal Investigation Branch (CIB) corresponds to what we generally call the detective division or bureau. Each district and division (or equivalent) has a complement of detectives, although at the district level they are generally assigned to specialized squads such as fraud or drugs. In the larger districts the CIB commander is a chief superintendent, or superintendent, who acts as a regional commander.

The regular task of conducting criminal investigations is carried out chiefly at the division level or its equivalent. Units below the division level may sometimes have detectives assigned if warranted by local conditions, as for example, the Queenstown subarea. In any event, detectives are responsible directly to the commanding officer of the unit to which they are assigned.

As in probably every police agency the average policeman prefers assignment as a detective to uniform duty. The procedure for becoming a detective in New Zealand is in sharp contrast to the majority of our own police departments, where transfer from uniform to detective status all too often results from political pressure or nepotism.

In New Zealand the constable aspiring to be a detective must have a minimum of two years' street experience, preferably more. He makes his initial application to his district commander. He is then interviewed by a district CIB man. If, in the opinion of the interviewer, the applicant is suitable, his file goes to the director of CIB. If the director agrees, in due course, the applicant is directed to attend a four-week Induction Course (basic detective course) of 20-25 students. The responsibilities of the instructors, in addition to teaching, include observing and assessing the candidates.

Shortly before the end of the session, the director of CIB visits the class to make his personal assessment. Those approved by him are given a trial as vacancies occur, for six months, during which they will have the status of constable.

If at the end of such six months the individual's supervisor recommends retention within CIB, and the director of CIB concurs, the constable designation is changed to detective constable. Thereafter, within 18 to 24 months, he must take the four-week detective course, an advanced course required of all candidates for detective. After at least two years as detective constable and satisfactory completion of both detective courses, there is another assessment and recommendation by his supervisor, and if the director of CIB concurs, the individual achieves detective rank.

Traffic

New Zealand is unique in that vehicle traffic regulations are enforced not by the police but by the Department of Transport. The police are authorized to serve a summons or make an arrest where the circumstances justify such action, but in an unusual situation enforcement is left to the Department of Transport. The police regard this as one reason why they generally maintain good community relations.

Juveniles

In New Zealand a juvenile is anyone under 17. From 14 to 17, a juvenile is designated as a "young person." Under 14, he is designated as a "child." Offenses committed by juveniles, regardless of age, are investigated by members of the patrol force and CIB, if needed as is generally the procedure here.

In each of the 16 districts of the New Zealand Police, and in some units below the district level, there is a Youth Aid Section. In addition, at the National Headquarters there is a Youth Aid Section within the Public Affairs Division which acts as coordinator of youth aid activities within the department.

The duties of the Youth Aid Section include: prevention patrol, especially of places known to attract undesirable individuals; cooperation with parents, social workers, clergymen, school personnel, and others interested in the rehabilitation of children and willing to assist them; referrals of children or parents in need of specialized advice to appropriate agencies: and maintaining knowledge of local youth, especially those who have been or are likely to be offenders.

Youth Aid Sections have participated in various programmes. For example, in Auckland the local section helps operate a Boys' Town modelled on Father Flanagan's Boys' Town. The sections also give talks in primary and intermediate schools.

A very important function of Yourth Aid Sections is their role with delinquents. In the case of "children" (under 14), the Youth Aid Section carries out a background investigation, interviews schools, social and welfare agencies, clergymen, and whoever else may have information on the child and its family, in order to make a recommendation concerning the action to be taken.

If the offense is petty, the usual recommendation is a warning. If it is more serious, the recommendation generally will be to refer the matter to the Children's Board, consisting of a member of the Youth Aid Section, a social worker from the Social Welfare Department, a welfare officer from the Maori Affairs Department, and a member of the public.

The parents are invited to attend the meeting of the Children's Board and discuss the child's problem and behaviour with the Board. The Board can counsel or warn the child and can, if needed, arrange for assistance from the Social Welfare of Maori Affairs Department, or for medical care. The Board will not consider the matter if the parent or child disputes the facts.

A child under 14 cannot be tried for any offense, although legislation is pending which would make would make it possible to try him for a homicide. But if it appears from the magnitude of an offense, or from a continued course of conduct, that the child is beyond the control of his parents, a complaint may be lodged against the *parents* in the Children's and Young Persons Court. If sustained, the child may be taken from the parents and placed under social control.

The Children's Board, as such, cannot consider cases of "young persons" (14-17). If the investigating officer believes the offense is sufficiently serious, he can make an arrest, in which event the Youth Aid Section merely records details of the offense and supplies details concerning the offender, if previously known. More commonly, the young person is released to his parents.

If an arrest is not made, a report is made to Youth Aid. Youth Aid conducts a background investigation and upon completion of the investigation places it on the agenda of the weekly conference held with the Department of Social Welfare. If a traffic offense is involved, the conference will include the Ministry of Transport (in New Zealand the traffic regulations are enforced primarily by the Ministry of Transport). If the offender is a Maori, the conference will include someone from the Maori Affairs Department. A magistrate sitting in the Children's and Young Persons' Court will not entertain the case unless such conference has been held.

The recommendation of the conference is submitted to the district commander. For a first offense, unless unusually serious, the customary recommendation might include prosecution or a referral to the Department of Social Welfare. In any event the district commander makes the final decision and may order a prosecution if he believes it warranted under the circumstances.

A new concept involves the creation of Joint Teams or J Teams. Each team comprises a member of the Youth Aid Section, an officer of the Maori Affairs Department, a social worker from the Department of Social Welfare, and may also include a representative of the community appointed by the Maori Affairs Department. Note that the composition of J teams is similar to that of Children's Boards, but there is no connection between these units.

The role of the J Teams is as yet unclear. In theory they initiate community action to deal with undesirable youth activity, give guidance and assistance to young people who are potential offenders, and identify the needs of young people and act as liaison with those who can assist in satisfying such needs.

The J Teams are given a great deal of autonomy, but are instructed that their efforts are not to be oriented on the basis of race, but on the basis of actual need. J Teams patrol places frequented by young people especially those catering to undesirable elements, maintain contact with leaders of gangs and groups having antisocial tendencies, advise and counsel young people who require it, and maintain close liaison with other police units, schools, and agencies which endeavour to assist in the development of young people.

There is now a new educational programme, sponsored by the Public Affairs Division at National Headquarters, designated as the Law Related Educational Programme. This is a combined effort of the police. Department of Transport, fire fighters, teachers and other public and private agencies to prepare a series of lessons in good citizenship for presentation in the schools, primarily from the fifth through ninth grades. The programme envisages different lessons for each grade level and presentation in some instances by representatives of agencies other than the Department of Education.

CANADA

Policing in Canada is carried out at the federal, provincial, and municipal levels. Actually the bulk of policing is performed by the Royal Canadian Mounted Police (RCMP). The RCMP not only enforce federal laws, but also perform provincial policing on a contract basis in eight of Canada's ten provinces, the exceptions being Ontario and Quebec. However, even in provinces policed by the RCMP, there are many cities that continue to have their own departments. A trend to regional policing is being encouraged.

Selection to the RCMP

An applicant for the RCMP is given a preliminary interview at the field office where he applies, and unless he is obviously unsuitable because of age, physique, lack of education, or other disqualifying factor, he is given an application form. The individual may receive an application at age 18 but cannot be appointed until age 19. No maximum age is specified, but no one will be appointed over the age of 50. The applicant must have a high school education or the equivalent. There are no longer height and weight requirements, but they are factors in determining an applicant's eligibility for appointment.

After the application has been completed, he is given a series of written tests covering math, geography, science, social studies, grammar, spelling, and general knowledge. He must also write a composition based on a topic he chooses from a number of topics offered by the examiner. The tests are given at the various detachment offices but are marked at the division headquarters.

The candidate must also undergo a "psychometric test." A number of the members of the RCMP with whom I discussed this test referred to it as a psychological test, but the RCMP does not at present carry out any psychological testing, as such. Actually the test involves two parts. The first part, consisting of 60 questions, tests the applicant's vocabulary, reasoning, and mathematical ability; the applicant is given credit for speed in finishing the test. The second part, consisting of 40 questions, is a logic test with questions like I is to 3 as a is to c, or man is to home as bird is to nest. There is no absolute pass/fail. The test measures intelligence but is definitely correlated to educational achievement. It is used as an important part of the selection process and play a role in selections for force-sponsored university attendance.

If the written tests and psychometric tests are satisfactory, the candidate's engagement process continues. He is called for a second interview, generally with a senior noncommissioned officer, and interviewed at length, sometimes as long as three hours. The interview covers his schooling, leadership, maturity, character, motivation, loyalty, driving ability and health. His family and employment record are discussed.

The interviewer seeks to ascertain if the candidate is a "loner," if he has been in trouble with the police; and if he has had a bad school attendance record, and if so why. Also examined are: the applicant's driving record; his athletic or fitness programme, if any; his work record (does he show constant change of jobs?); his attitude toward his bosses; his attitude toward the democratic system of government; his attitude toward the laws which he will be expected to enforce. If married, is there a harmonious relationship (the spouse is also interviewed). To what extent, if any, does the candidate provide financial assistance to members of his family, and what is his financial situation, including excessive debts.

The interview also covers the applicant's cultural interests. Does he read, enjoy music, play an instrument, draw or paint, keep abreast of current affairs, etc.?

The interview also delves into the individual's personal life; is there a steady girl/boy friend? Is there a trial marriage, and if so, is he willing to formalize the relationship? Are there any illegitimate children? The interviewer questions the candidate about his knowledge of the force, his willingness to work overtime, and whether he is aware he can be transferred anywhere in Canada.

A conviction for a minor offense will not automatically bar a candidate, but conviction for an indictable offense (roughly equivalent to our felony) will automatically disqualify. An arrest will not of itself bar the individual, but if it was for a serious offense, there will be a careful assessment of the circumstances to determine if there is sufficient cause for disqualification.

Selection is based on a rather involved point system. For example, in considering age, an individual over 40 receives no points, between 35 and 40 receives 10 points, between 30 and 34 receives 40 points, and under 30 receives 100 points.

For a man under 167.5 cm (just under 5′6″) or a woman under 162.5 cm per centimeter, until 172 cm for a male and 168 cm for a female score 100 points.

For education there is a sliding scale of 60 points for a high school graduate to 100 points for four years of college.

A college graduate may be hired as a regular member of the force or as a civilian member. If hired as a regular member, which carries greater benefits than a civilian, he must undergo the six-month basic training required of all recruits, as well as the six-month recruit field training at a division. the university graduate joins the department at the same basic level as the high school graduate.

The selection procedures of the RCMP seem to be effective because even though there are many applications, there are few vacancies, except for normal attrition.

Recruit Training

Recruits receive a six-month course of instruction at the RCMP Academy at Regina in the Province of Saskatchewan. In addition to the usual instruction in laws, evidence, arrests, report writing, etc., subjects include dictation, typing, and budgeting counselling (designed to assist the new constable with his financial problems).

Upon successful completion of the six-month recruit training the recruit is assigned to a division and then undergoes an additional six months of recruit field training within his division. Under the tutelage of a field trainer, a constable especially selected for this duty, the recruit has various tasks demonstrated to him, after which he is required to perform them himself in a satisfactory manner and satisfy the trainer that he can henceforth complete such tasks with only normal supervision. Typical tasks would be interviewing a witness, taking a statement, or preparing a report.

The recruit's performance is recorded in the Performance Record kept for each recruit, which lists the task a constable is most likely to encounter in his early service.

The completion of the two six-month periods of recruit training and field training ends the probationary period. Before the recruit is given a permanent appointment, his entire record is assessed, including his grades in recruit school, attitude, and potential to become a police officer.

Ontario Provincial Police

As I have indicated, the RCMP not only enforces the federal laws of Canada but also performs most of the policing at the provincial (approximately equivalent to our states) and municipal levels. Ontario is one of two provinces with own police agency. The Ontario Provincial Police (OPD) cover the entire province except for a few cities like Ottawa and metropolitan Toronto.

Promotions.[25] The current promotion procedures of the OPD might be of interest to American police administrations. Because of the rapidity of past and anticipated social change, coupled with the high rate of retirement in the senior ranks from now until 1985, it is believed that future high-level management potential must be identified and developed as soon as possible. In order to do this the OPD has developed an unusual and somewhat involved promotional process.

The first step is from constable to corporal. As vacancies arise, a qualifying examination is announced which any constable with five years' service is eligible to take. The test covers such subjects as criminal law, investigations, traffic, policy and procedure and problem solving. Those qualifying become eligible for "promotional assessment."

A supervising officer, at least two grades above the eligible, prepares the initial promotional evaluation. He describes in narrative form his assessment of the candidate on 16 separate qualities, including leadership, planning and organising, decision-making, public service motivation, learning ability, problem solving, communication skills, judgment under pressure, initiative, and interpersonal sensitivity.

He also makes an evaluation concerning the types of police work for which the candidate seems to possess or lack aptitude.

Finally, the supervisor makes a recommendation whether or not the eligible candidate should be considered for promotion. He must indicate that he has consulted other supervisors of the candidate and give their names and ranks.

The recommendation of the assessing officer than goes to a reviewing officer. If the recommendations of the assessing officer and reviewing officer are favourable, the documentation is sent to a Promotional Assessment Board.

There is a Board for each of the 17 field districts, composed of a superintendent as chairman, an inspector, a sergeant major and two noncommissioned officers, generally detachment commanders. Their jub is to sift through the recommendations which come from the various detachments within the districts in order to identify potential managers and administrators to be trained and developed for more senior administrative responsibilities. To be selected for development, candidates must have demonstrated high performance standards. The number finally selected is determined by the projects requirement for corporals.

The selections of the Boards are, in effect, an admission to the development programme. Each selection is given aptitude testing and career counselling. The career counsellor must divulge the results of the tests to the eligible, and the implications for career choices.

The management development program is designed to facilitate acquisition of a body of administrative knowledge and skills by the candidate through a combination of education and on-the-job training (OJT). The formal training is tentatively scheduled ad a 3-to 4-week junior command course. Course members will write an examination for each course attended.

On-the-job training consists of job rotation and operational exposure through work assignments in the candidate's present position. Each programme participant and his immediate supervisor must jointly identify opportunities for on-the-job development related to the newly gained knowledge.

The immediate supervisor of each participant fills out an assessment from each quarter. At the end of a year, the Career Management Branch makes recommendations for promotion to the commissioner, based on such factors as seniority, special skills and interests, and career planning and development.

The promotional procedures for ranks above corporal are somewhat similar, except that time in grade need only be a year instead of five years. Attendance at courses or prescribed home-study material and examinations are required. Of course, the ranks of the officers serving on the Promotional Assessment Boards will be correspondingly higher for each grade. Nor is there need for as many Boards in the higher ranks, since there are fewer candidates.

No one will be considered for promotion normally unless he has been recommended by Promotional Assessment Board. However, the Commissioner retains the prerogative of promoting a member of the OPC at any time.

Metropolitan Toronto Police

As students of administration are aware, many police departments endeavour to supplement their patrol force by utilization of auxiliary or reserve officers.

One of the best programmes is that of the Metropolitan Toronto Police (MTP) which has an active group of 250 auxiliary police, including about 60 females. The physical requirements are the same as for constables: males 5'8", 160 pounds, females 5"4", 110 pounds. The age limits are 21 through 65.

Prospective candidates must appear before a Selection Committee composed of MTP officers, each September. Successful candidates are assigned to a recruit class which begins in October and continues for 32 weeks, one night a week. The instruction includes the Criminal Code, provincial statutes, powers of arrest, the use of force, and first aid.

At the end of the course a written test is given. Those who pass are given an appointment certificate, issued uniforms, and given assignments to various districts.

Auxiliary policemen must attend training sessions twice a month and are expected to serve 12 hours a month with a regular constable, mainly on weekends in traffic and crowd control during parades and other special functions. Those with language capabilities are often used as interpreters. They are not armed.

Auxiliary policemen are not paid but are allowed 15 cents a mile for travel. For every five years service, they are awarded a maple leaf to be worn on the left sleeve of the uniform. In 1976, they gave 37,000 hours of service to the community.

Conclusions

Comparative studies can assist in the solution of our own problem by studying solutions which have been tried in other societies. It seems evident that. American policing can profit by a study of foreign police systems. Conceding that conditions differ from country to country, the following examples indicated that there is justification for research and experimentation along lines that have been adopted abroad.

Consolidation

It is questionable whether we need 17,000 police agencies in this country, many of which are understaffed, inadequately trained, poorly equipped, and generally incapable of delivering effective services.[26] Perhaps the English programme of amalgamation could encourage a more rapid trend to consolidation here, or at least a greater sharing of services.

Recruitment

Until recently there has been reluctance among American police departments to appoint persons under 21. Those agencies still hesitant to appoint applicants under that age might look at the experience of many other countries which indicates that individuals at age 18-1/2 can function effectively as police officers.

In connection with recruitment, stricter screening of applicants is desirable. The Royal Canadian Mounted Police by means of psychometric tests and intensive interviews have been highly successful in weeding out less qualified persons.

Training

The length and content of training are constant problems for police agencies. Although there has been some improvement in

American police training in recent years, some of the following training programmes abroad should interest our own police departments: assignment of graduates of the recruit school to selected senior police officers to train under their tutelage for a substantial period, such as six months in the Royal Canadian Mounted Police; intensive midmanagement and executive training courses as in England and Japan: requiring extension courses upon completion of the recruit school, as in New Zealand; emphasis on the martial arts, as in Japan.

Investigations

Our police agencies also benefit by looking at the selection and training of detectives in other countries. There are some who believe that no area of law enforcement in the United States is in greater need of improvement.[22] The English system of a month trial period followed by a 16-week training course at a detective training school would undoubtedly be an improvement over our present system which generally involves only a brief period of instruction, or simply on-the-job training.

Juveniles

In juvenile matters we might experiment with youth aid sections and children's boards, as in New Zealand. They should be particularly useful in cities with sizeable ethnic minorities.

Patrol

It is generally agreed that our traditional patrol techniques are not effective. It would be useful for American departments to consider the English unit beat system, the pivot patrols of New Zealand, or the equivalent of Japanese kobans.

Drug Control

We could learn from the Japanese approach to the drug problem which eliminates methadone and requires compulsory hospitalization of addicts and reporting for aftercare to special counsellors.

The above by no means exhaust the areas of interest for American police departments, but it clearly indicates that comparative police studies can be helpful in solving our own policing problems.

REFERENCES

1. *Uniform Crime Reports. FBI 1976*, Washington, D.C: U.S. Government Printing Office, Table 6, p. 105.

2. Letter, courtesy of Supt. A. Kirton, Surrey Constabulary, Surrey, England.

3. "Japanese Criminal Statistics, 1976," National Police Agency, Tokyo, Japan.

4. Source: *1977 Commercial Atlas & Marketing Guide*, Skokie, IL: Rand McNally & Co., p. 378.

5. *Ibid.*, p. 608.

6. *Ibid.*, p. 604

7. *Sourcebook of Criminal Justice Statistics* 1976, Albany, NY: Criminal Justice Research Center, Table. 8.1 I, p. 38.

8. Critchley, T.A., *History of Police in England and Wales*, 2nd ed. Montclair, NJ: Patterson Smith, 1972, p. 8.

9. *Ibid.*, p. 270.

10. Devlin, Sir Patrick, *The Criminal Prosecution in England*, New Haven, CN: Yale University Press, 1958, p. 31.

11. Miranda v. Arizona, 384 US 436, 16 L Ed. 2nd 694 S Ct 1602 (1966).

12. Skoler, Daniel L., "Research in Great Britain," *Police Chief* May 1969, p. 34.

13. Bayley, David H., *Forces of Order: Police Behaviour in Japan and the United States,* Berkeley, CA: University of

California Press, 1976, p. 87.

14. Clifford. William, *Crime Control in Japan*, Lexington, MA: D.C. Heath & Co., 1976, p. 80.

15. "Japanese Criminal Statistic, 1976," National Police Agency, Tokyo, Japan.

16. Uniform Crime Reports, FBI 1976, Washington, D.C.: U.S. Government Printing Office. p. 161.

17. *Australia National Times*, October 10-15, 1977, p. 15. See also Erika Young, "How to Get Lost and Still Win." *Garden Jet*, August-September, 1977, published by Japan Airlines, p. 28.

18. Police Training Regulations, Article 4, See *National Police Academy* issued by National Police Agency of Japan, p. 2.

19. Fukutake, Tadashi, *Japanese Society Today*, Tokyo: University of Tokyo Press, 1974, pp. 7, 39, 42, 45.

20. *Japan Daily Times*, September 17, 1977, p. 12.

21. "Keishicho: Metropolitan Police Department," Public Relations Section, Administrative Division, Metropolitan Police Department, Tokyo 1977, p. 24.

22. *Miami Herald*, February 22, 1978, p. 8B; see also Bayley, *op. cit.*, p. 62.

23. The principal sources for this section are *A Brief Account of Drug Abuse and Countermeasures in Japan*, Japanese Ministry of Health and Welfare, 1972 and 1977. The figures given are in the 1977 edition, p. 6.

24. The situation with respect to heroin seems to be deteriorating. *See Japan Times*, September 19, 1977, p. 2, claiming a growing use of heroin in Japan, and attributing it to the hallucinatory effects of stimulant drugs.

25. This section is based on the *Promotional Process Manual*, Ontario Provincial Police, issued November 1, 1976.

26. Wilson, O.W., and McLaren, Roy C., *Police*

Administration, 4th ed., New York: McGraw-Hill, p. 51.

27. *Ibid.*, p. 363; and Patrick Murphy and Thomas Plate, Commissioner: *A View from the Top of American Law Enforcement*, New York: Simon and Schuster, 1977, p. 187.

9

POLICE BEHAVIOUR AND ATTITUDINAL REFORM

Introduction

"Next to the blessings which a nation derives from an excellent Constitution and system of general laws, are those which result from a well regulated and energetic plan of police, conducted and enforced with purity, activity, vigilance and discretion."[1] Police has come to occupy a very prominent position among the institutions that have been recognised all over the world to be of importance in preserving democracy, freedom and liberty. The need of the hour is to transform the police into an effective instrument of social defence and social change. Unfortunately, no revolutionary change in the system of police functioning has been in evidence after the independence in India. Newspapers and periodicals are often carrying reports of incidents of police excesses, criticising police behaviour and depicting the Indian police as undemocratic, uncivilized and brute force. Acharya Kripalani has observed "We have not yet made any beginning in the last 30 years to train our policemen to abide by the law as behoves a democratic society". (Indian Express May 31, 1977). The rapid rate of industrialisation and urbanisation, the growing consciousness of the people, our Constitution, the fundamental rights, the emphasis on rule of law all these are factors which impose on all of us, particularly on the police, a new responsibility, a new obligation, a new sense of dedication to the cause of the Country. Police have to change alongwith the changing socio-economic-political scene of the country and, therefore, new training, behavioural orientation to the changing context and appropriate attitudinal change in police become absolutely necessary.

The Behavioural Movement

Modern behaviouralism which developed in the late 1930's and 1940's is concerned essentially with the scientific study of human behaviour in various settings. The behavioural sciences provide a necessary foundation for the study of organisational behaviour. In administrative studies, behaviouralism is considered to have started with Human Relation Movement of the 1930's and later developed, among others, by Chester Bernard and Herbert Simon. Herbert Simon has classified contemporary research in administrative behaviour as follows:[2]

(a) The study of bureaucracy (Robert Merton, Peter Blau and others using and improving upon the Weberian bureaucratic model;

(b) Human Relations study pertaining to motivation and job satisfaction (Chris Argyris, Douglas Mc Gregor, Rensis Likert, Warren Bennis and others);

(c) Motivation studies using the Bernard Simon equilibrium model; and

(d) Decision-making studies emphasizing primarily cognitive processes and the rational components of administrative behaviour."

3. Behavioural research indicates that obtaining group cooperation requires an understanding of the theories and principles that govern individual behaviour as well as those that relate to group behaviour in two organisational climates :

(i) behaviour in the formal organisation setting; and

(ii) behaviour patterns arising from peer pressure of the informal organisation.[3]

For example, transactional analysis provides an avenue of approach to better understanding of individual and group behaviour. The transactional analysis concept is built around three ego states the parent (ethics), the adult (reason) and the child (emotional expression and spontaneity) and is the study of behaviour related to "ego states" which are coherent systems of thought and feeling manifested by corresponding patterns of behaviour.[4] Parent behaviour represents the 'taught' concept of life, which over the years has solidified into values and habits; Adult behaviour represents the 'thought' concept of life and stems from an individual's ability to figure things out for himself enabling him to estimate probabilities and make decisions. and the child behaviour represents the 'felt' concept of life typified by joy or anger, excitement or moodiness. Transactional analysis provides us an avenue of approach to understanding our own dealings with others, as well as giving us a number of choices in responding to difficult life situations. The transactional analysis is not a panacea for every stress situation but it can be another effective tool for the police officer who understands the behavioural science theories and develops skill in its application to life situations. Human behaviour can be analysed and changed in organisation at six levels:

(i) Organisation in relation to its environment,

(ii) Functioning of the total organisation as a system,

(iii) Inter-team, inter-departmental and with inter-group relationships,

(iv) Intra-team behaviour and relationships,

(v) Inter-personal behaviour and relationship,

(vi) Intra-personal factors in behaviour.

The Behavioural Science seeks an understanding of human behaviour in its totality within—Socio-economic-political system of the country. Behaviour is visible and discernible response to stimulus, man's behaviour is in context of something with which be has come in contact event, person, situation. Organisational Behaviour is organisational performance actions and dealings with the people.

Organisational Behaviour in Police

Behaviour can be seen in the performance of an individual as it is the result of inter-action with his environment. A behaviour can be changed by:—

(a) A self awareness—Insight into self-Image sharing —Techinque of sharing self—awareness,

(b) Desired goal or a model,

(c) Strong desire to change,

(d) Facilites and environment to change,

(e) Feed-back from sincere and trust-worthy individuals, and

(f) Reinforcement—positive reinforcement.

Individuals living in society in fromal[1] informal organisations develop an organisational behaviour. Human behaviour is a dynamic entity and is of particular importance to the police where the human resources of the organisation interact directly in most of their of their activities with the masses of human beings outside. A conceptual scheme for understanding Organsational Behaviour is presented in Exhibit-1 (Attached).[5]

According to Keith Davis, fundamental concept of organisationl behaviour revolves around the nature of man (individual difference, a whole man, caused behaviour and human dignity) and the nature of organisation (Social systems and mutual interest). Behaviour is like a window which lets in light on to a person to reveal the hidden self, it is visible and discernible response to stimulus. Human Behaviour consists of a variety of observable activity which is closely linked with the mental life of an individual which influences substantially the overt behaviour. Though as individuals we are different and separate, each of us is moved by the same enduring principles, the same urges, the same needs. Organisations are constantly on move to revitalize, adapt, change, develop and grow in the face of innumerable changes that take place in the environment. In the past, behavioural scientists have tended to view police behaviour as a function of intrapersonal traits, such as authoritarianism, sadism and psychopathy.[6] Recent findings indicate that "policemen do not differ significantly from others of similar socio-economic background in authoritaranism." (Neiderhofer 1967). Unfortunately, almost all over the world police organisation behaviour is somehow identified with "Police Brutality," in dealing with certain citizens particularly those in the lower classes. The most common of these practices are :

(a) The use of profame and abusive language,

(b) Commands to move on or get home,

(c) Stopping and questioning people on the street or searching them or their cars,

(d) Threats to use force if not obeyed,

(e) Prodding with a nightstick or approaching with a pistol, and

(f) The actual use of physical force or violence itself'[7]

The third-degree interrogations and the use of physical brutality by the police are on the wane and better behavioural pattern is now clearly visible in the Society. In recent years many behavioural scientists have attempted to explain why police behave the way they do in performing their duties. According to Neiderhoffer, police officers are transformed into authoritarian personalities by virtue of the police role. Police develop a cynicism towards the public because their job throws them into contact with so many dishonest people and they begin to see everyone as dishonest and corrupt. James Wilson has observed that there are conflicting expectations from the police and this role conflict forces them to make certain compromises, accommodations and choices. The policemen face the dilemma of enforcing the law and at the same time maintaining order, they are expected to do both but order maintenance may at times require the officers to work outside the law ignoring a suspect's constitutional rights. Westley has found a police sub-culture of using violence to coerce respect. According to him "the most significant finding is that at least 37 per cent of the policemen believed that its was legitimate to use violence to coerce respect.[8] E. R. Stoddard (1968), L. Savitz (1970) and A.J. Reiss (1968) support the notion of a code of secrecy of policemen. Unfortunately, "Police outputs are hard to measure, many crimes are difficult to solve and impossible to prevent and some crime-suppression efforts may succeed, only in displacing rather than reducing the illegal behaviour Police administrators are more likely to be judged not by crime statistics but by the frequency of scandals, charges of corruption or abuse or political controversies; hence, the chiefs tend to practice defensive rather than service oriented administration"[9]. Police behaviour is generally reported to be rude and discourteous. According to Dr. P.D. Sharma some of the reason for the discourteous behaviour of police checked by the majority of members of the various sections of the community were as follows:

(a) Students: They are Power-drunk

(b) Intelligentia : They are illiterate and unfortunately placed

(c) Businessmen : They are corrupt

(d) Political leaders : They are agents of the ruling group

(e) Religious leaders : They are immoral

(f) Civil Servants : They do not have professional Ethics."

While analysing the police organisational behaviour Banton held that "the normal tendency of the police is to underenforce the law."[10] By under-enforce is meant making substantially fewer arrests than observed citizen behaviour in theory warrants. Drunkenness, assaults, malicious mischief, minor thefts and traffic offences are generally ignored by the policemen. In fact, "Police discretion is inevitable partly because it is impossible to observe every public infraction, partly because many laws require interpretation before they can be applied at all, partly because police can sometimes get information about serious crimes by overlooking minor crimes and partly because the police believe that public opinion would not tolerate a policy a full enforcement of all laws all the time."[11]

Since there are obvious differences in law enforcement styles across communities and countries, students of police behaviour can profit by directing their research towards an analysis of what effect the presence of large number of economic and racial minorities has upon the style of law enforcement in a given jurisdiction.[12] According to W. Cook, the process of law enforcement serves the interests of dominant groups in the society and either ignores or opposes the interests of those in lower social strata.[13] Police literature indicates that police discretion in making arrests is generally used to the disadvantage of minority groups. (Skolnick 1966, Goldman 1963; Wald 1967; Wilson 1968). There is some evidence that police subculture. develops to legitimize and keeps secret suppression of economic and racial minorities. (Reiss 1968; Westley 1970). According to John F Galliher, "much of the police behaviour seems most easily explained if one considers that whenever there is a conflict of interests between the dominant classes in a society or less powerful groups, the police protect the interests of the former and regulate the behaviour of the latter." Willian A Westley holds the view that police respond differently to different social classes, while police are afraid to brutalize the wealthy because of their political influence, police generally ill-treat the poor slum dwellers because the poor are generally seen as more disposed to law violation and conflict with the police. There is and appalling state of dishonesty and corruption in the police particularly at lower and middle levels. The Bihar Police Commission observed : "The tradition of corruption in the police is deep-seated and certain forms of corruption have come to be accepted by society as harmless." According to Shri S.C. Misra "The forms of corruption are very numerous. It manifests itself in every stage of the work of the police station. The complainant has often to pay a fee for having his complaint recorded. He has to give the investigating officer a present to secure his earnest. The Station House Officer has a specially rich vein in cases concerning disputes about land, water or crop and the management of cattle pounds."[14]

According to Skolnick, policemen have a working personality—a set of cognitive tendencies which influence their work. By virtue of enforcing the law the police become very supportive of the status quo and extremely politically conservative. "Police personnel are pro-status-quo both by temper and training". According to James H. Skolnick the dangerousness of the police mission as well as the requirements that officers use authority against civilians contributes to police solidarity "The reasoning is that the more hostility the police receive from the public, the more isolated they become and consequently the more dependent they become upon each other."[15] The same view is held, by Niederhoffer who refers to this police behaviour as the principle of equilibrium meaning that police are mainly concerned with protecting themselves from all criticism from whatever source.[16] Since the main task of the police brings police officers into a complex relationship with people-police behaviour as an individual or a group becomes very important. Police have to deal with religious tensions, caste tensions, language tensions, agrarian unrest, student unrest, status tension, organisational tension and various other types of group conflicts. Managements and resolution of conflicts have become a complex problem for the police. Police officers every day call upon their own knowledge of interpersonal skills many times in the course of a workday perhaps even to save their own lives.

The Concept of Attitude

The behavioural sciences have given a great deal of attention to attitude. The Scientists have studied the functions of attitudes, the ways in which they develop the conditions leading to change of attitudes and the resistance to change of attitudes. "An attitude is the predisposition of an individual to evaluate some symbol or object on any of his world in a favourable or unfavourable manner."[17] An attitude, according to James and Kelly is "an orientation towards or away from some object, concept or situation and a readiness to respond in a predetermined manner to these related objects, concepts and situations." The term attitude refers to the dispositions of men to view things in certain ways, it is "a mental or natural state or readiness organised through experiences, exerting a directive or dynamic influence upon the individual's response to all objects and situations with which it is related." According to Thomas and Znaniechki (1918) attitudes are individual mental process which determine both the actual and potential responses to each person in the social world. Thus attitude can be inferred by the actions. There are several situations and problems which are tackled by the police and their behaviour towards the members of the public and actions with reference to those situations disclose their attitudes. The basic factor which governs the behaviour of an individual or a group is thinking or outlook and that is what we know as the attitude. Attitude is a state of mind of individual towards a value. There are six possible values : theoretical, economic, aesthetic, social, economic and religious. A person's behaviour is conditioned by environment, mental import and biological import.

According to Katz attitudes perform four critical functions for the personality : adjustment, ego-defence, value-expression and knowledge. Together they furnish an understanding of the reasons that people hold the attitude they hold. One acquires his atitudes through his learning experiences and the major influences in attitude formation are the society (its customs, habits, traditions) the family, and the group membership of the socio-economic class. An organisation tends to shape its member and their attitude in its own image.[18] Allport has suggested the following three conditions for formation of attitudes:

1. "The accretion and integration learned in the course of growing up''.
2. "The influence of some dramatic experience or trauma."
3. "The adoption of ready-made attitudes" of parents, teachers and others.

Generally, attitudes are formed as human beings grown and the behaviour of elders, the atmosphere in the family, the customs observed in the family, the atmosphere of schools, the environment of the society where an individual grows, all these factors have considerable impact on the attitude formation. A child adopts generally ready-made attitudes from the mother, father, teachers, elder brother and sisters, and others with whom be comes in contact closely certain dramatic experiences and influences of childhood have deeper impact on attitude formation.

In general there are two ways to change attitudes : individual and programmatic. The individual approach can be accomplished through two methods : role changes and interpersonal contacts. The programmatic approach to attitudinal change embraces a host of training methods ranging from indoctrination to group discussion, lectures, syndicate study and sensitivity training. "The first and most critical step in initiating attitudinal change is to arouse a need for such a change. The next step is to show the person that suggested shift in attitude is beneficial to him and consistent with his other values or goals. The final step is to reinforce the newly acquired attitude through a system of rewards."[19] Attempts to influence people's attitudes in large number come mainly by way of channels of communications, books, group discussions, television, radio, newspapers, lectures, advertising etc.

Training for Attitudinal Change in Police

The Committee on Police Training having realised the importance of appropriate attitudes at all levels in the police have recommended inclusion of topics aimed at attitude fromation in the proposed syllabi right from Constable upot IPS Probationers. This need for attitudinal training felt by the committee will have to be shared by all trainers in various Police Training Institutions and recommendations have to be implemented at all levels in the right spirit. Inculcation of appropriate attitudes is a continuous process but the best results can only be achieved if this task is linked up with the basic and inservice training of all ranks in all police training institutions in the country. Gore Committee on Police Training has brought out the following seven recommendations :

(1) "Since the police have an accepted role to play in the establishment of conditions favourable for social growth and development, it is necessary for them to promote a feeling of confidence and security among the minorities and the weaker sections so that they can participate fully in and benefit from the national development effort."

(2) "There is need for a secular outlook and a sympathetic attitude in dealing with the victims of communal tensions and religious bigotry. The Law Enforcement Officers must inculcate a habit of prompt, vigorous and firm response whenever the secular concept is under threat. No aspect of the role of the police is more important than their active and purposeful participation in programmes of national integration based on the principles of equality and secularism."

(3) "The success of social legislation depends on the effectiveness of its enforcement and the police have a protective as well as a promotional role to perform in this sphere. They should be highly sensitive and familiar with the trends and process of social change and their implications for the society in which they live."

(4) "This new role requires the development of proper attitudes

and the ability to anticipate, analyse and take decisions to meet such difficult situations. The police officers must have a high degree of discernment and a knowledge in depth of society and its problems. His approach must be one of sympathy alongwith an abiding faith in law and orderly growth, Law has to be applied with a deep understanding of the changing needs of the society."

(5) "In the changed circumstances of our society, a wholly law and order oriented force has to be transformed ....The implications of this are that police officers must acquire a high degree of professional competance and develop an understanding of the social purpose of their activity, a sensitivity to trends and forces at work in the environment in which they act, attitudes in consonance with the concept of social justice with particular reference to the weaker sections of the society.''

(6) "It is, therefore, necessary to induct new concepts into police training programmes and to provide training material, which may make police officers aware of the tremendous problems of the minorities and the underprivileged classes and the need to deal with them with an understanding of the factors which give rise to particular situations."

(7) "Under these circumstances, the following considerations deserve special emphasis in the training of the police:

(a) Loyalty to the Constitution, commitment to the goals of the nation and the concept of an egalitarian society and the need for national integration.

(b) Awareness of the problems that arise in the wake of the development process including conflicts, social disorganisation, scarcity, and controls, regional imbalances etc.

(c) A deep awareness for comprehending and reacting to complex situations.

(d) Development of analytical and innovative skills since situations will continue to change and no ready made solutions can be prescribed.

(e) A new orientation in dealing with masses, who come from various strata of society divided among many contours such as religion, caste, region and income, as may lead to correct response in individual cases."

Police training has to build and sustain an attitude of service to the poor and the down-trodden and to bring about a behavioural orientation in police to the democratic ideals of service in the welfare state. "Police is an agency of the Govt., designed to stand between the powerful and the weak, to prevent oppression. Only a police force, which understands correctly its role in the society identifies itself with the aspirations of the people it serve, and its actions according, can win the faith and respect of the people."[20]

Areas where attitudinal change needed

Although this could be a separate subject for research in depth, some of the areas that can easily be identified are :

(a) The attitude of police officers at police station, and police outposts when people visit police stations to give complaints for registration.

(b) The attitude of police during investigation of cases, before arrest or house search etc.

(c) The attitude of police, after arrest, in police station during investigation.

(d) The attitude of police towards the poor, the ill-clad villagers and the weaker sections during police bandobast of VIP and public meetings.

(e) The attitude of police in offering bails particularly to the economically poor and the weaker sections of the society.

(f) The attitude of police during surveillance over the political suspects.

(g) Attitude of police towards minorities during communal tensions.

(h) Attitude of police towards weaker sections of the society when cases of atrocities are brought to the notice of the police.

(j) Attitude of the police in enforcing social legislation such as Abolition of Bonded Labour Act, Protection of Civil Rights Act and others.

Jawaharlal Nehru rightly instructed to policemen when he said : "Never allow the common man take the idea that he is being treated with discourtesy and contempt. This is of the highest importance in a democratic set up."[21] The civil service and the police must be committed in the constitution. Commitment is "a state of the inner being of man, a value achieved and seeking expression in outlook, action, attitude and behaviour outside." The policeman today must have a fully awakened social consciousness of his new role in building a real social democratic republic. Policemen like other Govt. servants should be committed in the sense "that should be loyal to the guiding principles of our constitution and the objectives which have been adopted by Parliament."[22]

Concluding Remarks

Some states like Maharashtra have started special Behavioural Reorientation courses for middle level police officers. S.V.P. National Police Academy, Hyderabad has also revised the syllabi of IPS Probationers for implementing the recomendations of the Gore Committee on Police Training Officers of the rank of S.P. and above are now quite conscious and aware of social implications of the police role and some visible impact in attitude is visible. There is considerable talk today regarding the need to policemen's attitudes and police training institutions have, therefore, included the "Principles of Police Conduct" and "Police Community Relations" as subjects in all their training programmes. But unfortunately, no attitudinal change is noticed in policemen's behaviour at lower and middle levels. A trainee leaves a training institution full of entusiasm and the right attitude but he cannot translate the attitudes into practice as the climate in the field inhibits it. Organisational environment has to be conducive for proper attitudinal change in policemen particularly at lower and middle ranks.

Changed attitude by itself, leads to little good unless it is followed by change in individual behaviour which is directly affected by the organisational climate. ''If training is to produce any useful results there has to be linkage between the 'Training'and the 'world of work' .....Bringing about attitudinal change through training institutions may be futile if the environment after training was unable to sustain it."[23] A more frank and free opinion has been given by Dr. P.D. Sharma who observed that the survey results in general are a pointer towards the futility of training programmes as an instrument of attitudinal change or attiteud building of the lower functionaries in the police hierarchy.[24] However, there is no denial to the fact that there is an immediate need for inculcation of appropriate attitudes in all the ranks of the police and it is hoped that National Police Commission will give due attention and make suitable practical recommendations for intensifying behavioural orientation and appropriate attitudinal change in Police.

REFERENCES

1. Colquohoun—Delhi Police Commission Report. V/I 1966—68.
2. Herbert Simon—Administrative Behaviour—International Encyclopedia of Social Sciences I, p. 74—79.
3. Donel F Favreah and Joseph E Gillespie Modern Police Administration.
4. Eric Berne—Games People 1964 and Transactional Anaylsis in Psychothereaphy, 1975.
5. Sri G.V. Sarveswara Rao—"Introduction to Organisational Behaviour" SIET Institute Publication-Introduction to Organisational Behaviour—Selected Readings—Vol. I.
6. Phillip A Mann—Psychology of Police Organisation—Reward Structure and group Dynamics in Power and Authority in Law Enforcement—Edited by Terry R Armstrong & K M Cinnamon, p. 104.
7. Albert J Reisis Jr. Police Brutality—Answer to Key

Questions—The Ambivalent Force—Perspectives on the Police—Edit. Arthur Neiderhoffer & A Blumberg, p. 354.

8. William A Westely—Secrecy and the Police Social Forces 34 (March) 254—257.

9. James Q Wilson—Preface to "Varieties of Police Behaviour" 1568 P.VIII

10. Banton—The Policeman in the community p. 127-136.

11. James Q Wilson—Varieties of Police Behaviour p. 7.

12. John F-Gallipher—Explanation of Police Behaviour in The Ambivalent Force—Perspectives on the police. Edited by Aruthur. Niederhoffer & Blumberg 1976, p. 7.

13. W Cook—''Policeman in Society: Which side are they, on?" Berkely Journal of Society 12 Summer, pp.117-129.

14. Sri S. C. Misra—Police Administration in Inida, p. 269-70

15. Jerome H Skolnic-Justice without Trial, 1966, pp. 53-58.

16. Niederhoffer—Behind the Shield—The Police in Urban Society, 1967, p. 13-15.

17. Daniel Katz—The Fundamental Approach to the Study of Attitudes—in "Psychology in Administration", 1963, p. 253.

18. Ivar Berg—"Do Organisation Change People" in Industrial and Big Business—ed. "Leonard Sayles, 1963."

19. Paul M Whiscnand—Police Supervision-Theory and practice—p. 38.

20. Working Papar on Seminar on "Role of police in Redress of Grievances of Weaker Sections of the Society." SVP, NPA, Hyderabad, 75, p. 6.

21. Jawharlal Nehru and Public Administration—Indian Institute of Public Administration, New Delhi, 1975, p. 63.

22. Smt Indira Gandhi—Address in Lok Sabha on March 1970 Indian Journal of Public Administrations, July-Sept. 1971.

23. S.G. Gokhale—Police : Attitudes, Training Institute, Organisational Climate, N.P.A. Magazine Vol XXIII Nov. 1973, p. 59.

24. Dr. P.D. Sharma—Indian Police—A Development Approach 1977, p. 84.

10

ECONOMIC CRIME AND ITS CONTROL

A Case Study

I

Current Significance

Economic crime and its control and prevention continue to represent a pressingly *problematic field and a topic of current interest* in our society. This is shown by the increased amd mutually beneficial sharpening of perception in science, legislation, police investigation and sentencing practice. The 13th International Congress on Penal Law, which was held in Cairo last year and which gave detailed attention to the conception and principles of economic criminal law in one of its sections[1] demonstrates this.

The reasons for the special sensitivity towards, and the increase in awareness of, the dangers posed by economic crimes are to be found in the extent of damage suspected, in the potential for abuse, in the involvement of members of the middle and higher classes as well as in the presumption of wide victimization. Particularly at times and in economic systems that are characterized by extensive opportunities for abuse through the existence of a large number of trustees of alien property we must reckon with greater attention on the part of organs of social control so that dangers and disappointment are held within limits.

II

Theoretical Attempts at Definition

Although we speak of ''economic crime'' and prosecute

"economic crimes" (not to speak of administrative offences in the economic field). Police *Criminal Statistics do not make use of the concept of "economic crime"*, not even as a selected group of offences. The position is similar in regard to justice administration statistics. It is only the Federal Survey of Economic Crimes on a Uniform Basis." Carried out by public prosecuting authorities since 1974 and evaluated on behalf of justice departments by the Max Planck Institute in Freiburg that gives us an idea of the extent, the structures and the development of the serious economic crime that is investigated and prosecuted.[2] The conceptual and steering basis for action here is the catalogue of economic crimes as contained in the jurisdiction provisions of section 74c of the Courts' Constitution Act.

To some extent—that is to say in police literature—doubts have been expressed regarding the possibility of finding common *immanent criteria for a precise conceptual definition.*[3] Even so traditionally firmly structured types of offences like bribery, fraud or breach of trust—which are obviously also committed outside the economic field—give rise to the question as to the circumstances that procure the lable "economic crime" for these offences. Differences in the answers given to this question emerge in the form of *uncertainty* in literature and crime investigation and prosecution, for example in the assignment of economic offences to specialized public prosecuting authorities or to courts dealing with such offences. This uncertainty is also apparent in the classification of police criminal statistics, as already mentioned. The controversy associated with attempts at definition goes back to the beginnings of the development of an economic criminal law at the end of the twenties. In the light of varying criminal policy consequences some practitioners still call for a firm definition. The difficulty involved in this task is enhanced when it becomes clear that penal provisions from more than 200 Federal Acts are ascribed to the realm of economically criminal conduct, so that the stress here falls not on the Criminal Code but on secondary criminal law.

III

Pragmatic Concept of Crime

Finding a solution can thus only lie in pragmatic action. A

strategy of this kind not only makes a *typological classification* according to the direction of attack and the mode of victimization possible but also enables links to be established with legislative and procedural tasks as well as with those relating to police tactics and justice organization. In spite of a certain amount of mutual permeation, economic crimes may roughly be divided into four groups of offences in the light of the *protected fields* concerned (the national economy, business, public finance, the general public, consumers and contracting parties).[4]

1. Offences against the banking and stock exchange system, against the credit system, the insurance system and freedom of competition, including breach of trust and insolvency offences as well as violations of copyright and trade mark rights.
2. Tax and duty evasion, customs offences, subsidy fraud, inducement and bribery.
3. Violations of youth protection and labour protection legislation as well of social security law; offences involving consumer edibles, passing off, and consumer and environmental offences;
4. Fraud and profiteering.

Individual interests worthy of protection come to the foremost conspicuously in the fourth group. This also has an effect on the investigation and prosecution of crime. On the other hand, the other three groups are mainly distinguished for the supra-individual or general nature of the fields protected.

By contrast with conventional crime, in relation to which roughly 80 to 90 per cent of all information is laid by private persons, economic crime mainly involves so-called *surveillance or control offences*. Generally, this applies to the whole spectrum of economic crimes, although only in an attenuated form of serious economic crime.[5] At any rate secondary analyses of court records of serious economic crime have shown that information is laid for breach of trust by private persons in only 70 per cent of cases and for credit fraud in only 42 per cent of cases. According to the Federal Survey of Economic Crimes the state was harmed in more than one-third of all cases in 1983, and in a further 10 per cent of cases social institutions were harmed. By contrast individuals and extraneous enterprises suffered unlawful harm to their property in one quarter of the cases and employers in 4 per cent of the cases. The special character of economic criminal offences is also apparent here, namely, that where the offender-victim relationship disappears,6 greater efforts on the part of the administration towards prevention and on the part of the police and public prosecutors regarding investigation and prosecution are necessary to make up and compensate for the lack of control by an individual victim.

Consideration of this kind probably also contributed to the creation of 74c *of the Courts' Constitution Act* with its special arrangement for judicial handling of serious economic crimes. The catalogue or crimes listed, however, also includes offences like fraud, breach of trust, profiteering, inducement and bribery, all of which are not—of necessity—special economic crimes. Hence the special arrangement in 74c is expressly made dependent on the additional criterion that "for evaluation of the case special knolwedge of economic life is necessary".[7] New problems of differentiation, however, arise through the addition of this criterion, so that we are left with the *decisive question as to the distinguishing features.* As a result one of the research problems to be investigated in the secondary analyses of court records was the question whether it is possible to find criteria capable of making the catalogue in 74c of the Courts' Constitution Act more definite or even superfluous. These studies have yielded the following criteria regarded as relevant by prosecutors.[8] The number of individual cases, the degree of harm caused, the number of victims harmed, the duration of proceedings and the calling of experts. Surprisingly, the question whether the accused committed the offence in his capacity as holder of an economic post was not considered to be decisive. The criterion was only applicable to fraud and breach of trust. Thus, it may ultimately be doubted whether a practicable differentiation of economic crime is possible at all within the framework of Section 74c of the Courts' Constitution Act.

IV

Structure of Economic Crime and Difficulties of Investigation and Prosecution

The rating of individual groups of offences or fields of crime can be determined by considering the *extent*, the *degree of gravity* and the *intensity of victimization and harm* of the offences concerned as well as the characteristic traits of the delinquents and the possibilities of control. According to the Federal Survey about 95 per cent of the work of specialist prosecuting authorities is taken up with offences listed inthe catalogue in Section 74c of the Courts' Constitution Act.[9]

If we were to generalize on the basis of these findings, *everyday economic delinquency* including administrative offences would be left out of the picture.[10] In this respect reference must be made particularly to offences involving consumer edibles and to modes of conduct associated with unfair competition, the focal point of non-punishable economic offences.[11] It must be borne in mind that serious economic crimes only amount to about 15% of all registered economic crimes and that, taken as a whole, the total number of economic crimes in relation to all crimes registered (including traffic delinquency) hardly amounts to more than 3 to 5 per cent.[12] Nevertheless, this relatively insignificant number of offences is offset by an *extremely high degree of offence potential*. This finding may be illustrated by the fact that in regard to serious economic crimes.

- relatively few criminal trials are conducted (1983 : 3,747), and
- a relatively small number of accused (1983 : 6,423) are identified, although those identified,
- account for a large number of invidual cases (1983 : 163,472), whereby
- a large number of people suffer harm (1983 : 34,598 in relation to one-fifth of all cases with relevant data), and
- altogether a high degree of damage to property is caused (1983: 6, 9 billion marks).

Already the fact that annually public prosecutors have to examine altogether 10,000 possible statutory offences in roughly 3,700 investigations shows that the prosecuting authorities have to evaluate these investigations not only from one, but usually from several, criminal law aspects. Even bribery, inducement or credit fraud may coincide with other offences and not infrequently give way to the latter on account of substantive principles regulating concurrence of offences or for the sake of principles of procedural economy. Accordingly, the structure of serious economic crime is mainly distinguished by the fact that the *offences concerned display complex features with many different combinations of definitional elements.*[13]

The difficulties that arise here for *crime solving (including proof), prosecution, and conviction and sentence* are quite obvious, and so is the *need for the specialist knowledge.* Serious economic crimes, moreover, usually occur in ways that outwardly appear to conform with the law. The legality of external conduct may almost be described as the protective mantle of economic crime.[14] The high-grade economic and technical quality of delinquency thus calls for specific technical training and specialization of the investigating and prosecuting authorities. Nevertheless, the calling of experts, in particular of accountants and tax advisers, often cannot be dispensed with. This applies especially to book-keeping and to balance sheets. On the other hand, new weak points also emerge: specialist and technical knowledge must be supplemented by knowledge of criminal law and criminal procedure so that investigation does not bypass the elements of criminal offences and the function of expert opinion in criminal procedure is not neglected.[15] Furthermore, the numher of experts available and the time at their disposal are limited. Questions relating to costs may also become problematic where investigation is extensive. Hence, as far as possible recourse must usually be made to the staff of public prosecuting authorities and the police.

V

Particular Forms of Criminal Activity

Economic crime shows a special tendency towards organised interdependence. The Federal Survey has shown us that about three quarters of all cases of serious economic crime are committed under the cloak of a private firm or of a commercial firm, principally in the form of a limited liability company, a trading company or a limited liability partnership. Here more than elsewhere—apart from so-called organized crime—we encounter a kind of "associative crime."[16] Hence in about 85 per cent of all cases a link can be established between the crime committed by the principal person accused and the duties he performed in the enterprise. Some lines of business are obviously more susceptible than others, or — to put it more guardedly — they are more likely to have to face privately initiated control through the laying of an information. In comparison with their share in the economy, some branches are more severely affected — above all banking and credit (by four times as much), building and real estate (by three times as much) and also transport and travel. The relative proportion of harm caused is obviously also determined by this greater strain.

International correlations are strikingly frequent as regards serious economic crime. In conformity with their considerable criminal quality economic criminal offences may not only transcend national borders unimpeded but may also use these very borders for their own purposes. On an international level offences of this kind—committed at a distance—display a special degree of efficiency and acquire an increased level of protection against prosecution.[17] This applies, for example, to international financial offences like dealings in foreign capital investments, arranging stock exchange business[18] and causing harm to banks. International complications arise above all in regard to tax offences, customs contraventions, violations of exchange regulations and of provisions relating to economic communities.[19]

Specific problems of fact and law obstruct investigation and prosecution where an accused is to be extradited or a witness interrogated abroad or where other investigations must be carried out —searches and seizure, etc. Legislation, varying frequently from country to country, is also problematic. Thus, the call for harmonization of European legal systems, for supra-national commissions to act as prosecuting authorities and for improved legal assistance between states is understandable.[20] However, *tension between the interest in supra-national criminal prosecution* on the one hand *and national sovereignty* on the other must also be taken into account. This tension can only be overcome through greater political co-operation in the international field.

Today special attention must also be given to the diverse attacks *on computer systems* over the past two decades that have constituted a threat both to individual firms and national economies in the USA, in Japan and subsequently to an increasing extent in Europe, too.[21] Of central importance here are the cases of so-called "computer manipulation", i.e. the alteration of data, carried out, especially by employees of the enterprise harmed for the sake of personal enrichment.[22] This fatal link between criminal inventiveness and technical progress has posed completely new problems for criminal law. However, there has been no indication of cases of computer crime either in the ten-year evaluation of the Federal Survey of serious economic crimes or in the secondary analyses of court records in about 5000 selected trials. Nevertheless, the occurrence of fraudulent computer manipulation within the framework of the Federal Survey obviously cannot be ruled out—it is simply not on record. Still we may say that computer offences of which there is official knowledge may still be classed among the extremely rare occurrences.

VI

Procedural and Substantive Innovations

Although the need for control of economically detrimental phenomena received only scant attention for years, there was a marked change in this situation during the seventies. The legislature became alarmed principally on account of scientific investigations confirming that there is an exceptionally high degree of offence potential in the held of economic crime with enormous damage in figures running into the billions.[23] As a result the German legislature decided *in the seventies to introduce a number of procedural and substantive innovations.*

To begin with, in 1971, the legislature created a legal framework in the Courts' Constitution Act for establishing special courts to deal with economic crimes. The intention behind this step was that of criminal offences where "for evaluation of the case special knowlege of economic life is necessary'' should be aided in an appropirate manner and dealt with more quickly. To achieve this goal the judicial handling of such offences was to be placed in the hands of judges with special knowledge and experience in the field who would be in a position to broaden and deepen their expertise.

With the passage of the *First Statute for the Control of Economic Crime* on September 1, 1976 (BGB1 1. 2034) the Federal legislature took further action by modifying substantive criminal law in order to check circumstances detrimental to the economy.

However, this statute was a first step only, for it was only partly capable of eliminating the shortcomings of existing legal provisions. Consequently, it is understandable that the German legislature has already set about introducing the *Second Statute for the Control of Economic Crime.*[24]

This *draft* is intended to link up with reform deliberations to date and in particular, to take account of the consequences of future economic and technological phenomena.[25] Thus, certain kinds of computer manipulation not punishable in the past are to be covered in future by an independent criminal offence of computer fraud (planned as Section 263a of the Criminal Code). In addition, forgery of stored data (planned as 269) and deception in data processing (planned as 270) are to be criminalized. For protection against capital investment offers lacking in seriouness a new offence precedent to fraud has been proposed, i.e. an offence of so-called ''capital investment fraud''(planned as Section 264a of the Criminal Code). Incorrect statements made in prospectuses, representations or summaries of assets and liabilities and intended for a wide circle of people are to be resisted by this offence. Finally, criminal law protection against embezzlement of pay is to be strengthened (in a new Section 266a).

This draft has not managed to silence those voices that have expressed misgivings in principle against the criminal law as an appropriate weapon for use in the fight against economic crime.[26] Consequently, *doubts* regarding the claim that socially harmful conduct in the economic field can be penalized and effectively with criminal law measures cannot be overlooked.[27]

However, great the tasks and the difficulties involved might be, they do not leave room for any doubt that we are here concerned with socially and economically harmful *problems* of a considerable dimension that have to be *mastered by means of criminal law measures as well.* Controversy only blows up as regards the extent to which "criminal law as instrument of economic policy" is capable of, and indeed may, be put to use.[28] Hence mobilization of the potential for effectively combating economically and socially harmful conduct is almost regarded as the "acid test of the criminal law system".[29] This view obviously applies to all areas relevant to the criminal law. It applies to legislation as well as to investigation and prosecution and also to conviction and execution of sentence. Moreover, it also includes science itself. Criminology and criminal law rightly see modern economic crime as a challenge.

VII

Reforms in Investigation

In contrast to the usual mode of reform, which begins with the introduction of new statutory offences and not infrequently goes no further, reform in the field of economic criminal law moved in the opposite direction. *First* came *organisational reform* and only then came innovations within the field of substantive criminal law. Those administering the law in practice mainly contributed to thisdevelopment.[30] On the basis of years of experience and difficulty, an attempt was made to compensate for traditional inadequacies in crime solution and prosecution by increasing the degree of *specialization* and *concentration* within the statutory framework available. The most significant reward reaped from this development has been the formation of specialist prosecuting authorities since the sixties.[31] Effective organs were to bring about more vigorous activity on the part of prosecuting authorities vis-a-vis the police and the experts, in order to create a kind of "equality of arms" vis-a-vis economic delinquents. In concrete terms this was intended to involve a curtailment of investigations by more intensive, more thorough and quicker solution at a concomitantly sound rate of solution in order to achieve more effective control of economic crime.[32]

This made it necessary for investigating and prosecuting authorities to operate in a certain manner. Whilst general (i.e. non-specialist) prosecuting authorities usually give the police wide room for manoeuvre when *carrying out investigations,* public prosecutors involved in cases of economic crime often lead the investigation personally. They hold interrogations themselves, take part in searches and to some extent evaluate the evidentiary material themselves. The police-regularly receive instructions regarding their investigations so that specially close ties are established with public prosecutors.[33]

These organisational reform measures were, however, not conceived in isolation. Instead they were embedded both in substantive innovations and in *accompanying of self- and external control within the economy.*[34] Relatively encouraging possibilities of protection for banks through investigations of creditworthiness are apparent. Banks have the staff and the technical means to order a comprehensive examination or creditworthiness before giving credit.[35] This becomes more difficult, however, in regard to businessmen and especially as far as private customers are concerned. Hence the notion has surfaced that economic crime not only encourages a certain category of offender but also puts a specific group of victims at a disadvantage.

VIII

Results of Innovations, Conclusions for Those Administering the Law in Practice and Challenges addressed to Criminal Policy

It we consider the efforts made to control economic crime since the last World War—and in particular the endeavours of the last fifteen years — we may draw the following conclusions, expressed here in terms of nine theses:

1. Investigation of economic crime that has come to the attention of the authorities shows that although economic crimes numerically do not exceed 3 to 5 per cent of the total number of crimes committed, their offence potential is nevertheless extremely high in view of the extent of the harm involved and the range of victimization. Nothing has happened in the last decade to alter this fact, as we see from the *relative*

constancy of serious economic crime as demonstrated by the Federal Survey of Economic Crimes on a Uniform Basis.

2. Corresponding efforts to control economic crime within a comparable space of time were noless significant. Besides organizational innovations, special reference must be made to reforms in economic law and in economic criminal law. Reform continues — as illustrated by current deliberations regarding the draft of a Second Statute for the Control of Economic Crime.

3. On the whole, it may be said of the reforms carried out that the organizational measures affecting investigation and prosecution have proved to be the most important for controlling economic crime. On the other hand, however, innovations in substantive criminal law have lagged behind in importance. This outcome is understandable since — as in the similar case of traffic and environmental crime - it is crucial particularly in the case of economic crime that the investigating and prosecuting authorities are not content merely to react but also to take action in advance.

4. Nevertheless, we should not fail to realize that there are also inadequacies here. Regarding specialization and concentration, *the courts dealing with economic offences and the police continue in their "need to catch up"*. Although the police in particular repeatedly drew attention to the high significance of economic crime as long ago as the fifties and early sixties, they have largely lost their earlier advantage in terms of knowledge and experience in resisting economic crime.

5. As far as the police's need for catachingup is concerned, it is not primarily a matter of better training in economic law and business administration (book-keeping) but indeed also applies to legal knowledge of economic criminal law. In particular the difficult, and thus not easily undestandable, *criminal offences* of subsidy fraud and credit fraud are still largely *assessed erroneously*.

6. In the light of the situation as described the *main task* of the police probably does not lie in prevention or even in prognostic evaluation of the development of economic crime in the future, but *first of all* in firm and effective *repression* and in the prophylaxis indirectly made possible thereby.

7. The efforts required on the part of investigating and prosecuting authorities—especially the police — have to be reckoned as all the greater since *hope of co-operation from within the economy itself* in the fight against economic crime must be limited only. For reasons well-known the business world is reluctant to co-operate actively in the suspension of economic crime by the police or through the criminal law. This applies particularly to areas of competition. If this were not the case, information would be laid under the Unfair Competition Act more frequently and objections to criminalizing fraudulent tenders would be more modest.

8. Some *forms of association* as for example the limited liability company or the limited liability partnership have long displayed *considerable susceptibility* to criminal abuse (according to the Federal Survey for the year 1983 more than 1000 cases still concerned criminal activities occurring under the cloak of a limited liability company).

9. Criminal law sanctioning of offenders who have committed economic crimes appears (internationally) to be comparatively lenient and has thus been the subject of considerable controversy for sometime. Nevertheless, it ought not to be overlooked that the ascertainable previous record of this category of offenders is on average highly insignificant so that the sentencing practice criticized here is *imaginable* in terms of general sentencing criteria.[36]

It can be shown that *too little use* is made of so-called "occupational prohibition." Since the early seventies it has been imposed on fewer and fewer occasions it constitutes an adequate remedy—similar to banning an offender from driving in a case involving drunkeness.

If we are to carry out a "success-rate check" of the manifold activities of the legislature, within the administration of justice, and of the investigating and prosecuting authorities, it will be found that there are sufficient indications for a generally positive assessment.[37]

This brings me to the recommendations that follow from the present state of research and from deductions clearly indicated.[38]

1. Controlling economic crime is labour-intensive and calls for a high degree of specialization. Hence, as a first step, *efficient, central*

and highly specialized police squads must be established so as to be better armed for controlling economic offences. Although generally there are central offices at police stations and in the State Crime Bureaux to deal with the suppression of economic crime, they have, however, obviously not turned out to be *adequate* in terms of their functions and their equipment so as to be on a par with specialist prosecuting authorities and, above all, to be able to meet the demands involved in their duties.[39]

2. Furthermore, *improved instruction and training* is *necessary* for police staff charged with the investigation of economic crime.

3. The legislature is called upon to pass *the Second Statute for the Control of Economic Crime as soon as possible* and, when doing so, to take the *criminilization of fraudulent tenders* into consideration.[40]

4. The *duration of proceedings* in serious cases of economic crime averages 500 days and is still too long. It ought, and also could, *be reduced* — inter alia through improved co-operation between the police and public prosecutors as well as through greater procedural economy, in particular partial termination of proceedings.

5. Greater control is necessary *with regard to international economic crimes.* This would be possible through *unification* of the relevant *legal provisions as well as* through an *improvement of extradition and legal assistance.* The difficulties involved in international co-operation in the area of so-called fiscal offences are not overlooked here.

6. As regards serious economic crimes — and at least those punishable with imprisonment — it ought to be compulsory for an *order* prohibiting the offender from continuing in his occupation (so-called ''*occupational prohibition*'') to be imposed on conviction. The improved basis provided by the Second Statute for the Control of Economic Crime for prohibiting the carrying on of a trade or business would not stand in the way of this step.

7. Furthermore, the *establishment of a bankruptcy register* for detection and suppression of economic crime might prove to be a sensible step,[41] particularly as entries in the so-called Central Trade Register have largely remained unproductive from the point of view of

control strategy.

8. In addition, *civil and administrative legal provisions* within the whole field of economic law must be *improved* and

9. *Self-help to guard against* economic crime must be *extended* whether through the support of consumer protection organisations or of the business world itself.

IX

Summary and Prospects

Where do we stand now *and what remains to be done* to control economic offences ?

By way of conclusion it may be stated that there is now a sharper awareness of the growing risk and menace of economic crime. Different ways and means however have been selected for its repression—of a kind probably specific to the actual situation faced or the tradition followed. Ultimately there is agreement that the fight against economic crime calls for a *comprehensive* legislative *concept* reaching beyond the classical field of criminal liability. Hence, in German law, changes and extensions affecting the regulations of civil, administrative and tax law are built into this conceptions.

The *importance* of economic crime in the Federal Republic is apparent from the salient degree of harm caused, from the substantial numbers of registered cases and victims harmed, from the relatively small group of offenders as well as from the nature of associative crime. Tax and customs offences, insolvency crimes as well as fraud and breach of trust are indicative of the type of offence. Charging an exorbitant rent (contrary to Section 302a (1) of the Criminal Code dealing with the offence of "profiteering"), with holding social security contribution and criminal advertising recede in comparison. Offences involving consumer edibles - although qualitatively of substantial importance — occur mainly within the range of less serious offences (a well-known exception here was the Spanish salad-oil poisoning case of May 1981 with 270 deaths, 18,000 taken ill and more than 50 million dollars estimated for nursing costs). The significance to be attached to economic crime is, moreover, underscored by the frequent occurrence of offences displaying complex features with corresponding difficulties and time needed for investigation and with a high termination quoto in some cases.

After ten years of increased efforts to check serious economic crime a *provisional assessment* does not bring us to a positive conclusion only but — on account of the limited successes — gives cause for reflection instead. In making an assessment however, attention must be paid to the fact that the *results* of the reforms carried out in practice and introduced by the legislature can only be measured on an individual basis or are only open to partial evaluation. General preventive effects that might possibly carry greater weight are scarcely capable of illumination. What may tell in favour of a certain general preventive effect is the fact that practical and legislative measures that have sometimes been applied with strong commitment and with a visible external reference are keeping serious economic crime within limits. The relatively consistent number of accused over the past decade definitely not only reflects the unchanged capacity of the investigating and prosecuting authorities but is also an indication of the restriction of criminal practices in the economic field.

Furthermore, the measures taken by the state in relation to investigation and prosecution, to which I have already referred, have probably had repercussions on economic institutions so as to intensify *control within the economy* itself. It may be the case that these efforts have had their main effect in the area of unfair competition and fraud in accordance with the interests involved. Nevertheless, the unmitigated aloofness of the business world towards criminalization of socially harmful conduct within their field of operation may have actually partly stimulated and strengthened initiatives within the economy itself aimed at stemming the limiting violations with the aid of the civil law if necessary. This again shows *the lustre and the drabness of prophylactic measures taken within the economy* as well as of the problems connected with supra-individual legal interests. Economic institutions mainly become active when it is a question of concrete individual interests and enterprises.[43] This fact not only has an effect on controlling activities within the economy but also influences the prospects for state crime control in this area. In concrete terms this means that information laid, and proceedings initiated by private persons are of importance for the prosecution of economic offences. This also finds expression in the reluctance of a usury victim to go to a reputable credit institution and to lay an information against the usurer.[44] The administration of criminal justice depends on the confidence reposed by jeopardized or victimized citizens in effective investigation and prosecution. However, as soon as the party harmed fails to function as an initiator of proceedings, as an informant or as an informal actor in social control through the criminal law, the legislature, the police and the administration of criminal justice must make increased efforts to compensate for the control deficit through intensive surveillance and through special expertise.

The *legislature has* also *acknowledged* this task. It is rightly asserted that the credibility of the administration of criminal justice might be prejudiced by the fact that petty offences are punished without delay whilst major economic and tax offences are no longer investigated, prosecuted and controlled by the authorities responsible but are merely "administered". Furthermore, there is not unjustified complaint that criminal justice only indicts these who have failed, but not the successful insofar as they have made themselves criminally liable. Hence cansideration must be given to the possibility of reducing the scope of proceedings through partial termination if necessary as well as to the possibility of extending the period of limitation.[45]

We are still far removed from a satisfactory solution to all the problems involved, that is to say from a situation which would allow us to be content with what has been achieved. Even if we do not fail to acknowledge the importance both of a necessary strengthening of public awareness of legality and of improving the provisions of civil, administrative and tax law, the *main emphasis in the fight against economic crime continues to lie within the realm of criminal law.* Implementing the norms on which the criminal law is based is above all the duty of the police and the courts. Whether they succeed in this task is not only the acid test for criminal law and criminal policy but also for equality and justice in our society itself.

REFERENCES

1. To this item see the German contributions by M. Heinz: *Konzeption und Grundsatze des Wirschaftsstrafrechts* (einschlieblich Verbraucherschutz), *Kriminologischer Teil*; H. Otto, loc. cit., *Dogmatisher Teil* I; U. Weber, loc. cit., *Dogmatischer Teil* II, altogether in ZStW 96 (1984), pp. 417-451, 339-375, 376-416.

2. A data classification and a longitudinal analysis are now under consideration: cf. K.-H. Liebl: *Die Bundesweite Erfassung von Wirtschaftsstraftaten nach einheitlichen Gesichtspunkten 1974-1981, Ergebnisse und Analysen*, Freiburg 1984.

3. In this sense for example P. Poerting: *Begriff und Besonderheiten der Wirtschaftskriminalitat aus kriminalpolizeilicher Sicht.* [In:] P. Poerting, (ed.): *Wirtschaftskrminalitat, Teil,* I. *Schriftenreihe des Bundeskriminalamts,* Vol. 52, Wiesbaden 1983, pp. 9-49.

4. To this item see E. Lampe: *Wirtschaftsstrafrecht. Handworterbuch der Wirtschaftswissenschaft*. Stuttgart et al. 1981, pp. 310 ff.

5. Cf. F. Berchkauer: *Die Strafverfolgung bei schweren Wirtschaftsdelikten,* Freiburg 1981, pp. 102, 279.

6. G. Kaiser: *Kriminologie — Ein Lehrbuch.* Heidelberg 1980, p. 477.

7. A sound jurisdiction gives reasons for the regularization of Section 74c Courts' Constitution Act. Because the usually rather difficult economic criminal cases should be dealt with by judges with a particularly good knowledge of the economic field, specific groups of offences were built. This catalogue of offences has become meaningful although it has no legal definition, and is only a product of organizational measures.

8. Cf. G. Kaiser, M. Sickenberger et al.: *Anschlu- und Vertiefungsuntersuchungen zur Bundesweiten Erfassung von Wirtschaftsstraftaten nach einheitlichen Gesichtaspunketen. Forschungsbericht Teil I: Betrug, Untreue, Wucher, Vorteilsgewahrung und Bestechung als Wirtschaftsstraftaten.* Bonn 1984, p. 249.

9. See Berckhauer f.n. 5, p. 41.

10. J. Fehervary: *Wirtschaftskriminalitat.* [In:] W.Blankenburg et al., (eds), *Die Staatsanwaltschaft im Proze strafrechtlicher Sozialkontrolle.* Berlin 1978, pp. 268-301.

11. G. Sieben, P. Poerting: *Zur praventiven Bekampfung von Wirtschafrsdelikten.* [In:] Schimmelpfeng GmbH (ed.), *Beitrage uber Wirtschaftskriminalitat.* Frankfurt/M. 1979, pp. 113, 119.

12. According to P. Lascoumes et al.: *Justice penale et delinquance d'affaires.* Paris 1979, p. 14, the situation is similar in France.

13. See Berckhauer (f.n. 5), p. 41, as to the most current combinations of offences; for an entirely different view cf. in particular U. Weber. [In:] *Straftrecht.* Besonderer Teil: *Wirtschaftsstraftaten,* ed. by Arzt et al. Bielefeld 1980, pp. 9, 12.

14. W. Zirpins: O. Terstegen: *Wirtschaftskriminalitat.* Lubeck 1963, p. 143.

15. D. Rauen: *Wirschaftskriminalistische Buch— un Betriebsprufung.* [In:] Poerting (f.n. 3), p. 213.

16. E. Heinitz gives an historical review in his expertise about "Is it recommendable to provide for a legal punishableness of artificial persons?" at the occasion of the 40t German Lawyers Conference (*Verhandlungen des 40. Dt. Juristentages Vol. 1.* Tubingen 1953, pp. 65 ff.) With reference to crimes committed by private or commercial firms and to organised crime in light of the ruling law, see in particular B. Schunemann: *Unternehmenskriminalitat un*

Strafrecht. Cologne et al. 1979, pp. 13 ff., 61 ff.; relating to fraudulent and irregular practices within the European Community cf. the *Annual Report of the European Court of Audit for the year* 1980: Amtsblatt der Europaischen Gemeinschaften, 24 (1981), pp. 61 ff.

17. Cf. P. Bernasconi: *Wirtschaftskriminalitat — Internationale Verflechtungen. Kasuistik, Rechtshilfe und Praventive Bekampfung.* [In:] *Wirtschaftskriminalitat. Wissenschaftliche Beitrage zum 50jahrigen Bestehen der Neutra Treuhand AG. Zurich* 1982, pp. 66 ff., 97.

18. To this item cf. K. Lackner, C. Imo: *Zum Vermogensschaden bei betrugerischen Manipulationen mit* Warenterminoptionen. MDR 1983, p. 969.

19. Referring to casuistry in general Bernasconi (f.n. 17), pp. 69 ff.

20. Cf. M. Meisenberg: *Strafprozessuale Probleme bei der Bekampfung der Wirtschaftskriminalitat*; [In:] R. Belke, J. Oemichen (eds): *Wirschaftskrinalitat. Aktuelle Fragen des Wirtschaftsstrafrechts in Theorie und Praxis.* Bamberg 1983, pp. 183-207 (199 ff.); K. Oehlke: *Internationaler Rechtshilverkehr und Auslandsermittlungen.* [In:] Poerting (f.n. 3), p. 141; furthermore S. Frohlich: *Eroffnungsansprache.* [In:] *Wirschaftskriminalitat,* ed. by Bundeskriminalamt Wiesbaden 1984, pp. 9 ff. (14); W. Schenider: *Rechtpolitische Aspekte der Bekampfung von Wirtschaftskriminalitat,* ed. by Bundeskriminalamt Wiesbaden 1984, pp. 67 ff. (78).

21. The dangers of crime commitment in the area of data processing are being studied systematically by the Institute of Criminology and Economic Penal Law of the Freiburg University since 1974: cf. U. Sieber: *Die Freiburger Untersuchungen zur Computerkriminalitat;.* [In:] *Freiburger Universitatsblatter* Serial No. 77 (1982), (*Wirtschaftskriminalitat*), p. 29, with further references.

22. Cf. Sieber (f.n. 21), p. 29; idem: *Gefahr und Abwehr der*

Computerkriminalitat. [In:] Belke, Oehmichen (f.n. 20), pp. 97 ff.; cf. also K. Tiedemann: *Computerkriminalitat und Mibbrauch von Bankomaten. Wertpapier-Mitteilungen* 1983, pp. 132 ff.; also K. Bauknecht: Computer-Kriminalitat. [In:] Neutra AG (f.n. 17), pp. 99-112; Th. Lenchner: *Computerkriminalitat und Vermogensdelikte.* Heidelberg et al. 1981; G.Stratenwerth: *Computerbetrug.* SchwZfStR 1981, pp. 229-234.

23. Cf. amtliche Begrundung zum 2. WiKGE (explanatory preamble to the Draft of a Second Statute for the Control of Economic Crime). Bundestags-Drucksache 9/2008, 12 und 10/318, p. 12; also Minister of Justice Engelhard in Recht 9 (1983), p. 71, each containing references to the corresponding research studies conducted by the Max Planck Institute for Foreign and International Penal Law in Freiburg.

24. Bundesministerium der Justiz (ed.): Bekampfung der Wirtzchaftskriminalitat. Schluberich der sachvertandigenkommission zur Bekampfung der Wirschaftskriminalitat (Reform des Wirtschaftsstrafrechts) uber die Beratungsergebnisse. Bonn 1980, p.28; see also R. Wassermann: *Strategien zur Eindammung der Wirtschaftskriminalitat.* [In:] *Beitrage uber Wirtschafskriminalitat.* (f.n. 11), pp. 44 ff.; furthermore, Schneider (f.n. 20), pp. 71 ff. The law on environmental protection (Sections 324 ff. Penal Code) and problems of its enforcement stay out of consideration. To this problem, in the place of many authors, see K. Tiedemann: Die *Neuordnung* des *Umwelstrafrechts,* Berlin et al. 1980.

25. Cf. *Draft of a Second Statute for the Control of Economic Crime* (with explanatory preamble). Bundestags-Drucksache 9/2008, and precisely to this item M. Mohrenschlager: *Der Entwurf eines Zweiten Gesetzes zur Bekampfung der Wirtschaftskriminalitat* (Stand: April 1982). [In:] Belke, Cehmichen (f.n. 20), pp. 315- 340 (315 ff.).

26. Cf. K. Volk: *Strafrecht und Wirtschaftskriminalitat - Kriminalpolitische Probleme und dogmatische Schwierigkeiten.* JZ 1982, pp. 85 ff.; against him J. Baumann: *Strafrecht und Wirtschaftskriminalitat; Eine wegen des E eines* 2. *WiKG notwendige Erwiderung. JZ* 1983, pp. 935 ff.

27. Critical above all M. Schubarth: *Wissenschaft und Gesetzgebung zum Wirtschaftsstrafrecht.* ZStW 92 (1980), pp. 80-106 (90); also sceptical K. Lackner: *StGB. Strafgetzbuch mit Erlauterunge.* 14th ed. Munich 1981, Vorbemerkung 1 f. vor Section 263.

28. H. Otto. *Strafrecht als Instrument der Wirschaftspolitik. MschKrim* 63 (1980), pp. 397-407 (400).

29. In this Line H. Jung: *Die Bekampfung der Wirtschaftskriminalitat als Priifstein des Strafrechtssystems.* Berlin et al. 1979. pp. 20 f.

30. With respect to historical antecedents see Berchhauer (f.n. 5), pp. 13 ff.

31. References in Berckhauer (f.n. 5), p. 14.

32. See f.n. 31.

33. Cf. P. Schweinitzer: *Die Zusammenarbeit von Polzei und Staatsanwaltschaft aus kriminalpolizeilche Sicht* [In:] Poerting (f.n. 3), pp. 111-120 (114); furthermore, H. Franzheim, H. Stullenberg: *Illegale Arbeitsvermittlung _ Ein Dauerbrenner? Eine Analyse aus strafrechtlicher und priminalisaticher Sicht.* Kriminalistik 36 (1932), pp. 556 ff.; H. Franzheim: *Die Zusammenarbeit von Polizei und Justiz bei der Verfolgung von Wirtsehaftsstraftaten aus der Sicht der Justiz.* [In:] Wirtschaftskriminalitat (f.n. 20), pp. 171 ff. (176); critical K. Gemmer: Polizeiliche Bekampfung der *Wirtschaftskriminalitat—Erfahrungen und Perspektiven.* [In:] *Wirtschaftskriminalitat* (f.n. 10), p. 57.

34. See W. Heinz: *Die Bekampfung der Wirtschaftskriminalitat mit strafrechtlichen Mitteln—inter besonderer*

Berucksichtigung des 1. WiKG. GA 1977, pp. 204 f.; G. Weinermann: *Das modernisierte Wirtschaftsstrafverfahren.* [In:] *Beitrage uber Wirtschaftskriminalitat* (f.n. 111), pp. 55 ff.; Lampe (f.n. 4), p. 235.

35. P. Ignee : *Bekampfung der Wirtschaftskriminalitat* durch Mittel Auberhalb des Strafrechts. [In:] Belke, Oehmichen (f.n. 20). 208- 232 (220).

36. To this item especially K. Tiedemann: *Die kriminologische Erforschung der Wirtschafsikriminalitat.* [In:] *Wirtschaftskriminalitat* (f.n. 20), pp. 113 ff. (126). and R. Wassermann: *Kritische Uberlegungen zur Bekampfung der Wirtchafts kriminalitat.* [In:] *Wirtschaftskriminalitat* (f.n. 20), p. 87.

37. Cf. Wassermann (f.n. 36), p. 93.

38. Similar opinion in Wassermann (f.n. 36), p. 94.

39. Conceivable would be the constitution of a team "under one roof", on the model of the Central Office (Zentralstelle) at Ludwigsburg with regard to the prosecution of violent crime; cf. Franzheim et al., (f.n. 33), p. 176.

40. Schneider (f.n. 20), p. 74.

41. Cf. E. Kube: *Pravention von Wirtschaftsdeliten. Utopie oder reelle Chance*? [In:] *Wirtschaftskriminalitat* (f.n. 20), p. 142.

42. Cf. Ignee (f.n. 35), p. 211.

43. Cf. the findings of Sieben, Poerting (f.n. 11), pp. 116 ff., 119. R. Muller, H.-B. Wahnitz: *Wirtschaftskriminalitat*, Munchen 1982, p. 95 reprehend very rightly the still missing, but necessary provisions for a formal demand for punishment according to Sections 12 ff., 22, of the Unfair Competition Act.

44. G. Kohlmann: *Wirksame strafechtliche Bekampfung des Kreditwuchers.* Tubingen 1974, p. 4; R. Sturm: Die

Neufassung des Wuchertatbestandes und die Grenzen des Strafrechts. JZ 1977, pp. 84-87 (85); Heinz (f.n. 34), p. 229; Otto (f.n. 28), p. 406, and H. Trondle: *Strafgestzbuch und Nebengesetze.* 40th ed. Munchen 1981, Section 302a marginal note No. 2.

45. Wassermann (f.n. 36), pp. 87 ff.

11

ECONOMIC CRIME IN INDIA : A RECAP OF THE STOCK SCAM

Indias biggest financial scandal, with its widening net of individuals and institutions, is still being unravelled four months after first reports of collusion between bank executives and brokers dealing in government securities hit the headlines in April 1992. All the acts and players and the forces behind them are yet to be pieced together, though much headway has been made by the RBI Enquiry Committee and CBI investigations into the "Stock Scam", as it is called, with the latest count of funds siphoned off at over Rs. 35 billion.

A scandal of this magnitude has naturally startled the Parliament, apart from shaking the confidence of people in the banking system and of millions of investors in India's principal stock market at Bombay whose dizzy rise in the early months of 1992 was as much perplexing to financial wizards as ordinary investors looking for modest gains.

After much uproar and opposition charges of ministerial involvement in the scandal, Parliament constituted a Joint Committee of 30 members—20 from the Lok Sabha and 10 from the Rajya Sabha—for a through probe and report before the end of the next session (November-December, 1992). Mr Ram Niwas Mirdha a Congress member of Lok Sabha and former Minister is chairman of the Joint Parliamentary Committee (JPC).

While administrative and legal steps are under way, a Parliamentary probe, to which Government was initially reluctant, should help to lay all the cards on the table, fix responsibility whatever the position the person occupies, and clear the decks for future reform.

Terms of Reference : Joint Parliamentary Committee

The terms of reference of the Joint Committee of both the House are as follows :

(i) To go into the irregularities and fraudulent manipulations in all its aspects and ramifications in transactions relating to securities, shares, bonds and other financial instruments and the role of the banks, stock exchanges, financial institutions and public sector undertakings in transactions relating thereto, which have or may come to light.

(ii) To fix responsibilities of the persons, institutions or authorities in respect of such transaction.

(iii) In the above context, to identify the misuse, if any, of and the failures/inadequacies in the control mechanism and the supervisory mechanism.

(iv) To make recommendations for safeguards and improvements in the system for elimination of such failures and occurrences in future.

(v) To make appropriate recommendations regarding policies and regulations to be followed in future.

The debates in Parliament before it moved to set up the Committee were marked by strong denunciations of the "laxity" in supervision by the Reserve Bank and strident demand for the resignation of the RBI Governor Mr. Venkataramanan and also of the Finance Minister Dr. Manmohan Singh, the latter by owning "moral responsibility." The Prime Minister Mr. P.V. Narsimha Rao has declared that on the basis of his information, no Minister is involved and "if any one of them is involved, he will not be in my Ministry".

He assured Parliament on August 3 that nothing would be allowed to come in the way of complete investigation and the guilty

*Paper written in 1994.

would be punished. "there is no question of any attempt to protect the guilty, no matter who the individual or what his position in Government or society".

That the opposition contentions were not entirely groundless were highlighted by the sudden resignation of the Commerce Minister Mr. P. Chidambaram who, as a Minister, with his wife had made investment in the Bangalore-based Fairgrowth Financial Services Ltd. (FGFSL), which figured in the second interim report of the RBI Enquiry Committee headed by Mr. R. Janakiraman, Deputy Governor of RBI.

A more serious development to follow Mr. Chidambaram's resignation was the easing out of Mr. V. Krishnamurthy, Member, Planning Commission (former Chairman of Maruti & SAIL) in the last week of July in view of his connections with FGFSL. Within a few days, CBI registered a case of corruption against Mr. Krishnamurthy as also against. K.J. Investments, a company managed by his sons, and Mr. Harshad Mehta, the bull operator and the central figure of the Rs. 3500 crore scandal. Charged with misuse of his official position to get a loan for his family concern, Mr. Krishnamurthy and his son Mr. Chandra Krishnamurthy were arrested and remanded to custody, Mr. Krishnamurthy has denied the charges and maintained that he is not responsible for actions of his sons pursuing their businesses. The matter will now go before the courts.

Role of Reserve Bank of India

Apart from political dimension, the scandal has brought into serious question the supervisory role of the central bank authority, RBI, in the months preceding the surfacing of the manipulation and fraud in securities dealings involving the State Bank of India and a few other public sector, private and foreign banks. Although RBI seemed to be aware of the violation of its guidelines to Banks issued in July 1991 on the subject, it was not until the end of March 1992 that RBI took up scrutiny of SBI transactions. It was not until after the shortfall in Government securities held by SBI was reported by a Bombay newspaper that the Governor set up the Janakiraman Committee to investigate into the possible irregularties in the funds management by banks and financial institutions, particularly in relation to dealings in government securities and public sector bonds.

The Committee was asked specifically to enquire into the extent of non-compliance by banks and financial institutions with RBI guidelines and into the inadequacies in systems and procedures in force in these institutions, suggest corrective steps, determine the extent of malpractices and where funds have been allowed to be used for speculative transactions by brokers and other intermediaries deriving undue benefits through unauthorised access to borrowed funds of the banks and financial institutions.

Details of various types of transactions in securities undertaken by banks, guidelines/instructions issued to banks particularly the RBI guidelines issued in July 1991 and the Indian Banks Association guidelines of May 1991 on issue of BRs (Banker's Receipts) are given in Annexure I.

Janakiraman Committee

According to the first interim report of the Janakiraman Committee, RBI had started making enquiries into the securities transactions of some of the banks since January 1992. Towards the end of March, information was also received that SBI had purchased a large quantity of Government securities on a "ready forward" basis one day prior to the date on which the coupon rate of Government of India securities was raised. SBI was advised on April 2, 1992 to furnish to RBI a statement of the investments held by it as on it as on March 31, 1992. The bank's response was that only the statement as at the end of January 1992 was available. It was observed that the bank was unable to furnish the statement, as it had not reconciled the balance of securities held by it as shown in its books, with the actual balance held in the Subsidiary General Ledger (SGL) Account with the RBI beyond November 1991. It is in this context that the Janakiraman Committee set about its task. It was the period when the BSE Sensitive index was rising to close at an all time high of 4, 467 by April 22, when it came to be seen as the result of billions of rupees being diverted from the banking system into the stock market.

The Janakiraman Committee, in its first report toward the end of

May, found that the National Housing Bank (NHB), State Bank of Saurashtra, SBI Capital Markets Ltd. and Standard Chartered Bank had together made payments of Rs. 1795.66 crores for purchase of investments for which they did not hold either securities, SGL forms or BRs. In the second category, the Standard Chartered Bank, Canbank Financial Services Ltd. (Canfina) and Canbank Mutual Fund were holding BRs/SGLs issued by the Bank of Karad Ltd. and the Metropolitan Cooperative Bank, for which the issuing banks did not appear to have sufficient backing. The amount involved was put at Rs. 1282.97 crores.

The total problem exposure of the banks/FIs identified thus came to over Rs. 3078 crores. The Committee also established that the transactions put through the intermediation of NHB, and which are outstanding, were prima facie connected with the broker Mr. Harshad Mehta and his associate concern Growmore Research and Assets Management Ltd. A large number of transactions undertaken by SBI on its own investment account (about Rs. 17000 crores during July 1,1991 to April 6, 1992) had been put through Mr. Harshad Mehta, and several of the latter's transactions appeared to have been put through in an irregular manner. Other brokers linked with the transactions at other banks included Mr. Hiten Dalal and Mr. A.D. Narottam. "There has been a systematic diversion of funds from the banking system to the individual accounts of certain brokers and this diversion is presumably represented by the transactions for which the banks and subsidiaries are not holding BRs or are holding BRs of doubtful value.

The Committee came to the disturbing conclusion that there had been "collusion" between the officials of SBI, the largest public sector bank, and Mr. Harshad Mehta based on the fact that the aggregate balance in respect of Government loans in SBI's Investment ledger would not tally with the relative balances appearing in the books of the Public Debt Office (PDO) in the Reserve Bank of India. Besides SBI, UCO Bank (United Commercial Bank) has also been under scrutiny. The Bank of Karad was found to have issued BRs of the value of Rs. 750 crores without any backing or against non-existent securities.

In its second report, (July 1992) the Janakiraman Committee had revised the total size of the problem exposure in securities transactions to a total of Rs. 3542.79 crores. The details are as follow:

		(Rs. in crores)
(i)	Total value of investments made by banks and institutions for which they do not hold any securities, SGL transfer forms or BRs.	1967.84
(ii)	Total exposure against BRs/SGL transfer forms issued by Bank of Karad or Metropolitan Co-op. Bank.	1470.12
(iii)	The estimated shortfall in the securities held by Andhra Bank Financial Services Ltd.	104.83
		3542.79
Less :	Value of securities reportedly seized by Standard Chartered Bank from M/s. Hiten P. Dalal	350.00
		3192.79

The break up of total value of investments made by the banks and institutions as in para (i) above for which they do not hold either securities, SGL transfer forms or BRs has been estimated by the Committee as under :

(Rs. in crores)

	Bank/ Institution	*Acquisition Cost*		*Bank/Institution payment was made*	
1.	National Housing Bank (NHB)	1271.20	i.	State Bank of India (SBI)	707.56
			ii.	ANZ Grindlays Bank	506.55
			iii.	Standard Chartered Bank (Stanchart)	55.18
			iv.	Canfina	1.91
					1271.20
2.	State Bank of	174.93	i.	SBI	99.11
			ii.	NHB	75.82

Saurashtra (SBS)			174.93
3. SBI Caps	121.36	SBI	121.36
4. Stanchart*	400.35	Under Investigation	
	1967.84		

* As indicated by the Bank.

The total exposure against BRs/SGL transfer forms issued by Bank of Karad Ltd. (BOK) and the Metropolitan Cooperative Bank Ltd. (MCB) (for which those banks do not appear to have sufficient backing) held by banks/institutions as in para (ii) above has been estimated by the Committee as under :

	Bank Institution	*Acquisition cost (Rs. in crores)*	*BR/SGL Issues*
1.	Canfina	435.31	Bank of Karad
2.	Canbank Mutual Fund	102.97	-do-
3.	Stanchart	355.94	-do-
		575.90	Metropolitan Co-op. Bank Ltd.
		1470.12	

A summary of the findings of the Committee' Report (July) is given in Annexure II.

In the light of the earlier report of the Committee, the Reserve Bank issued new guidelines (See Annexure III). The Committee had observed that it was necessary that there should be daily verification of all securities held in the SGL accounts of all banks in the aggregate and that on a weekly basis the PDO (Public Debt Office) submit to the Department of Banking Operations and Development (DBOD) of the RBI a report giving bank-wise details of all SGLs returned for want of sufficient balance.

Thus, on the basis of the Janakiraman Committee's two reports, it is clearly established that there were irregularities involving a few thousand crores of rupees, a large part of the sums having to be incurred as losses from the Banks Financial Institutions Concerned, through violation of RBI guidelines and collusion between Bank Officials and brokers, mainly Mr. Harshad Mehta.

Unfolding of the Scam

On the basis of the first reports in the press, Government told Parliament on May 4, in the last week of the budget session, that "appropriate action" would be taken against all individuals found to have indulged in malpractices in security transactions of all major banks. At that, the securities scandal was assumed to be only of the order of Rs. 622 crores, an irregularity confined to the State Bank of India arising out of "possible collusion" between some SBI officials and a "major stock broker", subsequently identified as Mr. Harshad Mehta.

When more reports filtered in involving the National Housing Bank (NHB), its Chairman Mr. M.J. Pherwani resigned on May 9 and later he succumbed to a heart attack on May 21 at Bombay.

On May 11, the Finance Minister Dr. Manmohan Singh announced in the Lok Sabha that the Central Bureau of Investigation (CBI) had been asked to enquire into the involvement of SBI, United Commercial Bank (UCO) and the National Housing Bank in the stock-scam. At that stage, the Finance Minister did not accept the demand for a Parliamentary probe, but said stern action would be taken against all those found guilty through CBI inquiry.

This was followed by the publication on June 2 of the first interim report of the Janakiraman Committee which said there had been misappropriation of funds from the banking system to individual accounts of certain brokers and flouting of RBI guidelines on transactions in securties. It identified the banks and Fls which had exposures without sufficient backing by way of securities.

On June 3, CBI arrested Mr. Harshad Mehta and his brother, two SBI officials, the Assistant General Manager of NHB, and three other employees of Growmore Group of Companies of Mr. Harshad Mehta.

CBI raided 30 places in Bombay including the residences and offices of Mr. Mehta and his companies.

On June 6, the Government of India promulgated the Special Courts (Trial of offences relating to Transactions in Securities) Ordinance 1992, providing for a Special Court for speedy trial and the appointment of a Custodian. The following day, the movable and immovable assets of 31 individuals and firms were attached under an order issued by the Custodian Mr. A.K. Menon. The Special Court, headed by Mr. Justice S.N. Variava, sits at Bombay. The object of the ordinance is to help government recover dues of banks and FIs while punishing the guilty. Most of the arrested persons including Mr. Harshad Mehta and some bank officials are still in custody pending trial. More arrests followed including those of Mr. Bhupendra Dalal, a leading stock broker, on June 23. In all, properties of 39 individuals have been attached. CBI had raided 144 places, arrested 26 individuals till July 10, and registered 7 FIRs.

The following 17 companies and financial institutions were notified by the custodian, while adverse comments had been made in regard to 7 companies in the Janakiraman Committee reports.

A. Names of Companies/Financial institutions notified by the custodian under section 3(2) of the special court (Trial of offences relating to transactions in securities) ordinance 1992.

1. Sunrise Enterprises
2. Growmore Research & Assets Management Ltd.
3. Growmore Leasing & Investments (Pvt.) Ltd.
4. Growmore Exports (Pvt.) Ltd.
5. Aatur Holdings (Pvt.) Ltd.
6. Harsh-Estates (Pvt.) Ltd.
7. Cascade Holdings (Pvt.) Ltd.
8. Orion Travels (Pvt.) Ltd.
9. Fortune Holdings (Pvt.) Ltd.
10. Treasure Holdings (Pvt.) Ltd.

11. Velvet Holdings (Pvt.) Ltd.
12. Eminent Holdings (Pvt.) Ltd.
13. Pallavi Holdings (Pvt.) Ltd.
14. Zest Holdings (Pvt.) Ltd.
15. Topaz Holdings (Pvt.) Ltd.
16. Divine Holdings (Pvt.) Ltd.
17. Fairgrowth Financial Services Ltd.

B. Names of companies on which adverse comments have been given in the interim reports of the committee to enquire into the securities transactions of the banks and financial institutions

1. SBI Capital Markets Ltd.
2. Canbank Financial Services Ltd.
3. Andhra Bank Financial Services Ltd.
4. All Bank Financial Services Ltd.
5. Growmore Research & Assets Management Ltd.
6. Fair Growth Financial Services Ltd.
7. Mazda Industries & Leasing Ltd.

On the administrative side, the Chairman of the State Bank of India Mr. M.N. Goiporia, who was on the verge of retirement, was asked to proceed on leave along with the Deputy Managing Director of SBI. The service of Mr. Margabandhu, Chairman of UCO Bank were terminated. The Chairman of Bank of Karad and two of its directors were removed while the Managing Director of Canbank Financial Services was asked to proceed on leave. Several other officers of banks have been suspended while those arrested are tacing charges before the Special Court.

On July 8, the Finance Minister in a statement in Parliament when it met for the monsoon session, reported on the developments in the "Scam", and announced Government proposed to establish a Supervisory Board consisting or four of five fulltime members with the

Governor of RBI as Chairman in order to strengthen supervision over banks and Fls, and ensure compliance with regulations and guidelines. Surprise inspections would be part of the Board's operations. The Board will have an Advisory Council with eminent persons in the fields of banking, auditing, law, economics and management. Government is also considering the establishment of a Special Bureau on Frauds to deal with serious frauds in banks and Fls.

In his statement Dr. Manmohan Singh said unscrupulous brokers, in collusion with certain bank officials, manipulated securities transactions of banks and other financial institutions for their own purposes in a variety of ways and in clear violation of the established rules, guidelines and prudent business practices. Banks funds ostensibly intended for purchase by one bank from another bank of government securities, PSU bonds, Units etc. and call money loans of one bank from another bank have been siphoned into the accounts of brokers. In another kind of manipulation, credit has been extended to the brokers through transactions engineered to represent discounting of bills, rediscounting of bills or ready forward deals in shares. The total amount of transactions for which the banks and financial institutions involved do not have security backing is now estimated at about Rs. 3542 crores. Against this, the Janakiraman Committee has identified securities worth Rs. 350 crores held by one of the banks, so that the net problem exposure is estimated at Rs. 3192 crores.

"The transactions resulting in this large level of problem exposure have been in fliagrant and deliberate violation of established rules and guidelines. It is also clear that there has been a serious failure of internal control systems in the banks involved but for this, the senior management of the banks should have become aware of these irregular transactions at much earlier stages. This internal control failure seems to have occurred in all three segments or our banking sector : nationalised banks, private sector banks and also foreign banks." The Finance Minister said these developments revealed "serious deficiencies in the operation of our banking systems. The fraudulent manipulations which have resulted in large scale mis- appropriation of bank funds, require prompt corrective and panel action."

The Government is according top priority to recovering the

amounts, punishing the guilty and restoring the basic confidence in the financial system.

Income Tax Departmant Action

Income-tax Authorities have continued their investgations into the Harshad Mehta Group for tax evasion and a large number of searches/surveys have been conducted. Assets seized aggregated to approximately Rs. 72.5 crores. Provisional attachment has been ordered under section 281B of the It Act for 37 immovable properties with the approximate market value of Rs. 25 crores and shares with market value of the order of Rs. 500 crores as on 28.2.1992. The current value of these shares has to be ascertained. Intensive investigations have been initiated in some other groups of brokers including Bhupen Dalal, A.D. Narottam, Hiten Dalal and connected cases like T. B. Ruia, Dhanraj Mills etc., the Finance Minister said.

The Ministry of Finance took up with the Securities and Exchange Board of India the issue of action to be taken against brokers found guilty of stock exchange irregularities. Subsequently the Bombay Stock Exchange Board suspended the main share brokers involved.

RBI has issued new instructions to regulate transactions in securities by banks and a special cell in RBI would also scrutinise these reports. RBI is modifying its inspection procedures providing for detailed annual inspection of all banks with focus on financial evaluation.

Lack to computerisation and reliance on manual processing in the Public Debt Office is one of the factors making it difficult for the banks to set up effective internal control systems to supervise Government securities trading. A process of computerisation of the Public Debt Office has been initiated. Certain officials in the the Public Debt Office have been suspended and the matter is being investigated.

Steps to Counter Malpratices

Steps are also being taken to improve trading practices in the stock exchanges, with a view to ensuring greater transparency in transactions and eliminating manipulation of stock prices' and insider trading. To this end, the Securities and Exchange Board of India was given statutory powers with effect from 30th January, 1992. Amendments of the SEBI Act are currently under consideration with a view to strengthening SEBI further in order to increase its effectiveness in achieving its objectives. Government has also decided to set up a new Stock Exchange at New Bombay which will act as model Exchange. It will be completely automated in terms of both trading and settlement procedures and would provide access to investors from all over the country. Government have also decided to set up a national Clearing and Settlement System with a Central Depository Trust and a Securities Facilities support Corporation which would be entrusted with the task of establishing and maintaining the network among exchanges.

Dr. Manmohan Singh said it could be asked whether the scam could have been prevented through greater vigilance and better supervision. There is no doubt that better systems of internal control, or even greater efficiency in operating the existing system, would have enabled the top managements of the banks to have a better feedback on day to day operations, which could have identified the irregularities earlier. The statutory audits in the banks should also have identified some of these problems earlier. The fact that this did not happen underscores the need for thorough-going reforms and modernisation of the banking system and its procedures.

On RBI's role, Dr. Manmohan Singh said "In retrospect it is clear that RBI's supervisory function was not as effective as it should have been. It hould be noted, however, that it is the RBI's own investigations that led to the unearthing of these irregular practices in the banks which had evolved over several years." RBI had directed the banks to submit compliance reports on its guidelines and had subsequently received such reports from most banks indicating that their procedures were in line with the July 1991 circular. Subsequent developments showed this was not the case.

The Reserve Bank of India subsequently did undertake inspection of the bank of Karad, the Andhra Bank and the Bank of Madura and these investigations did throw up evidence of continuing irregularities.

The Narasimham Committee has made a number of

recomendations for reform of policy and procedures in the banking sector aimed at creating a more efficient banking system which can serve the needs of a rapidly modernising economy. It has also recommended creation of a separate supervisory authority under the aegis the the Reserve Bank of India. Government propose to act expeditiously on all these recommendations.

The Government attaches high priority to implementing the various recommendations of the Narasimham Committee aimed at financial sector reform. The irregularities and frauds that have come to light are in no way due to financial liberalisation. On the contrary, they have surfaced under a regime of apparently tight regulation of banking activity. Over regulation of bank interest rates and an excessive per-emption of bank resources into low interest assets has contributed to some extend for bank managements looking to non-traditional banking activity to bolster bank profits. Steps taken recently by the Government to rationalise interest rates and to reduce the statutory liquidity ratio will help to correct these imbalances.

Bank of Karad

Due to large-scale irregularities in the securities transactions undertaken by the Bank of Karad Ltd. on behalf of certain brokers, a huge financial liability much beyond its capacity to fulfil, would have devolved on the bank and the Bank's continuance would have been further prejudicial to the interests of the public and depositors. The Reserve Bank of India moved the High Court, Bombay, under Section 38 of the Banking Regulation Act, 1949, for the winding up of the Bank of Karad Ltd. The Bank has been placed under provisional liquidation as per the orders of the Bombay High Court, with effect from the close of 27.5.1992.

The Janakiraman Committee had identified an amount of Rs. 894.22 crores for which the Bank of Karad has issued BRs/SGL transfer forms and for which that Bank does not appear to have sufficient backing. These BRs/SGL transfer forms are held by the CaNBANK Financial Service Ltd., Canbank Mutual Fund and Standard Chartered Bank.

Role of Foreign Banks

The Reserve Bank of India has in the wake of the Scam appointed auditors to conduct special audit of treasury/investment operations of four foreign banks, Standard Chartered Bank (Stanchart), Citibank, ANZ Grindlays Bank and the Bank of America.

In regard to Grindlays Bank, NHB had issued certain cheques crediting Rs. 506.54 crores in favour of ANZ Grindlays Bank covering certain underlying security transactions. The cheques on realisation were credited by Grindlays Bank was advised by RBI that it would be liable to repay the amount to NHB. Grindlays Bank has offered to make necessary provision without prejudice to their legal rights and contentions.

In the case of Stanchart, this bank also deposited in the account of the broker firm (Growmore Research and Asset Management Co. Ltd) of Mr. Harshad Mehta the sum of Rs. 55.10 received from NHB. This apart, the total exposures of Stanchart against BRs/SGL issued by the liquidated Bank of Karad and Metropolitan Cooperative Bank (for which these banks did not have sufficient backing) amounted to Rs. 931.84 crores. Senior Executive of Stanchart said here on August 6 that the Bank would try to recover at least part of the loss of 162 million pound sterling (over Rs. 800 crores) it lost in the "Scam".

Sum-Up

The securities scandal of this magnitude could not have occurred at a more awkward situation, when the country is seeking to gain international confidance and investment flows in support of its broad range of structural reforms, of which the financial sector is regarded as the fulcrum. Stock market crashes and financial scandals recur in other parts of the world, where the economies are in a more developed state and could withstand temporary shocks. In India, in will take a long time for restoration of people's confidence in the banking system. The investor sentiment has been considerably dampened and the stock markets are going through a period of cull. While the artificial boom of early 1992, due to siphoning of funds from the banking system, had to undergo strong correction the markets have also been affected by spells of closure with brokers, agitation against the requirement of registration with the Securities and Exchange Board of India (SEBI) and with the determination yes to be made about "tainted shares". Overall, investment activity is at a low ebb. Foreign investors, while praising the new liberalisation policies, continue to put India on "watch list" and would await a thorough cleaning up of the financial system before making their decisions.

Fortunately, no sense of panic on the part of depositors was triggered off by the stock-scam, though the reputation of several leading public sector bank with SBI in the lead, has been tranished in the process. The Finance Minister has asseted that the scandal had nothing to do with the Government's liberalisation policies and that it has only lend a new sense of urgency to reform of the financial sector especially prudential regulations being put in place. Structural Adjustment loan from the World Bank for financial sector reform has been put on hold for the present.

A combination of systemic failures and collusion with brokers at the level of banks/financial institutions as well as laxity in supervision on the part of the Reserve Bank have contributed to the scandal. That a bull operator could exploit the mechanism of securities transactions to divert massive funds to the stock market to push up the prices of selected shares, which led to the rise of BSE Sensitive Index by 1500 points in two weeks, has laid bare the fragility of the system.

The banks already in poor health because of low profitability have to maket provision for losses from their normal operations as well as for the exposures in the securities transactions. It is not going to be easy for all the banks to raise capital from the market by offering equity and this would necessarily lead to some restructuring of the banking system in the months to come. Much would depend on the outcome of the Joint Parliamentary Committee's labours while proceedings before the Special Court could drag on for months.

JPC REPORT ON SECURITIES SCAM

The Joint Parliamentary Committee (JPC) report on the securities scandal of 1991-92 is landmark in the history of the Indian Parliament. The 30-member JPC headed by Mr. Ram Niwas Mirdha had two basic terms of reference. To determine who was responsible for the securities scandal and why the scam occurred and to "suggest such corrective steps as may be necessary to have a more efficient and accountable system in the future.''

The unanimous JPC report was submitted to both houses of Parliament on December 21, 1993, after a 16-month enquiry by the Committee, in which all political parties were represented. The report blamed commercial banks, the stock market, the financial institutions and the Reserve Bank of India, as well as the Ministry of Finance and other economic ministries, in varying degrees. The report also found "some evidence of collusion of big industrial houses" in the scandal.

Functionally, the JPC found that there was not adequate accountability of banks, brokers, public sector undertakings and ministries. It also found that "supervision failed from top to bottom." Commenting on the moral dimension of the scandal, the Committee said there was a "distressing lack of fibre on the apparatus of governance."

On the size of the scam, the Committee gave three figures: the Janakiraman Committee's figure of Rs. 4,024 crore, the CBI's figure of Rs. 8,383 crore and of the Office of the Custodian's figure of Rs. 3650 crore. The aggregate value of transactions ran into some Rs. 12,00,000 crore of which the foreign banks were involved in Rs. 6,82,427 crore worth of transactions between April 1991 and May 1992.

The JPC placed the "criminal misuse of public funds" in the scandal at Rs. 8,383 crore. The securities fraud was the product of collusion between men holding the highest offices of trust in the Finance Ministry, the RBI, nationalised banks, foreign banks and in the brokering community. Clearly, it took place in a milieu of loose regulations and ineffective supervision, where opportunities for arbitrage were huge and widespread. A few brokers found ways of moving funds swiftly, activating the securities market to unnatural levels and diverting funds from there to fuel an artificial stock market boom. In this task, they found willing collaborators among the officers of the banks and the public sector undertakings, some of whom sought private benefit, while others went in to make money for their own institutions.

The foreign banks, with their skills in deploying and switching funds swiftly, were major players. So were the Government—owned banks which were under pressure and found the highly profitable areas of portfolio management schemes (PMS) and even playing the chaotic securities market too tempting to stay away from. Indeed, it would seem that even as the artificially propped up system was heading for an inevitable collapse, so long as it operated, several institutions made huge profits and got out unscathed.

Responsibility Identification

In determining who was to blame, the Committee sought to fix two types of responsibility. The first was that of functionaries entrusted with the task of supervision, and here it concluded that there was a breakdown of the supervisory mechanism at all levels and places. The overall constructive and political responsibility was laid at the door of Finance Minister Manmohan Singh, though there was no suggestion that he was personally responsible. The report came down heavily on Mr. B. Shankaranand as Petroleum Minister during the period and Mr. Rameshwar Thakur, than Minister of State for Finance, former RBI Governor S. Venkitaramanan and two Deputy Governor Mr. Amitava Ghosh and Mr. R. Janakiraman. The second type of responsibility related to the collusion between the brokers, public sector undertaking managers and the managers and staff of banks.

In striving to reach a consensus on the major issues and personalities, the Committee made compromises along the way. It did not seek to quantify the cost of the scam for the country—how much money was involved and where it went. The report left three jobs undone and called for special action. These were the Goldstar case, where a special probe was sought; the tracing of the scam money by a special Finance Ministry team and a Central Bureau of Investigation (CBI) probe into the alleged coupon rate hike leak.

The multi-party Committee held 96 sittings, lasting over 400 hours to produce the report. The main report ran into 344 pages (Volume I). The report had five additional notes. One by a joint opposition team, including members from the Bharatiya Janata Party, Janata Dal, CP (M), CPI, Samajwadi Janata Party and the DMK, called for separate parliamentary probes into the Mehta payoff case; an alleged forgery case concerning Tripura Governor Romesh Bhandari, lacunae in the functioning of investigative agencies; audit of public funds and banking institutions and co-operation with the Committee, and powers of parliamientary committees.

Another by three Janata Dal members blamed the Finance Minister for the scam, accused witnesses of suppression of facts, and sought a special probe into the role of industrial houses in the scam.

The note by Mr. Gurudas Gupta of the CPI singled out Finance Secretary Montek Singh Ahluwalia and former Finance Secretary K.P. Geethakrishnan, and said their role had been ignored. Of the two notes by a group of Congress members, one spoke of contradictions in Mr. Mehta's deposition in the payoff case involving the Prime Minister and the other said the Bhandari case did not fall within the purview of the Committee. One note by Mr. K.P. Unnikrishnan (Congress-S) argued against any lapse by Mr. Venkitaramanan or Dr. Manmohan Singh.

The exhaustive JPC report was in two volumes, which together had 474 pages. The second volume consisted of appendices including circulars, income tax assessments, letters and ministerial communications. The main report consisted of 262 pages and 18 chapters.

The JPC report made clear that there were more fundamental and crucial questions concerning the non-functioning of regulatory mechanisms of the banking system and the complete absence of any sense of accountability among the bank executives—from the lowliest co-operative banks to the highest echelons of even the Reserve Bank of India. The report pointed out that the scam peaked at about the same time as the controls on the economy were being lifted as part of the economic liberalisation programme in 1991. The lesson that emerged was that economic liberalisation meant absence of controls, not absence of regulation and supervision.

To quote one of the most cogent sections of the report: "The most unfortunate aspect has been the emergence of a culture on nonaccountability which permeated all sections of the Government and banking system for years... grave and numerous irregularities persisted for so long that eventually (they)... came to be regarded and defended as 'market practice'. It is abundantly clear that the scam was the result of failure to check irregularities in the banking system, and also liberalisation without adequate safeguards... Accountability was largely absent, punishment for a wrong committed was rare, an ethos of non-implementation prevailed all around...That supervision failed from top to bottom is self-evident."

"The scam is basically a deliberate and criminal misuse of public funds through various types of securities transactions...with the aim of illegally siphoning off funds of banks and public undertakings (PSUs) to suspect brokers for speculative returns," the JPC report said. Why did the scam happen at all? The administered interest rates and an over regulated banking system found a way to earn high rates of interest (which were over 20 per cent) by "converting asset" through the issue of false bankers receipts (BRS) and deploying them in the stock market through helpful and unscrupulous brokers.

The JPC recommended that a separate Board of Financial Supervision be set up under the Reserve Bank of India to ensure effective supervision of banks.

Debate or Report

Both houses of Parliament discussed the JPC report on December 29 and 30, 1993.

Besides the demand for the resignation of the ministers indicated in the report, the discussion also focused on the manner in which the financial system can be ruined when left to the mercy of politicians, bankers, brokers, industrial houses and government officials.

The outcome of the debate in Parliament on the JPC report was no unfavourable as feared in some quarters. In fact,. the proceedings were not as stormy as anticipated and Prime Minister P.V. Narasimha Rao and other Government spokesmen gave the assurance that those found guilty during the period of the scam would be punished. Further, steps would be taken to reorganise the entire banking system and the supervisory machinery of the RBI.

Dr. Manmohan Singh submitted his resignation on December 23, two days after the JPC report was tabled in Parliament. His resignation evoked widespread reaction with several political leaders and trade and indstry circles asking the Prime Minister not to accept it. Mr. Rao on December 31 formally turned down Dr. Singh's resignation, setting at rest the week-long uncertainly about his continuance in the Cabinet. The Prime Minister observed that after taking everything into consideration, including the "enormous agenda of work that the Government had mandated itself to address," it would not be appropriate for Dr. Singh to resign.

Replying to the JPC debate in the Lok Sabha, Dr. Singh defended himself and the Government and promised quick action to consider implementing the recommendations of the JPC report. Dr. Singh and two other ministerial colleagues who came in for criticism in the JPC report did not resign as the Government accepted collective responsibility and the developments during the period of the scam attributed to system failure and not in any way to lack of timely directives from the authorities concerned.

Report

Ministers, brokers, bankers, bureaucrats, investigating agencies, and to a lesser extent, business houses, were all indicated by the Joint Parliamentary Committee for their role in the Rs. 8,383.32 crore securities scam, described as a "criminal misuse of public funds."

The object failure of supervisory mechanisms in the Finance Ministry, Reserve Bank of India, individual banks, collusion between brokers, public sector undertakings PSUs and bankers, came in for stinging criticism in the JPC report.

The conduct of Health Minister B. Shankaranand for investing funds as Chairman, Oil India Development Board while holding the Petroleum portfolio was adversely commented upon. Dr. Manmohan Singh came in for gentle chiding even as the Jpc expressed unhappiness about the role played by Mr. Rameshwar Thakur while he was Minister of State for Revenue.

In the case of the RBI, Mr. S Venkitaramanan (former Governor), Mr. Amitava Ghosh and Mr. R. Janakiraman (former Deputy Governors) and Mr. N.D. Parameshwaran (former chief of the Department of Banking Operations and Development) came under fire.

With the JPC going along with the CBI conclusion that no case was made out in the Rs. 1 crore bribery charge levelled against the Prime Minister, Mr. Rao was been given a clean chit.

The Committee called for a multi-agency inquiry into the Rs. 2 crore "dubious" loan extended by Mr. Hiten Dalal, stock broker, to Goldstar Steel & Alloys Ltd in which Mr. P.V. Prabhakar Rao, son of the Prime Minister, is a director.

According to the report, the investment decisions taken by Mr. Shankaranand had created doubts that some institutions had received "preferential treatment". The Committee said it was its "sad duty to conclude" that Mr. Shankaranand, as OIDB Chairman, did not discharge his responsibilities in "consonance" with the high office held by him.

"What has caused considerable concern to the Committee is that OIDB did not possess either the securities or any stamped receipts in respect of the investments made by them. More astonishigly, these funds of OIDB were widely used in making investments in equities of private sector companies."

Referring to the failure of the Finance Ministry in adhering to its own instructions and in exercising greater supervision of banking and securities transactions and the relative unconcern in the Ministry about rising share prices, the report said: "In the light of the above, the Committee feels that the responsibility and accountability of the Finance Minister to Parliament cannot be denied.

Finance Minister's Statement

Commenting the Finance Minister's statement on March 28, 1992, to presidents of stock exchanges, the Committee observed: "However, it is said that the spurt in share prices or the abnormal behaviour of the stock market had not been discussed, despite the fact that he was stated to be greatly concerned about the rising share prices and had remained alert to the behaviour of the stock market from even as early as September 1991.

On Dr. Singh's statement, that he did not lose his sleep over the rise and fall of the share market, the report said: "Similarly, the Committee would like to observe that it is good to have a Finance Minister who does not lose his sleep easily, but one would wish that when such cataclysmic changes take place some alarm would ring to disturb his slumber."

The Committee expressed its "unhappiness" about Mr. Thakur keeping a file containing details about income-tax raids on stock broker Harshad Mehta, pending from April 4 to May 6, 1992. Expressing unhappiness over this delay, the Committee found "The MOS (R), Mr. Thakur, signed and forwarded this note...only after news of the scam broke out in the press and was referred to in the Houses of Parliament."

Interestingly, Mr. P. Chidambaram, former Commerce Minister, who resigned after admitting that he possessed promoter quota shares of Fair Growth Financial Services Ltd. (FGSL), was virtually exonerated.

There was no reference to him in the JPC report. The former Minister, who had sent in his resignation to the Prime Minister voluntarily shortly after the scam broke out, had given evidence before the Committee.

The report blamed the RBI management squarely for the bank's contribution to the scam. "If the RBI had not turned a blind eye to the massive irregularities in the baking transactions between July 1991 and April 1992 when thousands of crores of bank funds were diverted to the stock market it would not have been possible for some brokers to play havoc with the system."

"Shri S. Venkitaramanan, as the Governor of the Bank during this crucial period, must be held no less responsible. The suggestion to treat the foreign banks differently, the delay in the issue of the circular of July 1991...the delay in the issue of the bill discounting circular for 22 months, his recommendation to appoint people in top positions which proved to be a liability, subsequently, display of unusual interest in the account of HSM (Harshad Mehta), his acts of omission and commission cannot be overlooked in any of their ramifications.

"Similarly, the large number of SGL bouncings, the deficiencies in the functioning of the PDO (Public Debt Office) and the goings-on in both SBI and NHB (National Housing Board) of which he was a Director clearly indicate that there was dereliction in performing his duties by Deputy Governor, Shri R. Janakiraman.

"In turn, Mr. Amitava Ghosh as Deputy Governor must be held primarily responsible for the continuing irregularities in the banking sector, ignoring the various inspection reports prepared by the teams of RBI inspectors like the Augustine Kurias reports...and for being casual in his approach to his duties.

"Shri N.D. Parameswaran, the Chief Officer of DBOD should also be held responsible for the lapses of the DBOD. He also need not have played any role regarding the account of HSM."

Calling for penal action against foreign banks, including the suspension of their licenses, the JPC said they acted in an "unbecoming manner". "In the process they have thrown over board all principles of prudence and safety in management of funds..."

"Both the RBI and the Ministry of Finance, by not taking any deterrent action against them (foreign banks) early enough, enabled the foreign banks to exploit the situation and commit large-scale irregularities in total violation of the guidelines laid down by RBI."

A sample of the JPC's views on the role played by banks is available in the comments on the State Bank of India. "The SBI is the premier retail bank of the country. Its very name confirms its status and standing. The Committee, however, finds that its officers have done everything to rob it of its status...The SBI hierarchy from top to bottom was casual in its approach, negligent in the performance of its duties and unpardonable in its collusion with brokers. The Committee feels that the whole matter required to be inquired into with a view to punishing the guilty.

About the influence exercised by brokers like Mr. Harshad Mehta, the report quoted Mr. R. Sitaraman, then in SBI, as saying: "At that time his (Mehta's) stature was such that had I opened my mouth they would have simply thrown me into the Arabian Sea and that too would have been all right in those days."

The JPC recommended that a team comprising specialists in the field of accountancy, taxation and criminal investigation be formed under the charge of the Finance Ministry to probe the end-use of scam monies. A CBI probe into the "coupon rate hike" was also called for.

RBI and Public Debt Office

In the case of Mr. R. Janakiraman, the report said the large number of bouncing SGL forms, the deficiencies in the functioning of the Public Debt Office and the goings-on in both the State Bank of India and the National Housing Bank of which he was a director clearly indicated that there was dereliction in performing his duties.

In the case of Mr. Ghosh, the JPC noted that he was deputy-governor in charge of the Department of Banking Operations and Development (DBOD) for 10 long years. "He must be held primarily responsible for turning a Nelson's eye to the continuing irregularities in the banking sector, ignoring the various inspection reports prepared by the team of RBI inspectors in his approach to his duties." The JPC also indicated Mr. N.D. Parameshwaran, the chief officer of DBOD, saying he should be held responsible for the lapses of the department and that he need not have played any role regarding the account of Mr. Mehta.

On the question of SGL accounts, the JPC said that the number of SGL forms with the PDO. Bombay, had grown steadily, from 160 in 1987 to 455 upto June 1992. Similarly, SGL transfer froms received had also grown from 3,902 in 1987, to 4,871 in 1988, 5,778 in 1989 to 6,434 in 1990, 12,383 in 1991 and 5,623 during the first semester of 1992.

The Committee found that in the securities transactions of the banks involved in the recent irregularities a common feature was that SGL transfer forms of several banks were not honoured due to insufficient balance in their respective SGL account with the PDO, Bombay.

The bouncing in the SGL accounts had taken place in Andhra Bank, UCO Bank, Standard Chartered Bank, Anz Grindlyas, Bank of Karad, Bank of America, Citibank, Bank of Madura, Canfund and Canfina.

In the absence of any enabing provision in the Public Debt Act, 1944, and the PDO manual to penalise defaulting banks, the Central Office (Department of Government and Bank Accounts) advised the PDO on March 11, 1991, to write D.O. letters to the chairman of such banks and suitably advise the DBOD in the matter.

The JPC said that no concrete action was, however, taken by the Central Office on the statements pertaining to the quarters ending September 1991, December 1991 and March 1992, on the plea that the impact of the measures could not be assessed correctly for the first quarter as the D.O. letters were issued only on August 22, 1991, while the statements for the subsequent quarters were received only after the irregularities surfaced.

Apart from delays in computerising the PDO, a draft amendment to the Public Debt Act, given to the RBI in February 1992, was submitted to the Government only in August 1992.

The Committee noted while junior officers of the RBI had been regularly filing inspection reports pointing out numerous irregularities, the top management failed to act over a period of several years. The Committee wanted stern action taken against officials involved in the RBI scrutiny of PMS operations of Vijaya Bank during August-September 1989. The RBI also undertook the scrutiny of the bills portfolio of Vijaya Bank during January-February 1990. Although serious irregularities were noticed during these scrutinies, the chief officer of DBOD, told the JPC that though he had recorded a note that scrutiny of a few banks in specific areas like bills, PMS, investments including call money operations and securities transactions was required, no action had been taken by the people concerned.

The Committee said while foreign banks had treated the RBI in a casual manner, there were no traces of strong action against them. It specifically cited Citibank as prime culprit in this respect. "It is the excessive accommodation shown to foreign banks by the top management of RBI that imparted arrogance to these banks to describe as 'market practice' what was in fact blatant flouting of RBI directives. The foreign banks eventually emerged as the originators as also the biggest players in the scam."

The report noted that serious irregularities in the bill discounting operations of some Indian and foreign bank (with active involvement of the Reliance group and the Vijay Mallya group) had been detected as early as 1990, but the circular relating to bill discounting facilities was issued only on July 28, 1992, after a "characteristic delay of 22 month's'' after the scam came to light.

The JPC found that because of the fragile foreign exchange situation and the balance of payments crisis, the RBI had not been assertive enough in the action taken against foreign banks, and recommended strict action without any delay.

It also found that the nominee directors on the RBI board had neither noticed the irregularities nor effectively discharged their role on the board of nationalised banks and recommended that the RBI nominees be dispensed with.

Banks' Placidity

The JPC indicted banks for slack internal inspection machinery and lack of proper vigilance. It specifically pulledup the Reserve Bank of India and the State Bank of India, among others, on various lapses in their functioning.

The Committee said that the internal inspection machinery of banks and their subsidiaries was not updated to cope with the new areas into which they were venturing. While powers were delegated, responsibility was not assigned and there was very little accountability of staff for mistakes and irregularities. Information systems, which are vital to the banking industry, were mainly dysfunctional.

In a sharply critical chapter, the Committee stated that "no senior official appearing before the committee ever admitted to knowing what was happening in their banks; all wrongs were invariably transferred to the misconduct of officials lower in the rung."

The RBI was castigated for "an inordinate delay" in finalising the report on the management audit of SBI conducted by it. The report, although finalised by the inspecting officer and submitted to the deputy governor on November 30, 1991, was finalised and issued to the SBI only on November 13, 1992.

The report detailed deficiencies in internal control and supervision in banks and financial institutions in the following areas:

1. The segregation of duties between persons responsible for entering into deals, persons having custody of investments and persons responsible for recording the transactions in the books.

2. The periodic reconciliation of investment account and its independent verification.

3. Controls over issue of SGL forms and BRs and record keeping in this respect.

4. Controls for verification of the authentically of BRs and SGL forms and confirmation of authorised signatories.

5. Procedures for confirmation with counterparts, brokers' contracts as also of overdue BRs.

6. Segregation of responsibilities of persons handling the banks' own investments and those dealing with client's accounts.

7. Fixation of exposure limits.

8. Reporting system, and

9. Laying down of instructions relating to investment in securities in the Manual.

The Committee also said that the vigilance departments of some of the banks under examination did not do what they were supposed to. "Neither the top management of the banks nor the boards paid sufficient attention to vigilance matter."

The vigilance system of public sector banks/financial institutions was found to be totally unsatisfactory, the report said.

The Committee noted serious weaknesses in the internal control systems of the banks, especially on the treasury and investment side.

It said that since no comprehensive document containing all directives, guidelines, circulars issued by the RBI existed for reference, such a compendium should be brought out son and kept up to date.

The Committee stated that there was no satisfactory mechanism in most banks to follow up the suggestions in the reports of the internal inspection department. Proper follow-up action was also needed on the inspection and other reports issued by RBI. It suggested that a Committee of Board of Director, which may include the Chairman, nominees of RBI and the Government and a chartered accountant, be constituted to oversee follow-up action.

The Committee pointed out deficiencies in the way several banks made investments in securities, deficiencies relating to handing of BRs and SGL transfer forms.

The JPC also stated that most banks did not have any proper system of reporting to top management about details of transactions in securities, details of bouncing of SGL transfer forms issued by other banks etc.

It also said that many banks had not formulated and got approved internal exposure limits for transaction including exposure limits on the volume of transactions through individual broker, and the maximum amount of outstanding BRs to SGLs issued by other banks which can be accepted by the bank. Even where exposure limits were fixed they were breached with impunity.

The Committee gave detailed examples of irregularities in the approval of investment transactions in SBI.

Andhra Bank/ABFSL: The bank was castigated for failure of internal control at its Fort Branch at Bombay.

"ABFSL had made a total investment of Rs. 1717.52 crore with the FFSL Ltd. which formed about 43 per cent of its total investment. This disproportionate share of business going to FFSL was only detected on June 16, 1992...well after the scam had broken out." The reason for this as stated before the Committee was that "there was no day-to-day reporting system or day-to-day consultation."

Canara Bank, CANFINA and CMF have also been pulled up for deficiencies in internal control.

National Housing Bank: The irregularities committed by Mr. C. Ravi Kumar, who was in charge of the Funds Management Board is one of the examples of failure of the reporting system in the NHB.

NHB was pulled up for various other failures in internal working.

Referring to specific cases, the Committee stated that the SBI's apex vigilance department at Bomaby failed miserably in detecting the irregularities being continuously committeed on a large scale at the apex level in Bombay itself.

In Andhra Bank, officials involved in the irregularities were being investigated and reports were awaited.

In the case of ABFSL, apart from the CBI inquiry, no departmental action like vigilance inquiry was undertaken by the bank against the erring officials. The irregularities that occurred were not thoroughly examined no were any comprehensive reports prepared, the committee said.

Foreign Banks Indictment

The JPC came down heavily on foreign banks and even recommended "suspension of their licenses keeping in view the extent of irregularities indulged into by each of them." This is besides the stringent penalties which the JPC recommended against these banks.

Since some foreign banks had violated the banking laws of both India and their own country, the JPC recommended that "legal action should be pursued in India and the foreign country concerned." Citibank, ANZ Grindlays, Bank of America and Stanchart have been named as the major violator of banking laws and guidelines.

The JPC recommended a special scrutiny by RBI in all foreign banks involved in the irregularities. The Committee said RBI should even consider the question of disallowing repatriation of profits made by foreign banks through irregular securities transactions and other mal-practices.

The JPC observed that all four foreign banks mentioned by it had shown a spurt in profits from 1990-91 onwards. The quantum rise in their profits, besides being attributable to the sharp rise in the volume of these trarsactions, were also due to the irregularities committed during the process, the JPC report observed.

In this respect, Citibank and Bank of America came in for special criticism. The JPC report said Citibank did a complete volte face in its second deposition. Initially, the bank had made assertions before the Committee that it had committed no irregularities. Later, during the second deposition, Citibank officials said that lapses in implementation had come to light.

With regard to Citibank, the JPC report said: "The information available with the Committee believes the spontaneity of action as claimed by Citibank with regard to removal of some of its officers. In the case of A S Thyagarajan, senior Vice-President, who was looking after investment and other corporate areas of the bank he was relocated outside India at the instance of RBI when it came to its notice that Thyagarajan was interfering with the ongoing investigation of the bank."

Going into Bank of America's role, the Committee said: "The gross violation of RBI instructions on securities transactions by BOA led the inspecting officer of the special scrutiny team to seek RBI orders regarding disallowing the bank to remit to its head office profits earned from securities transactions during 1991-92."

In the case of Stanchart, the Committee observed that the irregularities in securities transactions were in the knowledge of the top management of the bank when these were conveyed to its London head office by one of its officers, namely Prakash Yardi, Assistant Manager, as early as September 1990. The bank did not take a cue from this warning the report said.

It said the Committee had been informed that the Securities and Exchange Commission (SEC) of the US had written to SEBI on the possible violation of US banking laws by American banks operating in

India.

SEC had also written to SEBI suggesting investigation into securities transactions of the American banks, the report said.

The JPC also observed that all the four foreign banks involved in irregularities had their own well laid out procedures for internal control but all these rules and regulations seem to have been followed more in breach than in observance.

For instance, the books of ABZ Grindlays showed non-updating of BR exposure records, non-maintenance of list of authorised signatories and inaccurate monitoring of positions by dealers. During a special audit of Citibank, it was seen that in many cases the names of brokers had not been fed in the computers though the bank officer concerned indicated the name of the broker in a deal slip.

Scrutiny of Citibank documents showed that the bank was using the words 'dummy customer' in a large number of cases involving huge amounts. Further, "the Committee was amazed to note that even in large banks of international standing like SCB the demarcation of responsibility between the front office and back office got diffused and controls totally weakened.

The report pointed out that all foreign banks had regularly used PMS customer accounts for skimming profits over above the benchmarks indicated to the customer.

"An interesting feature about certain PMS accounts managed by Citibank was that out of the total portfolio funds deployed with the bank almost 30, per cent have in directly come from Citibank itself. For instance Citibank would subscribe to 17 per cent PFC bonds worth Rs. 150 crore on the condition that the money would be placed back by PFC in PMS at an interest rate of 14.25 per cent," the Committee noted.

Investigating Agencies

Lack of coordination among the investigating agencies handicapped the investigation of scam related cases, the JPC said.

It also charged the Central Board of Direct Taxes with not

examining the role of industrial houses with respect to the scam.

CBDT officials, during oral depositions before the JPC, had said that though the activities of every industrial house were scrutinised in details, no specific steps regarding their involvement in the scam had been taken.

The Committee maintained that there were several instances in the investigations which clearly brought the failure of the CBI, the CBDT and the Enforcement Directorate to ensure co-ordinated action, despite serious concern expressed at various levels.

As a result, the Enforcement Directorate was unable to take any action or prevent Nirañjan Shah from leaving the country after the income-tax authorities raided his premises on May 30 and 31, 1992. This was because the information in this connection reached them only on June 2, 1992.

Similarly, the report pointed out that the CBI failed to take up action on the basis of information furnished by the CBDT. The delay in setting up the coordination committee of the three agencies only highlighted their failure to ensure organised action, the report said.

This aside, the Committee came down heavily on the CBDT for its failure to initiate proper follow-up action in scam-related cases.

In the case of the Harshad Mehta group, searches were first carried out in September 1990. However, the department failed to launch a single prosecution for various defaults and levied only a paltry penalty of Rs. 6.4 lakh. Moreover, no action was taken against the officers responsible for various lapses.

The Committee noted that even after the second raid on the group in February 1992, there was no coordinated approach and no serious efforts were made to introduce systems and procedures to ensure expeditious finalisation of assessments, especially in big cases involving huge revenue.

The JPC found that the assessment of various brokers for the year 1990-91 had only been completed in March 1993 and in some cases even the assessments for this and earlier years were still pending finalisation.

The Committee urged the government to ensure that the CBDT stuck to its deadline of completing the investigation of scam-related cases in 1993-94. In addition, follow-up action should be expedited.

In the case of the CBI, the Committee observed instances of inordinate delay in making preliminary enquiries and the non-registration of regular cases by the CBI in spite of sufficient evidence to support it.

Brokers

The JPC report revealed violation of rules by banks in favouring certain select brokers. Among the brokers named were the broking firms of Harshad Mehta. N.K. Aggarwala & Co., H.P. Dalal, Somayajulu & Co., Batliwala & Karani and V.B. Desai & Associates.

The report stated that of the Rs. 7,43,604 crore securities transactions conducted by the banks and financial companies during April 1991 to May 1992, 58 per cent were handled through brokers. Some of these brokers cornered nearly 20 per cent of the total business.

The report established the manner in which the banks in general colluded with some unscrupulous brokers and extended undue advantage to them, disregarding the rules.

The report stated that the close nexus between certain PSUs, banks and brokers enabled the latter to have unauthorised access to funds. That, in turn, led to diversion of huge public funds from the banking system to the brokers, thereby enabling them to manipulate the market.

The banks failed to evolve any clear-cut policy regarding the role of brokers in securities transactions, including their selection, fixing the limit over the quantum of business, nature of transactions and the system of reporting.

The report said it was regrettable that no corrective measures were taken even after the matter was raised by RBI during the inspections since 1986. The report said the RBI, though seized of the problem, for long did not take any action nor deem it fit to lay down any guidelines for regulating the investment function till June, 1992.

As a result, even brokers new to this field were able to exploit the loopholes to their advantage.

Given this diversion of funds to brokers, the huge sums of money paid to them as brokerage, and other mal-practices indulged in by them, the Committee considered whether there was any need for banks to use the services of brokers for interbank transactions.

The report said the banks needed to trade in securities mainly for SLR purposes. The short-term requirement of the banks in this matters could be met by the Discount and Finance House of India (DFHI), which had developed a secondary market in treasury bills for different maturity periods.

The RBI also announced in Apirl 1993 the proposal to set up a Securities Trading Corporation of India for the development of a secondary market in government securities and public sector bonds, it said.

Since there were few players holding government securities to any appreciable extent (RBI commercial banks and LIC reportedly hold 88 per cent of the government securities) and those required to trade in them were also few, the Committee recommended that the government and the RBI consider the need for brokers in such transactions.

Notes of Specific Members

Not satisfied with the findings of the Joint Parliamentary Committee (JPC) in regard to the alleged Re.1 crore pay-off to Prime Minister P.V. Narasimha Rao by Mr. Harshad Mehta, 13 members of the JPC belonging to the Opposition parties demanded a further detailed investigation under the Commission of Enquiry Act.

In other separate notes attached to the report, members of the Committee called for a law against insider trading, statutory audit of banks by the Comptroller and Auditor General of India (CAG) and a probe into the nexus between industrial houses, politicians and bureaucrats. One member also drew attention to the fact that the JPC had not looked into the issue of possession of promoter quota shares by senior officials of the Government and financial institutions.

As regards the allegation about the pay-off to the Prime Minister, the 13 members have said that though all concerned had tendered written evidence before the Committee, no witnesses other than Mr. Harshad Mehta had been called for oral evidence. The response of the CBI to both the investigation and to enquiries by the Committee "was not marked by any degree of purposefulness or despatch.

"The CBI was not entirely forthcoming in sharing information with the Committee. It would dilate on shortage of staff and overwork. It would even talk of its mandate being particularly related to public officials and not politicians. It tended to be excessively legalistic. Its enquiry into the allegation was conducted in a manner that was unnecessarily and unduly secretive. It arrived at its conclusions with unnatural haste," the members said.

"We are thus led to the view that in this entire matter of allegations of payment of Re. 1 crore by Mr. Harshad Mehta, there is need for further detailed investigation under the Commission of Enquiry Act. We also hold that the findings of such enquiry ought thereafter be submitted to Parliament within six months of institution," the joint note said.

The note was signed by Mr. Jaswant Singh, Mr. Ram Naik, Mr. T.N. Chaturvedi, Mr. Harin Pathak, Mr. Sushil Chandra Varma, Mr. Nirmal Kanti Chatterjee, Mr. Rabi Ray, Mr. George Fernandes, Mr. Jaipal Reddy, Mr. Gurudas Das Gupta, Mr. Murasoli Maran, Mr. Sukomal Sen and Mr. Digvijay Singh.

A similar recommendation was also made for an enquiry into the allegation about Mr. Romesh Bahandari's efforts at obtaining affidavits relating to the Committee's work.

As if a counter to this point, a separate note by the Congress members was appended, suggesting that in view of the contradictions in the depositions of Mr. Harshad Mehta and on the basis of records available to the Committee, there was no truth in the allegations of a pay-off. In the case of allegations against Mr. Bhandari, the same members said the subject did not fall within the purview of the Committee's terms of reference.

The joint note also comes down heavily on the CBI for the

"selective subjectivity exercised in the discharge of its responsibilities and obligations in investigating the securities and banking transaction matters. The premature retirement of Mr. K. Madhavan of the CBI at a crucial stage of the investigation still remains unsatisfactorily explained and needs to be further examined," the members said.

"In addition and for example the CBI's enquiry into the matters of Goldstar, ABFSL, Mr. Hiten Dalal have been far from satisfactory. The CBI has also failed to carry conviction about its handling of Mr. Mohan Khandelwal, inclusive of the manner in which a bag full of jewellery reportedly siezed from a driver working for Mr. Khandelwal and the hasty and surreptitious manner in which the entire matter was hushed up has left a great deal to be desired."

The members also recorded that Mr. Madhavan's reported assertions of important persons of India being paid abroad through some accounts remained largely unsatisfactorily explained. "The Chairman and the Committee repeatedly asked the CBI to look into the alleged nexus between politicians/ ministers and industrial houses as well as to identify the ultimate houses as well as to identify the ultimate recipients/repository of the scam funds. This was not done."

Another suggestion from these members was that statutory audit of banks and the Reserve Bank be undertaken regularly. The Comptroller and Auditor General was recommended strongly as the body to undertake the audit, as opposed to the Committee recommendation for the creation of a centralised authority for the task.

For Favours Done

In a separate note by Mr. Geroge Fernandes, Mr. Rabi Ray and Mr. Jaipal Reddy, it was mentioned that another area of investigation had to be the nexus between industrial houses and politicians and bureaucrats. In this context, the note mentioned that Mr. S.L. Khosla, who took up employment with Reliance Industries immediately after he retired as Chairman of the Oil and Natural Gas Commission, was not the only case of bureaucrats who had cultivated links with industrial houses by doing favours for them when in Government service reaping benefits after retirement.

These three members also called for legislation to ban insider trading since a lot of illegitimate money was generated by some of the unscrupulous among the industrial houses. Pushing or bringing down share prices through insider trading was also tantamount to cheating the shareholders and instances had come to notice during the investigations into the scam of how share prices of certain companies were pegged high for a certain period before fresh issues in order to cheat new investors, the members said.

In another separate note, Mr. Gurudas Das Gupta specifically mentioned that he had evidence that former Finance Secretary. K. P. Geethakrishnan had promoters quota shares, among others, in DCM Toyota, Modi Xerox, Indo Matsushita, Ramganga Fertilizers and India Glycol. Others who have been found to be holding such shares include Mrs. Janaki Kathpalia, former Additional Secretary in the Ministry of Finance, her husband, Mr. Ravi Kathpalia, Controller General Accounts, Mr. G.C. lyer, Additional Comptroller General of Accounts, and Mr. I.T Vaz and Mr. P.B. Kulkarni, both of RBI.

Finance Ministry Criticised

Mr. Das Gupta was also unsparing in his criticism of the Finance Ministry and said its role in sponsoring and perpetuating the scam had not been adequately dealt with." The mischiefs of Mr. Montek Singh Ahluwalia (then Secretary, Banking and Economic Affairs) have been ignored."

Mr. K.P. Unnikrishnan, in a lengthy note, drew attention to the fact that the Committee did not go deep into the question of the missing millions and instead got involved in pursing certain cases of "individual responsibility" beyond the limits warranted by the evidence or terms of reference.

Annexure-I
MEMBERS OF JPC

The Committee Members

The 30-member Joint Parliamentary

Ram Naik

Harin Pathak

Committee consisted of 20 members from the Lok Sabha and 10 from the Rajya Sabha. They are:

SC Verma (all BJP)
George Fernandes
Ravi Ray (both J.D.)
KP Unnikrishnan (Cong-S)

Lok Sabha	**Rajya Sabha**
Mani Shankar Aiyar	S. S. Ahluwalia
Basava Rajeshwari	H. Hanumanthappa
P.C. Chacko'Kamal Chaudhury	Jagesh Desai
Kamal Chaudhary	
Ram Niwas Mirdha	R N Yadav (all Cong.)
Murli Deora	Dipen Ghose (CPI-M); replaced by S. Sen (CPI-M)
Debi Prosad Pal	S Jaipal Reddy (JD)
Sriballav Panigrahi	"Murasoli" Maran (DMK)
Shravan Kuman Patal	T. N. Chaturvedi (BJP)
P. M. Sayeed (all Congress)	Yeshwant Sinha (JDS); replaced by Digvijay Singh
B. V. Raju (Telugu Desam-V)	Gurudas Dasgupta (CPI-M)
P. G. Narayanan (AIADMK)	
Nirmal Chatterjee (CPI-M)	
Nirmal Chatterjee (CPI-M)	
Jaswant Sing	

Annexure-II
PROCEDURES OF SECURITY TRANSACTION

Banks have been undertaking transactions in securities (i) on their own Investment Account (ii) on account of PMS Clients" Account in their fiduciary capacity and (iii) on behalf of their other constituents including brokers purely as an agency function.

The investment portfolio of banks (in respect of their own Investment Account) primarily comprises Government and other Trustee securities (except a very small fraction consisting of PSU bonds, shares and debentures which would have devoloved on them on account of their underwriting commitments) which are intended to comply with the SLR requirements. Therefore, in the normal course banks' transactions in securities on their own Investment Accounts are expected to be in government and other Trustee securities. Further, since bulk of the protfolio comprises Central Government securities, a major portion of the securities transactions among banks is expected to be put through their respective SGL Accounts maintained with PDO of the RBI.

However, composition of the portfolio in respect of PMS Clients' Account is expected to generally consist of high coupon bearing capital market instruments like PSU bonds, corporate debentures and shares. Accordingly, the transactions on account of PMS Clients' Account are expected to be primarily in the above securities and in the absence of SGL Account facility for them, transactions are expected to be on actual delivery basis.

The transactions in securities on behalf of their other constituents like brokers undertaken as an agency function would be both in Trustee securities and other corporate bonds, debentures and shares because the broker client may be dealing in both Trustee securities as well as corporate bonds, debentures and shares.

Banks' transactions in Trustee securities are generally on outright basis and ready-forward basis. The outright deals would also in the nature of switch deals. Outright sales are undertaken generally when the bank has surplus SLR security and it wants to get rid of the security because of its low yield and its opportunity cost in higher than the yield and it is in a position to book the loss arising thereform. Similarly, when a bank is ahort of SLR security and it has longterm funds, it prefers to buy a security on an outright basis, whereas when the bank does not have any surplus SLR security, as a long-term funds, it prefers to buy a security on an outright basis, whereas when the bank does not have any surplus SLR security, as a long-term strategy of improving the overall yield from its SlR securities held in its investment portfolio, by deliberately booking a loss at the short-end, the bank may undertake a switch deal by selling a low coupon security and buying a high coupon security, provided it is a position to book the loss arising out of the sale. However, given the maturity pattern of their resources and uncertainty about their future requirement of SLR securities, the banks have been generally managing their short-term cash requirements either for maintenance of CRR or for other purposes and SLR requirements, by entering into ready-forward (buy-back or repose) deals in SLR securities. In this type of transaction, a bank buys/sells a SLR security ready with the undertaking to sell back/buy back the same security on the specified future date (normally a fortninght and rolled over from fortnight to fortnight) at a mutually agreed pre-determined rate. The rates agreed upon (ready and forward rates) have no relevance to the market rates of the security but are related to the callmoney rate prevailing on the date of putting through the first leg of the transaction, as this type of transaction is basically a found management/SLR management exercise (i.e. raising funds against a SL R security which is in excess of the SLR requirement or temporary borrowing a SLR security for a cost). Thus, the difference between the ready and forward rates in a ready forward deal is supposed to represent the cost of funds. Thus, by this method, a bank which has a surplus security but wants cash prefers to borrow temporarily because it would be cheaper as compared to call-money borrowing as it has an additional cost of maintenance of CRR thereon. It may not like to sell the security outright because it may not be sure about its future SLR requirements and in such a situation, if it is required to buy outright later on to comply with future SLR requirements, it may have to pay a higher price. Insofar as buying the security ready is concerned, it may be short for complying with SLR requirements and it may have no long-term resources to buy outright or it may not be sure about its future requirements and therefore, it prefers to buy short and roll over. Further, raising funds may be costlier than buying it on a ready forward basis. Earlier, as there was no short-term maturity SLR securities available to banks to enable them to use such securities for short-term management of their cash/SLR securities requirements, (before the intorduction of

182 days Treasury Bills), the banks have been permitted by the RBI to undertake ready-forward deals in Trustee securities among themselves. However, RBI has prohibited banks from entering into such ready-forward deals whith their non-bank clients. In fact, as in 1988, the RBI had instructed the banks that ready-forward deals should be undertaken only among banks and that too only in approved trustee securities and that no ready-forward deals should be undertaken in public sector bonds and Units of Unit Trust of India (UTI). The RBI had also clarified to the banks that they should not enter into any ready-forward deals even with financial institutions and bank subsidiaries. Normally, all the deals in securities are expected to be settled between the parties to the deal either through their SGL Accounts maintained with PDO (where SGL Account facility is available) or by physical delivery of securities. Even the ready-forward deals which are very short-term in nature are expected to be settled through their respective SGL Accounts with PDO because normally these are only among banks and that too in Government securities. Use of BRs (which represent a certificate issued by the selling bank to the effect that it has been holding the relevant securities on behalf of the buyer bank for value received and would be delivering the same within a very short period) is expected to be in exceptional circumstances when the seller bank is not in a position to give physical delivery of the security either on account of delay on the part of the issuer of security to issue the scrips or because the security is held by the selling bank at a place other than the place at which the transaction has taken place and it is likely to take some time to transfer the security from the place where it is held to the place where delivery is to be given. In any case, BRs are expected to be used only in such exceptional circumstances and that too only in the case of such securities for which no SGL Account facility is available and the BRs issued are expected to be liquidated within a very short time by physical delivery of securities.

Banks while undertaking the business of their clients including brokers as an agency function are expected to collect the instruments on behalf of their broker clients to the account of the brokers maintained with them and receive or give physical delivery of securities kept with them for safe custody against payment, strictly as per their specific instructions, and are not expected to commit themselves on behalf of their broker clients by issuing their own BRs./SGL forms.

During the course of inspection/scrutiny of securities transactions of some banks it came to the notice of the RBI that some banks had been freely issuing BRs in respect of their sale transaction in securities irrespective of whether SGL Account facility was available in respect of that particular security, some banks had been issuing of that particular security, some banks had been issuing their own BRs against the BRs of other banks held by them and that some of the banks were unnecessarily committing themselves on behalf of their borker clients by issuing their own BRs covering broker transactions. With a view to cautioning the banks in general about the undesirable systems followed by some banks while undertaking transactions in securities, particularly issue of BRs and undertaking of broker business, in July 1991, vide then Deputy Governar, Shri A. Ghosh's D.O. letter DBOD. No. FSC. 46/C: 469-91/92 dated 26 July 1991 addressed to all the Chairma/Chief Executive of commercial banks, the RBI had advised the banks to frame and implement a suitable investment policy to ensure that operations in securities are conducted in accordance with sound and acceptable business practices and while evolving the investment policy with the approvals of their respective Boards, to keep in view the following guidelines :

(i) Under no circumstances, the banks should hold a oversold position in any security, that is to say, that no sale transactions should be put through without actually holding the security in its investment account.

(ii) All the transactions put through by the banks either on outright basis or on ready-forward basis and whether through the mechanism of SGL Account or BR should be reflected on the same day in their investment accounts and accordingly for SLR purposes, wherever applicable.

(iii) Transactions between banks should not be put through the brokers' accounts.

(iv) For issue of BRs, the banks should adopt the format prescribed by the Indian Banks' Association (IBA) and strictly follow the guidelines prescribed by them in this regard (copy appended) and banks should issue BRs covering their own sale transactions only and should not issue BRs on behalf of their constituents including brokers.

(v) Banks should be circumspect while acting as agents of their broker clients for carrying out transactions in securities on behalf of brokers.

(vi) Any instance of return of SGL form from the PDO of the RBI for want of sufficient balance in the account should be immediately brought to the notice of RBI with the details of the transactions.

The IBA Rules on BRs mentioned earlier, inter-alia provided as under:

(a) The BR should be issued in the prescribed format only. Receipt issued in any other format should not be accepted.

(b) Normally, no BR should be issued where SGL facility is available.

(c) A separate BR should be issued for each type of security.

(d) BR is non-transferable.

(e) BRs should be issued serially numbered on security paper.

(f) BR must be exchanged with actual scrips as early as possible and in any case within 90 days of issue.

(g) BR should be signed by two authorised signatories whose signatures should be registered with the buyer-bank to verify the signatures.

(h) BR can be accepted from any of the following institutions:

(i) All member bank of the IBA.

(ii) Financial institutions like IDBI, IFCI, ICICI, NABARD, UTI, GIC, LIC

(iii) Public Sector Undertakings.

(iv) Any other institution specified by the IBA/RBI.

The RBI had also issued guidelines and prudential exposure limits to be followed by banks for undertaking underwriting of corporate shares, debentures and PSU bonds and other commitments in the nature of safety net for public issues of convertible debentures and shares and devolvements arising therefrom, advising them to make periodical review of such business and apprise their respective Boards. As far back as in October 1986, the RBI had issued a Memorandum setting out guidelines/safeguards to be followed by banks in granting advances against corporate shares and debentures to different types of borrowers and the maximum advance that could be granted to different types of borrowers. In 1989, the RBI had instructed the banks that they and their subsidiaries should not finance badla transactions. In the light of the steep rise in the prices of corporate shares durng the second half of 1991, the RBI Governor during his Credit Policy meeting with the Chairman/Chief Executives of banks had instructed that banks should limit their aggregate advances against corporate shares and deventures to the level which prevailed as on 7 October 1991. Subsequently, in the light of the unprecedented rise in the prices of shares during March/April 1992, the RBI Governar during his Credit Policy meeting with Chairmen/Chief Executives of banks held on 22 April 1992 had instructed the banks that while they should continue with the earlier cap on aggregate lendings against shares and debentures, in the case of advances against shares and debentures to individuals, they should like the margin requirements to 75 per cent.

The RBI had also issued detailed guidelines to banks and subsidiaries for providing Portfolio Management Services (PMS) to their clients which inter-alia stipulate that PMS should in the nature if investment consultancy for a definite pre-determined fee not related to actual yield on the portfolio, purely at customers' risk, without guaranteeing any pre-determined minimum return on the portfolio. As per RBI guidelines only such banks which have the necessary experties to provide the PMS on their own should undertake the activity, maintain client-wise record of portfolios, and should furnish the clients periodical statements or their portfolio. Any transactions between the banks' Investment Account and PMS Clients' Account should be at market rates.

As per the findings so far, the total value of investment made by banks and institutions for which they do not hold either securities, SGL transfer forms or BRs in the order of Rs. 1967.84 crores, of which the NHB's exposure-amounts to Rs. 1271.20 crores. Except for a sum of Rs. 400.35 crore of Standard Chartered Bank for which investigations are going on, the balance amount under this head had gone mainly for the benefit of the Harshad Mehta group. The problem exposure in the other set of transactions where the banks and institutions hold BRs Banker's Receipts and SGL (subsidiases General ledger) transfer form issued by the bank of Karad and Metropolitan Cooperative Bank, the two small sized banks which have since been taken into liquidation, amounted to Rs.1470.12 crores, of which the exposure of Standard Chartered Bank comes to Rs. 931.84 crores. Thus, the problem of exposure of Standard Chartered Bank is the highest at Rs. 1332.20 crores.

The Janakiraman Committee has also brought out certain irregularities in transactions relating to Fairgrowth Financial Services Limited. (Bangalore) and certain banks and institutions. Audit had then been completed in certain banks and institutions where these have been completed, there are some variations and other irregularities which are being looked into by the Committee.

While the preliminary investigation revealed that the diversion of bank funds was made possible through purchases made by banks/institutious where the cunter party was ostensibly another bank but the proceeds had actually been diverted to the broker's account, direct financing of brokers through the discounting of accommodation bills, the further scrutiny has revealed that certain other methods have been used for diversion of bank funds. These are as follows :

While banks/institutions have shown large payments as call money transactions, the funds have actually been credited to individual broker's accounts and on the due date the call loans have been repaid by debiting the broker's accounts. Banks have rediscounted bills of exchange but the proceeds and repayment have been routed through the broker's account.

In respect of the transaction between the State Bank of India and Shri Harshad Mehta, to the extent that there is no record in the books of the SBI for these transactions which however, are reflected in the PDO books, it appears that the broker has used the SBI Investment Account to finance his ready forward deals with other banks.

The Merchant Banking Subsidiaries of Public sector banks have received large amounts of intercorporate deposits and these funds have been made available to brokers under ready forward deals. The RBI is looking into the matter whether such investment could contravene the relevant provisions of the Companies Act. It is also observed that in a number of transactions, the rates at which the sale of investments have been booked are at considerable variance with the rates at which the counterparties had booked their purchases. Further, in serveral instances, the banks and financial institutions have issued SGL forms against SGL forms brought by brokers and this is within the full knowledge of the management.

Highlights

The Committee has highlighted certain irregularities in the transaction of banks relating to Public Sector Enterprise Shares.

The scrutiny has brought out certain significant trends in the securities transactions. During the period of 14 months between April 1, and end May 1992, the banks had entered into sales/purchase contracts in excess of 58,000 in number and 9 lakh crores in face value of underlying securities. Two-third^ of these transactions were entered into by only four foreign banks. Over 70 per cent of these transactions are in Units of UTI. The security transactions entered into by the banks have been prodominately of ready forward basis of which over 60 per cent were through the intervention of brokers. Of the total broker transactions, over 40 per cent were through the intervention of only for brokers. Over 20 per cent in number and 30 per cent in value of the transactions cannot be matched as the transactions have not appeared in the books of the counter party banks named by the reporting bank. This matter is being further looked into by the RBI. It is to be clarified that while this reconciliation is going on, it does not mean that the amount relating to these are outstanding. All that the Committee has brought out is serious deficiencies in the systems of internal control exercised by banks and institutions over the treasury operations. Already, based on the earlier report of the Janakiraman Committee, RBI had issued certain instructions in this regard. The RBI has also appointed Special Auditors to carry out detailed audit of the investments operations in four foreign banks which account for a large portion of the operations in securities other than Government securities, as also in the case of certain that public sector/private sector banks and institutions. The RBI will examine these points further and issue fresh instructions where necessary.

NEW RBI INSTRUCTIONS (June 20, 1992)

Investment Policy

Banks have been undertaking transactions in securities on their own Investment Account, on behalf of Portfolic Management Scheme (PMS) clients in their fiduciary capacity, and on behalf of other clients, either as custodians of their investments or purely as their agents. With the approval of their respective Boards, banks should clearly lay down the broad investment objectives to be followed while undertaking transactions in securities under each category mentioned above, clearly define the authority to put through authority, procedure to be followed while putting through deals, various prudential exposure limits, and the reporting system. While laying down such investment policy guidelines, banks should strictly observe the following instructions.

Ready-Forward (buy-back) Deals

(i) Banks are prohibited with effect from 22 June 1992, and until further instructions, from undertaking inter-bank ready-forward deals in dated government and approved/trustee securities. Existing deals in dated securities should be completed on due dates without resorting to any extension or roll overs. As such, inter-bank ready-forward transactions may henceforth be undertaken only in Treasury Bills (of all maturities).

(ii) All double ready-forward deals in government securities including Treasury Bills are strictly prohibited.

(iii) No ready-forward and double ready-forward deals should be put through even among banks and even on their own Investment Accounts in any other securities, such as public sector undertakings (PSUs) Bonds and Units.

(iv) Similarly, no ready-forward and double ready-forward deals should be put through in any security including government securities, on behalf of PMS Clients Accounts or on behalf of other constituents including brokers.

Transactions in Government Securities

(v) All transactions in government securities for which SGL facility is available should be put through SGL Accounts only.

(vi) Before issue of SGL transfer forms covering their sale transactions banks should ensure that they have sufficient balance in their respective SGL Accounts. Accordingly, under no circumstances, and SGL transfer from issued by a bank in favour of another bank should bounce for want of sufficient balance in the SGL Account. The purchasing banks should issue the cheques only after receipt of the SGL transfer forms from the selling banks.

(vii) The SGL transfer form received by purchasing banks should be deposited in their SGL Accounts immediately. No sale should be effected by way of return of SGL Accounts immediately. No sale should be effected by way of return of SGL form held by the bank.

(viii) SGL transfer form should be signed by two authorised officials of the bank whose signatures should be recorded with the respective Public Debt Office (PDO) of RBI and other banks.

(ix) The SGL transfer forms should be in the standard format prescribed by the RBI and printed on semi-security paper of uniform size. The should be serially numbered and there should be a control system in place to account for each SGL form.

Bank Receipts (BRs)

(xi) No BR should be issued under any circumstances in respect of transactions in government securities for which SGL facility is available.

(xii) Even in the case of other securities, BR may bc issued for ready transactions only, under the following circumstances::

(a) The scrips are yet to be issued by the issuer and the bank is holding the allotment advice

(b) The security is physically held at a different centre and the bank is in a position to physically transfer the security and give delivery thereof, within a short period.

(c) The security has been lodged for transfer/interest payment and the bank is holding necessary records of such lodgements and will be in a position to give physical delivery of the security within a shot period.

(xiii) No BR should be issued on the basis of a BR (of another bank) held by the bank and no transaction should take place on the basis of a mere exchange of BRs held by the bank.

(xiv) BRs may be issued covering transactions relating to banks own Investment Accounts only, and no BR should be issued by banks covering transactions relating to either the Accounts of PMS Clients or Other Constituents Account including brokers.

(xv) No BR should remain outstanding for more than 30 days.

(xvi) BRs should be issued on semi-security paper, in the standard format (perscribed by IBA), serially numbered, and signed by authorised officials of the bank, whose signatures are recorded with other banks. As in the case of SGL forms, there should be a control system in place to account for each BR form.

(xvii) Separate registers of BRs issued and BRs received should be maintained, and arrangements should be put in place to ensure that these are systematically followed up and liquidated within the stipulated time limit.

Internal Control System

There should be a clear functional separation of (a) trading, (b) settlement, monitoring and control, and (c) accounting. Similarly, there should be a functional separation of trading and back office functions relating to banks own Investment Accounts, PMS Clients Account and Other Constitutents (including brokers) Accounts. While providing portfolio management service to their clients, the banks should strictly follow the guidelines issued on the subject and PMS Clients Accounts should be subjected to a separate audit by external auditors.

Banks should put in place a reporting system to report to the top management on a weekly basis, the details of transactions in securities, details of bouncing of SGL transfer forms issued by other banks and BRs outstanding for more than one month, and review of investment transactions undertaken during the period.

It is reiterated that banks should not draw cheques on their account with RBI for third party transactions including inter-bank transactions. For such transactions bankers' cheques/pay orders should be issued.

The Internal Audit Department should audit the transactions in securities on an ongoing basis and monitor compliance with the laid down management policies and prescribed procedures and report the deficiencies directly to the top managements of banks.

Dealings Through Brokers

If a deal is put through with the help of broker the role of the broker should be restricted to that of bringing that two parties to the deal together.

While negotiating the deal, the broker is not obliged to disclose the identity of the counterparty to the deal. However, on conclusion of the deal, he should disclose the counterparty and his contract note should clearly indicate the name of the counterparty.

On the basis of the contract note disclosing the name of the counterparty, settlement of deals between banks, viz., both fund settlement and delivery of security, should be directly between the banks and the broker should have no role to play in the process.

With the approval of their top management, banks should prepare a panel of approved brokers which should be reviewed annually, or more often if so warranted. Clear-cut criteria should be laid down for empanelment of brokers, including verification of their creditworthiness, market reputation, etc. A record of broker-wise details of deals put through and brokerage paid, should be maintained.

A disproportionate part of the business should not be transacted through only one or a few brokers. Banks should consider fixing aggregate contract limits for each of the approved brokers, and ensure that these limits are not exceeded.

Audit, Review and Reporting

Banks should undertake a half-yearly review (as of 30 September and 31 March) of their investment portfolio, which should, apart from other operational aspects of investment portfolio, clearly indicate and certify adherence to laid down internal investment policy and procedures and RBI guidelines, and put up the same before their respective Boards within a month i.e. by end-April and end-October.

A copy of the review report put up to the bank's Board, should be forwarded to the RBI by 15 November and 15 may respectively.

In view of the possibility of abuse, treasury transactions should be separately subjected to a concurrent audit by internal auditors and the results of their audit should be placed before the Chairman and Managing Director of the Bank once every month. These audit reports should be sent to the newly constituted Cell on Supervision of Funds

Management Operations in Banks in the Reserve Bank of India. Department of Banking Operations and Development, Central Office.

A copy of the internal investment policy guidelines duly framed by banks with the approval of their boards should be forwarded to RBI certifying that it is in accordance with RBI guidelines.

The aforesaid instructions will be applicable mutatis mutandis to the subsidiaries and mutual funds established by banks, except where they are contrary to, or inconsistent with, specific SEBI or RBI regulations governing their operations.

Annexure IV

List of Persons/Companies whose properties have been attached by the Custodian

1. M/s Harshad S. Mehta, Proprietory Concern
2. M/s Ashwin S. Mehta, Proprietory Concern
3. M/s J.H. Mehta, Proprietory Concern
4. Mr. Harshad S. Mehta, S/o Shantilal Mehta
5. Mr. Ashwin S. Mehta
6. Mr. Hitesh S. Mehta
7. Mr. Sudhir S. Mehta
8. Mrs. Jyoti H. Metha, W/o SI. No. 4
9. Mrs. Deepika A. Mehta, W/o SI. No. 5
10. Mrs. Pramila H. Mehta, W/o SI. No. 6
11. Mr. Harshad S. Mehta, HUF
12. Aswin S. Mehta, HUF
13. Hitesh S. Mehta, HUF
14. M/s Sunrise Enterprises
15. Growmore Research & Assets Management Limited

16. Growmore Lasing & Investments (Pvt.) ltd

17. Growmore Exports (Pvt.) Ltd

18. Aatur Holdings (Pvt.) Ltd.

19. Harsh Exports (Pvt.) Ltd.

20. Cascade Holding (Pvt.) Ltd.

21. Orion Travel (Pvt.) Ltd.

22. Fortune Holdings (Pvt.) Ltd

23. Treasure Holding (Pvt.) Ltd

24. Valvet Holdings (Pvt.) Ltd

25. Eminent Holding (Pvt.) Ltd

26. Pallavi Holding (Pvt.) Ltd

27. Zest Holding (Pvt.) Ltd

28. Divine Holding (Pvt.) Ltd

29. Topaz Holding (Pvt.) Ltd

30. Abhay Dharamsinh Narottam (S/o Dharamsinh Narottam)

31. Hiten Prasan Dalal (S/o Prasan Jayantilal Dalal)

32. Shri C.L. Khemani, Dy. Managing Director (T&IM), SBI, Central Office, Bombay.

33. Shri A.N Bavadekar, Dy. Manager, Securities Division, Main Branch, State Bank of India, Bombay.

34. Shri R. Sitaraman, JMG-I Officer, Securities Division, Main Branch, State Bank of India, Bombay.

35. Shri Bhupen Dalal, Managing Director of M/s Champaklal Investment & Financial Consultancy Services Ltd. Bombay-21.

36. Shri J.P. Gandhi, Anita Building, Malabar Hill, Bombay.

37. Shri T.B. Ruia, 6A, Samundra Gurav, Worli Seaface, Bombay.

38. M/s Fairgrowth Financial Services Ltd., Bangalore-I.

39. Shri R. Ganesh, Asstt. Vice-President, M/s Fairgrowth Financial Services Ltd. Bangalore-1.

40. M/s. Dhanraj Mills (Pvt) Ltd., Lower Parel, Bombay-13.